MY SiDEWALKS ON
SCOTT FORESMAN
READING STREET
Teacher's Guide

Level D
Volume 2

Glenview, Illinois • Boston, Massachusetts • Chandler, Arizona •
Upper Saddle River, New Jersey

Copyright © 2011 by Pearson Education, Inc., or its affiliates. All Rights Reserved. Printed in the United States of America. This publication is protected by copyright, and permission should be obtained from the publisher prior to any prohibited reproduction, storage in a retrieval system, or transmission in any form or by any means, electronic, mechanical, photocopying, recording, or likewise. For information regarding permissions, write to Pearson Curriculum Group Rights & Permissions, One Lake Street, Upper Saddle River, New Jersey 07458.

Pearson, Scott Foresman, and Pearson Scott Foresman are trademarks, in the U.S. and/or other countries, of Pearson Education, Inc., or its affiliates.

ISBN-13: 978-0-328-45346-7
ISBN-10:   0-328-45346-3
4 5 6 7 8 9 10 V064 14 13 12

MY SiDEWALKS ON
SCOTT FORESMAN
READING STREET
Intensive Reading Intervention

A Safe Place to Learn

Fit Your Framework

NO MATTER HOW YOU FRAME IT, IT FITS.

My Sidewalks provides the essential elements of Response to Intervention (RTI) in a validated instructional design for accelerating reading achievement.

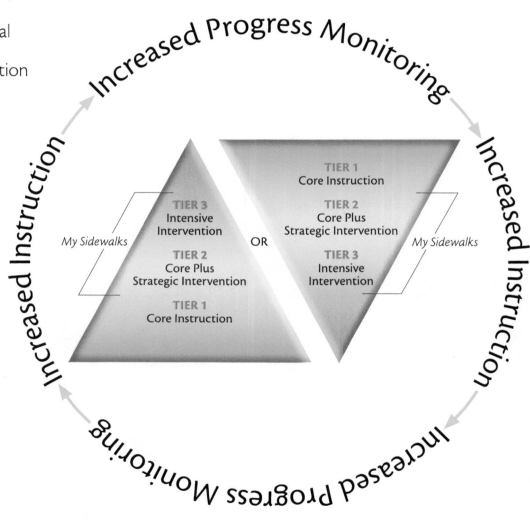

Increased Progress Monitoring

Increased Instruction

Increased Instruction

Increased Progress Monitoring

My Sidewalks

TIER 3
Intensive Intervention

TIER 2
Core Plus Strategic Intervention

TIER 1
Core Instruction

OR

TIER 1
Core Instruction

TIER 2
Core Plus Strategic Intervention

TIER 3
Intensive Intervention

My Sidewalks

Three Steps Toward Creating a Safe Place to Learn

1 SUSTAINED INSTRUCTION

My Sidewalks contains lesson plans for 30 full weeks. Every day, for 30–45 minutes, you can put your struggling readers—monolingual and English Language Learners—on solid footing. With instruction that is systematic and explicit, *My Sidewalks* helps you create a learning environment that is both consistent and predictable so your students can sustain progress every day. Your students will make strides with:

• Increased time on task
• Explicit teacher modeling
• Multiple response opportunities
• Tasks broken down into smaller steps

2 INTENSIVE LANGUAGE AND CONCEPT DEVELOPMENT

Research shows that a child's vocabulary entering first grade is a strong predictor of comprehension at eleventh grade. This is a critical area where Tier III students are deficient. *My Sidewalks* helps build a foundation for future comprehension success with daily, intensive language and concept development:

• Unit themes organized around science and social studies concepts
• Five to seven new vocabulary words tied directly to the week's theme
• Four weekly selections that build on the unit concept
• Concepts that connect from week to week

3 CRITICAL COMPREHENSION SKILLS

Along with daily vocabulary instruction, *My Sidewalks* provides explicit and systematic instruction on the comprehension skills and strategies researchers have identified as being the most critical for developing reading success:

• Drawing Conclusions
• Compare/Contrast
• Sequence
• Main Idea and Supporting Details

Components

Student Readers

My Sidewalks takes high-interest reading selections and puts them in an engaging magazine format. Every week, your Tier III students read four different selections that work together to develop a science or social studies concept. Week in and week out, these fiction and nonfiction selections help your students get a better understanding of the overall unit theme (the same themes and concepts found in *Scott Foresman Reading Street!*). 30 lessons, organized into 6 units. (5 units at Level A)

Teacher's Guides

My Sidewalks keeps your intervention instruction running smoothly. The Teacher's Guides contain everything you need for Tier III instruction. Complete lesson plans focus on high priority skills and provide daily routines with suggested time frames to help you keep your instruction focused and on time.
2 Volumes per level

Practice Books

Finally, a practice book written specifically for Tier III students. These consumable workbooks/ blackline masters give your students additional practice in phonics, comprehension, vocabulary, and writing. Books are available for each level and have multiple practice selections for every lesson. Plus, each page contains a Home Activity to strengthen the school-home connection. *A Teacher's Manual with answer key is also available.*

Benchmark Readers

What's working for your students? Which students need more targeted instruction? Accurately assess your Tier III students' progress with these unit readers. Each 8-page book contains examples of all the skills targeted in the unit so you can find out instantly whether a student is ready to transition out of *My Sidewalks* or still needs additional intervention.

Alphabet Cards

Help your Tier III students practice letter names and sounds with these colorful cards. *(Level A)*

Assessment Book

All your assessment needs, all in one book. Along with assessment instruction, you'll find progress-monitoring forms, placement tests, unit assessments in individual and group formats, and guidelines for students to exit *My Sidewalks*.

Finger Tracing Cards

Hands-on Tracing Cards allow students to connect sounds to letters while they learn their letter shapes. *(Level A)*

Manipulative Letter Tiles

Sturdy, plastic, manipulative tiles are easy for little fingers to practice word building. *(Levels A–B)*

Student Readers DVD-ROM

Recordings of the Student Readers read at a fluent pace give Tier III students complete access to every selection.

Sing with Me Big Book

Large, illustrated Big Books develop oral vocabulary and build background. Pages inspire small group discussions using vocabulary words and include songs that demonstrate the words in context. *(Levels A–B)*

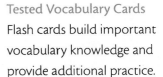

Sing with Me Audio CD

Song recordings accompany each Sing with Me Big Book. *(Levels A–B)*

Sound-Spelling Cards

Colorful cards with instructional routines introduce each sound-spelling in the intervention lesson. *(Levels A–C)*

Sound-Spelling Wall Charts

Large-size formats of the Sound-Spelling Cards are ideal for use in small-group instruction. *(Levels A–C)*

Tested Vocabulary Cards

Flash cards build important vocabulary knowledge and provide additional practice.

Welcome to *My Sidewalks*

This handy guide shows you how to provide effective instruction, manage your time, and help students catch up.

Write-On/Wipe-Off Cards

These cards have a write-on/wipe-off surface and writing lines for practicing letter forms, letter-sounds, spelling, and writing.

Level	Grade
A	1
B	2
C	3
D	4
E	5

Authors

My Sidewalks was created by the leading researchers in the area of reading intervention instruction. Their work has helped struggling readers and is the basis for the 3-Tier model of instruction.

"Research shows that for students to make significant progress, they need systematic and intensive instruction that is tailored to their current instructional level."

Sharon Vaughn

Connie Juel, Ph.D.
Professor of Education
School of Education
Stanford University

Jeanne R. Paratore, Ed.D.
Associate Professor of Education
Department of Literacy and
Language Development
Boston University

Deborah Simmons, Ph.D.
Professor
College of Education and
Human Development
Texas A&M University

Sharon Vaughn, Ph.D.
H.E. Hartfelder/Southland
Corporation Regents
Professor
University of Texas

Contents

Unit 4   Puzzles and Mysteries

Unit 5 Adventures by Land, Air, and Water

Unit 6 Reaching for Goals

Resources

Distinctions Between Levels

Understanding the Levels of *My Sidewalks*

The goal of the *My Sidewalks* program is to enable struggling readers to succeed with the reading material used in their regular classrooms. To achieve this, *My Sidewalks* focuses on accelerating students' acquisition of priority skills. Each level of *My Sidewalks* is designed to provide a year and a half of reading growth. Consequently there is an overlap of skills between one *My Sidewalks* level and the next.

These pages describe the skills students should have to successfully begin each level of *My Sidewalks* and what they will learn in that level. Use the Placement Tests to help you determine the correct level at which to enter each student.

To begin this level a child should know:	**In this level**, the instructional focus is on:
Early Reading Intervention (Grade K)	
	• Phonological and phonemic awareness • Letter names and sounds • Blending regular short-vowel words • Sentence reading
Level A (Grade 1)	
• Some phonological awareness	• Phonemic awareness • Letter names • Consonants: Individual letter-sounds, blends, and digraphs • Vowels: Short, long (CVC*e*), and *r*-controlled • Blending words and fluent word reading • High-frequency words • Oral vocabulary and concept development • Building fluency (40–60 WCPM) • Passage reading and retelling

To begin this level a student should know:	In this level, the instructional focus is on:
Level B (Grade 2)	
<ul><li>Letter names</li><li>Individual consonant letter-sounds</li><li>Some basic high-frequency words</li><li>And be able to read Benchmark Reader A2 with accuracy and comprehension</li></ul>	<ul><li>Phonemic awareness</li><li>Letter names and sounds</li><li>Blending words and fluent word reading</li><li>High-frequency words</li><li>Oral vocabulary and concept development</li><li>Building fluency (70–90 wcpm)</li><li>Passage reading and retelling</li></ul>
Level C (Grade 3)	
<ul><li>Consonants: Individual letter-sounds, blends, and digraphs</li><li>Vowels: Short and long (CVCe) and be able to distinguish between them</li><li>A wider range of high-frequency words</li><li>And be able to read Benchmark Reader B2 with accuracy and comprehension</li></ul>	<ul><li>Blending words and fluent word reading</li><li>Decoding multisyllabic words, including words with one or more affixes</li><li>Phonics: Vowels</li><li>Concept vocabulary</li><li>Building fluency (100–120 wcpm)</li><li>Passage reading and summarizing</li></ul>
Level D (Grade 4)	
<ul><li>Consonants: Individual letter-sounds, blends, and digraphs</li><li>Vowels: Short and long (CVCe) and be able to distinguish between them</li><li>How to decode regular VC/CV words with short and long (CVCe) vowels</li><li>Many high-frequency words</li><li>And be able to read Benchmark Reader C1 with accuracy and comprehension</li></ul>	<ul><li>Decoding multisyllabic words, including words with one or more affixes</li><li>Phonics: Less frequent vowel patterns, such as vowel diphthongs</li><li>Concept vocabulary</li><li>Building fluency (110–130 wcpm)</li><li>Passage reading and summarizing</li></ul>
Level E (Grade 5)	
<ul><li>Consonants: Individual letter-sounds, blends, and digraphs</li><li>Vowels: Short and long (CVCe) and be able to distinguish between them</li><li>How to decode regular VC/CV words with short and long (CVCe) vowels</li><li>Many high-frequency words</li><li>And be able to read Benchmark Reader D1 with accuracy and comprehension</li></ul>	<ul><li>Decoding multisyllabic words, including words with one or more affixes</li><li>Phonics: Less frequent vowel patterns, such as vowel diphthongs</li><li>Concept vocabulary</li><li>Building fluency (120–140 wcpm)</li><li>Passage reading and summarizing</li></ul>

Differentiating Instruction

The charts on these pages show instruction during a week in *My Sidewalks*. The charts can also be used as guides for **reteaching** or **accelerating** through parts of the lessons. In addition, the *If... then...* directions will help you identify how to customize instruction for your students.

Reteaching To meet the needs of the lowest performing readers, it may be necessary to modify the pacing and intensity of instruction. Activities shown in gray boxes on the charts may be repeated for these students.

Accelerating A child who shows mastery of skills following initial instruction may be ready for instruction at a faster pace with fewer repetitions. Activities shown in green boxes might be omitted for these students.

Levels A–B

	PHONEMIC AWARENESS	PHONICS	HIGH-FREQUENCY WORDS	CONCEPTS/ ORAL VOCABULARY	PASSAGE READING	FLUENCY	WRITING
Day 1	Phonemic Awareness	Blending Strategy	High-Frequency Words	Concepts/ Oral Vocabulary	Read a Passage	Reread for Fluency	
Day 2	Phonemic Awareness	Blending Strategy	High-Frequency Words		Read a Passage	Reread for Fluency	Write
Day 3	Phonemic Awareness	Blending Strategy	High-Frequency Words	Concepts/ Oral Vocabulary	Read a Passage	Reread for Fluency	
Day 4		Fluent Word Reading		Concepts/ Oral Vocabulary	Read Together	Reread for Fluency	Write
Day 5		Assess Word Reading	Assess Word/ Sentence Reading	Check Oral Vocabulary	Assess Passage Reading/ Reread		Write

☐ **Reteach**   ☐ **Omit for acceleration**

If... a child is struggling with word reading,
then... reteach Word Work activities and include More Practice extensions.

If... a child lacks oral language,
then... elicit extended language from the child, provide ample opportunities for the child to respond when building concepts, and expand the structured picture walks before reading each selection.

If... a child's reading is so slow that it hinders comprehension,
then... provide additional models of fluent reading, give more corrective feedback during fluency practice, and include More Practice extensions when rereading for fluency.

If... an English learner struggles with sounds,
then... repeat appropriate practice activities.

Levels C–E

	VOCABULARY	COMPREHENSION	PASSAGE READING	PHONICS	FLUENCY	WRITING
Day 1	Vocabulary		Read a Passage	Blending Strategy (Level C)	Reread for Fluency	Write (Levels D–E)
Day 2	Vocabulary	Comprehension Skill	Read a Passage	Phonics	Reread for Fluency	Write (Levels D–E)
Day 3	Vocabulary	Comprehension Skill Assess (Levels D–E)	Read a Passage	Phonics	Reread for Fluency	Write
Day 4	Vocabulary	Comprehension Skill/Strategy Assess (Levels D–E)	Read Together (Level C) Read a Passage (Levels D–E)	Phonics Review (Level C)	Reread for Fluency	Write
Day 5	Vocabulary	Assess Comprehension	Read Together (Levels D–E) Reread (Level C)	Assess Sentence Reading (Level C)	Assess Fluency	Write

If... a student is struggling with word reading, **then...** reteach Vocabulary and Phonics activities and include More Practice extensions.

If... a student lacks oral language, **then...** elicit extended language from the student, provide ample opportunities for the student to respond when building concepts, and expand the After Reading discussion for each selection.

If... a student's reading is so disfluent that it hinders comprehension, **then...** provide additional models of fluent reading, give more corrective feedback during fluency practice, and include More Practice extensions for fluency.

If... a student lacks comprehension and is unable to retell or summarize, **then...** reteach comprehension skills and strategies, provide additional modeling of retelling and summarizing, and give more corrective feedback during practice.

If... an English learner lacks English vocabulary for known concepts, **then...** say the unknown English word, have the student repeat it, and ask questions that will allow the student to use the word in a meaningful context.

Meeting ELL Needs

My Sidewalks was developed to provide intensive reading intervention for Tier III students struggling to read and write. The program has been designed to reflect current research on literacy instruction for English language learners (ELLs)—not as additional notes, but integral to all elements of instruction. From its original conception, instruction to meet the needs of both native English speakers and English learners (who have some basic English conversational skills) has been integrated into the curriculum, teaching practices, and learning activities. Since English language learners acquire literacy skills in much the same way as their English-speaking peers, both will benefit from the same good instructional practices.

Research Says "ELLs at risk for reading problems profit considerably in their literacy skills from systematic and explicit interventions that address the core reading skills of beginning reading: phonemic awareness, phonics, fluency, vocabulary, and comprehension. . . . Our work with ELLs suggests that postponing interventions to wait for language to become more proficient is not necessary, and supporting literacy acquisition in the language of instruction provided by the school for students at risk is beneficial." Vaughn, S., Linan-Thompson, S., *et al.* 2005. "Interventions for 1st Grade English Language Learners with Reading Difficulties." *Perspectives*, 31 (2), p. 31–35.

English language learners need. . .	My Sidewalks provides. . .
Phonemic Awareness	
• to develop familiarity with the sounds of English • to practice identifying, segmenting, and blending sounds in English words • to learn the sounds of English within words, in isolation and in meaningful contexts	• explicit and systematic modeling of sounds in words • scaffolded instruction that evokes active responses by children • ample practice identifying, counting, segmenting, blending, adding, and deleting sounds in words • clear lessons that tie phonemic awareness to phonics
Phonics	
• to learn the letters and letter-sound correspondences of English • to master identifying, segmenting, and blending the variety of sounds that letters represent in English words • to understand how to complete phonics activities • to use the phonics they learn—seeing, saying, reading, and writing words—with growing proficiency • to learn the sounds and spellings of written English words in meaningful contexts	• explicit phonics instruction with regular practice • routines for practicing the core English phonics elements • clear, step-by-step blending strategies understandable to students learning English as they learn to read • active learning—hearing, speaking, reading, and writing—that ties phonics to decodable text (Levels A–C) and to decoding of multisyllabic words in text (Levels D–E) • practice decoding and reading words related to concepts explored in oral language and texts

English language learners need. . .	My Sidewalks provides. . .

Vocabulary

<ul><li>to develop oral vocabulary in English, including words already familiar to English-speaking children</li><li>to learn functional English vocabulary, including high-frequency words</li><li>to encounter new words in meaningful oral and written contexts</li><li>to hear, see, and use new words repeatedly</li><li>to learn academic English vocabulary</li></ul>	<ul><li>multiple exposures to each vocabulary word</li><li>a routine for learning high-frequency words (at Levels A and B)</li><li>a routine for learning oral vocabulary (at Levels A and B)</li><li>a focus on words related to science and social studies concepts</li><li>multiple opportunities to practice using and producing oral and written vocabulary, including academic English</li><li>development of deep meaning for key concepts and words</li></ul>

Comprehension

<ul><li>to continually improve their comprehension of oral English</li><li>to read comprehensible texts and develop abilities to interpret more complex written language</li><li>to use their prior knowledge in order to comprehend texts</li><li>to acquire understanding of sentence structures and text organizations of academic English</li><li>to learn about cultural concepts embodied in the readings</li></ul>	<ul><li>an emphasis on oral language and concept development, to improve students' English proficiency and comprehension</li><li>an abundance of comprehensible reading materials focused on science and social studies concepts</li><li>modeling, instruction, and practice of priority comprehension skills and reading strategies, including prereading routines</li><li>explicit instructional routines that model new skills, build on students' prior knowledge, use visual elements to clarify ideas, and incorporate ample practice and review</li><li>exposure to the structures of English, text organization, and cultural concepts of the readings and lessons</li></ul>

Fluency

<ul><li>to hear models of fluent reading of instructional-level texts</li><li>to practice and improve their fluent reading</li><li>corrective feedback on their reading</li></ul>	<ul><li>teacher modeling to familiarize students with expressive, meaningful reading of instructional-level academic texts</li><li>engaging practice opportunities that include choral reading, paired reading, and reading with AudioText, which provide many models for building fluency</li><li>instruction in reading rate, accuracy, expression, and intonation</li><li>repeated readings and corrective feedback, to help students see words in context and pronounce them</li><li>progress monitoring and assessments to aid in fluency growth</li></ul>

Writing

<ul><li>to develop their English proficiency by writing as well as reading</li><li>to write about ideas related to reading topics</li><li>to practice communicating their ideas in English through manageable, interesting writing activities</li></ul>	<ul><li>opportunities to respond to literature about themes</li><li>scaffolded writing instruction including sentence frames for young children, manageable writing prompts for all students, and self-checking activities</li><li>feedback for writers from teacher and fellow students</li></ul>

Unit 4
Skills Overview

Why These Skills? *My Sidewalks* focuses on the priority skills students need in order to succeed at learning to read. **Priority skills** are the critical elements of reading—phonemic awareness (Levels A–C), phonics, fluency, vocabulary, and text comprehension. Scientifically based research has shown that these skills are the foundations of reading and must be taught in a systematic sequence.

		WEEK 1	WEEK 2
		5–30 **Perception**	31–56 **Wild Things**
Phonics	Decoding	Compound Words	Long *i* Spelled *igh, ie,* Final *y*
	Spelling	Compound Words	Words with Long *i*
Vocabulary	Concept	Can you always believe what you see?	Why do animals act that way?
Amazing Words	Vocabulary	*illusion, invisible, magician, mysterious, perception, vanish*	*communication, instinct, protect, relationships, response, sense, young*
Comprehension	Skill	Sequence	Compare and Contrast
	Strategies	Preview, Ask Questions, Use Story Structure, Summarize	Preview, Ask Questions, Use Story Structure, Summarize
	Writing	Response to Literature	Response to Literature
Fluency		Reread for Fluency Practice	Reread for Fluency Practice

WEEK 3	WEEK 4	WEEK 5	
57–82 **Secret Codes**	83–108 **Communication**	109–134 **Finding Clues**	
Consonant + *le* Syllables	Diphthongs *ou, ow*/ou/	Suffixes *-er, -or, -ish, -ous*	
Words with Consonant + *le*	Words with Diphthongs *ou, ow*	Words with Suffixes	
Why do we need secret codes?	**How can we communicate in different ways?**	**How do we solve a mystery?**	
conceals, creative, exchange, interprets, transmit, visible	*combine, conversation, dialect, phrase, region, shouts, symbols*	*convince, curious, diver, evidence, explorer, investigate, scrutiny*	
Compare and Contrast	Main Idea	Draw Conclusions	
Preview, Ask Questions, Use Story Structure, Summarize	Preview, Ask Questions, Use Story Structure, Summarize	Preview, Ask Questions, Use Story Structure, Summarize	
Response to Literature	Response to Literature	Response to Literature	
Reread for Fluency Practice	Reread for Fluency Practice	Reread for Fluency Practice	

Unit 5

Skills Overview

Why These Skills? *My Sidewalks* focuses on the priority skills students need in order to succeed at learning to read. **Priority skills** are the critical elements of reading—phonemic awareness (Levels A–C), phonics, fluency, vocabulary, and text comprehension. Scientifically based research has shown that these skills are the foundations of reading and must be taught in a systematic sequence.

		WEEK 1 5–30 **Emergencies**	**WEEK 2** 31–56 **Past Times**
Phonics	Decoding	Diphthongs *oi, oy*	Common Syllables *-ion, -tion, -sion, -ture*
	Spelling	Words with Diphthongs *oi, oy*	Words with Common Syllables
Vocabulary	Concept	What can we do in emergencies?	What surprises can the past hold for us?
Amazing Words	Vocabulary	*dangerous, destroyed, exciting, hazards, hero, profession*	*ancient, civilization, society, statue, theater, traditions*
Comprehension	Skill	Compare and Contrast	Compare and Contrast
	Strategies	Preview, Ask Questions, Use Story Structure, Summarize	Preview, Ask Questions, Use Story Structure, Summarize
	Writing	Response to Literature	Response to Literature
Fluency		Reread for Fluency Practice	Reread for Fluency Practice

WEEK 3	WEEK 4	WEEK 5
57–82	83–108	109–134
Adventures and Heroes	**Extreme Homes**	**The Moon**
Vowel Combinations *oo, ew, ue*	Vowel Sound in *ball* Spelled *a, al, au, aw, augh, ough*	Suffixes *-hood, -ment, -y, -en*
Words with Vowel Combinations	Words with Vowel Sound in *ball*	Words with Suffixes
How can adventures change us?	**What do people give up to live in certain places?**	**Why does the moon fascinate us?**
adventure, expeditions, forecasts, unfamiliar, wilderness	*adapted, architecture, burrow, extreme, homesteaders, prairie*	*astronaut, astronomers, craters, mission, myths, satellite*
Sequence	Main Idea	Draw Conclusions
Preview, Ask Questions, Use Story Structure, Summarize	Preview, Ask Questions, Use Story Structure, Summarize	Preview, Ask Questions, Use Story Structure, Summarize
Response to Literature	Response to Literature	Response to Literature
Reread for Fluency Practice	Reread for Fluency Practice	Reread for Fluency Practice

Unit 6
Skills Overview

Why These Skills? *My Sidewalks* focuses on the priority skills students need in order to succeed at learning to read. **Priority skills** are the critical elements of reading—phonemic awareness (Levels A–C), phonics, fluency, vocabulary, and text comprehension. Scientifically based research has shown that these skills are the foundations of reading and must be taught in a systematic sequence.

		WEEK 1 5–30 Opportunity Knocks	**WEEK 2** 31–56 Challenges
Phonics	Decoding	Short *e* Spelled *ea*	Vowels *oo* in *foot*, *u* in *put*
	Spelling	Words with Short *e*	Words with Vowels *oo*, *u*
Vocabulary	Concept	How can we be successful?	How can we overcome obstacles to reach our goals?
Amazing Words	Vocabulary	*circumstances, conviction, devised, model, procrastinates, suggested*	*achieved, furious, hurdles, perseverance, personality, timid*
Comprehension	Skill	Sequence	Draw Conclusions
	Strategies	Preview, Ask Questions, Use Story Structure, Summarize	Preview, Ask Questions, Use Story Structure, Summarize
	Writing	Response to Literature	Response to Literature
Fluency		Reread for Fluency Practice	Reread for Fluency Practice

WEEK 3	WEEK 4	WEEK 5	
57–82 **American Journeys**	83–108 **Grand Gestures**	109–134 **Space**	
Long *i: -ind, -ild;* Long *o: -ost, -old*	V/V Syllables	Related Words	
Words with Long *i,* Long *o*	Words with V/V Syllables	Related Words	
How can moving change our view of the world?	When do people choose to make sacrifices?	How do we reach for the stars?	
appreciate, awkward, barrier, immigration, international, occupations	*apply, determined, distinguishes, efficient, headway, progress*	*complex, futuristic, galaxy, scientific, telescope, universe*	
Draw Conclusions	Main Idea	Compare and Contrast	
Preview, Ask Questions, Use Story Structure, Summarize	Preview, Ask Questions, Use Story Structure, Summarize	Preview, Ask Questions, Use Story Structure, Summarize	
Response to Literature	Response to Literature	Response to Literature	
Reread for Fluency Practice	Reread for Fluency Practice	Reread for Fluency Practice	

Concept Development
to Foster Reading Comprehension

Theme Question: Is there an explanation for everything?

Concept: Puzzles and Mysteries

EXPAND THE CONCEPT

Week 1	Week 2	Week 3	Week 4	Week 5
Lesson Focus Can you always believe what you see?	**Lesson Focus** Why do animals act that way?	**Lesson Focus** Why do we need secret codes?	**Lesson Focus** How can we communicate in different ways?	**Lesson Focus** How do we solve a mystery?

DEVELOP LANGUAGE

Week 1	Week 2	Week 3	Week 4	Week 5
Vocabulary illusion invisible magician mysterious perception vanish	**Vocabulary** communication instinct protect relationships response sense young	**Vocabulary** conceals creative exchange interprets transmit visible	**Vocabulary** combine conversation dialect phrase region shouts symbols	**Vocabulary** convince curious diver evidence explorer investigate scrutiny
Background Reading "Let's Explore: Mystery Spots"	**Background Reading** "Let's Explore: Amazing Homes"	**Background Reading** "Let's Explore: Sports Signals"	**Background Reading** "Let's Explore: Communication"	**Background Reading** "Let's Explore: Dinosaur Hunters"

READ THE LITERATURE

Week 1	Week 2	Week 3	Week 4	Week 5
Biography "Harry Houdini Escapes" **Fantasy** "Inside a Top Hat" **How-to Article** "Disappearing Act!"	**Expository Nonfiction** "Keeping Baby Safe" **Legend** "Black Feather and the Ravens" **Expository Nonfiction** "Animal Expressions"	**Expository Nonfiction** "Codes for Kids" **Realistic Fiction** "A Case of Cat and Mouse" **How-to Article** "Leonardo's Secret Code"	**Expository Nonfiction** "Sending the Message" **Expository Nonfiction** "Trading Phrases" **Expository Nonfiction** "Do You Speak English?"	**Expository Nonfiction** "Monster Mysteries: Bigfoot and Nessie" **Mystery** "The Creature on Pine Tree Lane" **Expository Nonfiction** "The Bermuda Triangle Mystery"

TEACH CONTENT

Week 1	Week 2	Week 3	Week 4	Week 5
Connect to Science • Illusions • How Houdini Did It • Distracting an Audience	**Connect to Science** • Animal Characteristics • Animal Survival • Animal Habitats	**Connect to Social Studies** • Communication • Codes • Leonardo da Vinci	**Connect to Social Studies** • Regional Dialects • Evolving Means of Communication • British vs. American English	**Connect to Science** • Paleontology • Scientific Method • Raccoons • Bermuda Triangle

 Unit 4 develops the same concepts and content-area knowledge as in Scott Foresman's *Reading Street*, Grade 4, Unit 4.

Concept Development
to Foster Reading Comprehension

Theme Question: What makes an adventure?

Concept: Adventures by Land, Air, and Water

EXPAND THE CONCEPT

Week 1	Week 2	Week 3	Week 4	Week 5
Lesson Focus What can we do in emergencies?	**Lesson Focus** What surprises can the past hold for us?	**Lesson Focus** How can adventures change us?	**Lesson Focus** What do people give up to live in certain places?	**Lesson Focus** Why does the moon fascinate us?

DEVELOP LANGUAGE

Vocabulary dangerous destroyed exciting hazards hero profession	**Vocabulary** ancient civilization society statue theater traditions	**Vocabulary** adventure expeditions forecasts unfamiliar wilderness	**Vocabulary** adapted architecture burrow extreme homesteaders prairie	**Vocabulary** astronaut astronomers craters mission myths satellite
Background Reading "Let's Explore: Quick Thinking"	**Background Reading** "Let's Explore: Civilization"	**Background Reading** "Let's Explore: Adventure on the Job"	**Background Reading** "Let's Explore: How We Live"	**Background Reading** "Let's Explore: Phases of the Moon"

READ THE LITERATURE

Expository Nonfiction "Heroes Who Help"	**Expository Nonfiction** "Ancient Builders"	**Expository Nonfiction** "A Lesson in Adventure"	**Expository Nonfiction** "Living Down Under"	**Myth** "One Moon, Many Myths"
Realistic Fiction "Calling New Smokejumpers"	**Realistic Fiction** "It's Still Standing!"	**Realistic Fiction** "Wits Versus Wilderness"	**Narrative Nonfiction** "A Sea of Grass"	**Realistic Fiction** "Saving the Moon Tree"
Expository Nonfiction "Wildfires!"	**Expository Nonfiction** "Forever Sleeping Under Rome"	**Narrative Nonfiction** "Sea Turtle Adventure"	**Poetry** "Old Log House" "Houses"	**Expository Nonfiction** "Moon Facts"

TEACH CONTENT

Connect to Science • Emergencies • Medical Training • Wildfires	**Connect to Social Studies** • Ancient Civilizations • Native American Mound People • Greek Landmarks • Roman Catacombs	**Connect to Social Studies** • Adventurous Work • Outward Bound • Survival	**Connect to Science** • Earth's Resources • Climate • Adapting to Environments • Underground	**Connect to Science** • Moon Phases • Multicultural Moon Myths • Apollo 14 (1971) Moon Mission • Lunar Eclipse

Unit 5 develops the same concepts and content-area knowledge as in Scott Foresman's *Reading Street*, Grade 4, Unit 5.

Concept Development
to Foster Reading Comprehension

Theme Question: What does it take to achieve our goals and dreams?

Concept: Reaching for Goals

EXPAND THE CONCEPT

Week 1	Week 2	Week 3	Week 4	Week 5
Lesson Focus How can we be successful?	**Lesson Focus** How can we overcome obstacles to reach our goals?	**Lesson Focus** How can moving change our view of the world?	**Lesson Focus** When do people choose to make sacrifices?	**Lesson Focus** How do we reach for the stars?

DEVELOP LANGUAGE

Vocabulary circumstances conviction devised model procrastinates suggested	**Vocabulary** achieved furious hurdles perseverance personality timid	**Vocabulary** appreciate awkward barrier immigration international occupations	**Vocabulary** apply determined distinguishes efficient headway progress	**Vocabulary** complex futuristic galaxy scientific telescope universe
Background Reading "Let's Explore: The Ferris Wheel"	**Background Reading** "Let's Explore: The Secret of Success"	**Background Reading** "Let's Explore: Immigration"	**Background Reading** "Let's Explore: Grand Gestures"	**Background Reading** "Let's Explore: What's Out There?"

READ THE LITERATURE

Biography "They Didn't Give Up" **Realistic Fiction** "The Wright Report" **Poetry** "74th Street" "Ladder to the Sky"	**Biography** "Hurdles to Success" **Humorous Fiction** "Sammy the Sofa" **Expository Nonfiction** "Climbing to the Top of the World"	**Biography** "A Shooting Star from China" **Realistic Fiction** "Becoming an American" **Expository Nonfiction** "Traditional Clothing"	**Narrative Nonfiction** "Library Hero" **Expository Nonfiction** "A Simple Gift" **Expository Nonfiction** "A Birthday Give-Away"	**Expository Nonfiction** "Spaceships from Hollywood" **Realistic Fiction** "Searching the Universe" **Expository Nonfiction** "The Sounds of Space"

TEACH CONTENT

Connect to Social Studies • 1893 Chicago World's Fair • Seizing Opportunity Against Long Odds • Wright Brothers • Motivation	**Connect to Social Studies** • Thomas Edison • Persevere to Find Success • Civil Rights • Mount Everest	**Connect to Social Studies** • Immigration • Yao Ming • Cultural Exchange • Ethnic Clothing	**Connect to Social Studies** • Community Awareness and Action • Charities • Heifer International	**Connect to Science** • Telescopes • The Space Age • Outer Space and Science Fiction • Communication Satellites

Unit 6 develops the same concepts and content-area knowledge as in Scott Foresman's *Reading Street*, Grade 4, Unit 6.

Unit 4 Week 1 *Perception*

 Can you always believe what you see?

Objectives *This week students will...*

Vocabulary
- build concepts and vocabulary: *illusion, invisible, magician, mysterious, perception, vanish*

Phonics
- read compound words
- apply knowledge of word structure to decode multisyllabic words when reading

Text Comprehension
- use sequence to improve comprehension
- write in response to literature
- make connections across text

Fluency
- practice fluency with oral rereading

Word Work *This week's phonics focus is . . .*

Compound Words

Amazing Words Concept/Amazing Words *Tested Vocabulary*

The week's vocabulary is related to the concept of perception.
The first appearance of each word in the Student Reader is noted below.

illusion	something that looks different from what it actually is (p. 10)
invisible	cannot be seen with the eye (p. 18)
magician	someone who performs tricks (p. 10)
mysterious	hard to explain or understand (p. 13)
perception	understanding how something works (p. 9)
vanish	to disappear suddenly (p. 10)

Student Reader Unit 4 *This week students will read the following selections.*

8	**Mystery Spots**	Expository Nonfiction
10	**Harry Houdini Escapes**	Biography
18	**Inside a Top Hat**	Fantasy
26	**Disappearing Act!**	How-to Article
30	**4 You 2 Do**	Activity Page

Daily Lesson Plan

	ACTIVITIES	MATERIALS
Day 1	**Build Concepts** Weekly Concept: Perception Vocabulary: *illusion, invisible, magician, mysterious, perception, vanish* **Read a Passage** "Mystery Spots," pp. 8–9 Comprehension: Use Strategies Reread for Fluency **Write** Response to Literature	Student Reader: Unit 4 Routine Cards 2, 4, 5 Tested Vocabulary Cards Student journals Practice Book, p. 61, Vocabulary Student Reader DVD-ROM
Day 2	**Word Work** Phonics: Compound Words Vocabulary: Deepen word meaning **Comprehension** Sequence **Read a Passage** "Harry Houdini Escapes," pp. 10–12 Reread for Fluency **Write** Response to Literature	Student Reader: Unit 4 Practice Book, p. 61, Vocabulary Graphic Organizer 5 Routine Cards 1, 2, 3, 4, 7 Practice Book, p. 62, Compound Words Student Reader DVD-ROM
Day 3	**Word Work** Phonics: Compound Words Vocabulary: Deepen word meaning **Comprehension** Sequence **Read a Passage** "Harry Houdini Escapes," pp. 13–17 Reread for Fluency **Write** Response to Literature	Practice Book, p. 62, Compound Words Tested Vocabulary Cards Student Reader: Unit 4 Graphic Organizer 5 Routine Cards 1, 2, 3, 4, 7 Practice Book, p. 63, Sequence Student Reader DVD-ROM
Day 4	**Word Work** Vocabulary: Extend word knowledge **Comprehension** Skill and Strategy Practice **Read a Passage** "Inside a Top Hat," pp. 18–25 Reread for Fluency **Write** Response to Literature	Practice Book, p. 63, Sequence Student Reader: Unit 4 Routine Cards 2, 3, 4 Student Reader DVD-ROM
Day 5	**Read a Passage** "Disappearing Act," pp. 26–29 Comprehension: Sequence; Listening **Build Concepts** Vocabulary **Write** Response to Literature: "4 You 2 Do," p. 30 **Assessment Options** Fluency Comprehension	Student Reader: Unit 4 Routine Cards 3, 5, 6, 8 Fluency Progress Chart, p. 185 Practice Book, p. 64, Writing

See pp. xvi–xvii for how *My Sidewalks* integrates instructional practices for ELL.

Build Concepts

Amazing Words **Vocabulary**

| To Do | To Say | *10–15 minutes* |

Develop oral vocabulary.

See Routine Card 6 and p. 198.

Introduce the Concept/Amazing Words with an oral routine prior to displaying them in print. Page 198 in this Teacher's Guide provides specific guidelines for introducing each word.

Develop word meaning.

See Routine Card 5.

Discuss pp. 7–9.

Have students read p. 7 and then look at the pictures on pp. 8–9. **Look at the pictures. What do you notice?** (People seem to be leaning in strange directions.) **Can you use the word** *perception* **to describe what's happening?** (Example: Our *perception* that people are tilting may be mistaken.)

Scaffold instruction.

Create a concept web.

In the center of a web, write *Perception*. **This week's concept is** *perception*. *Perception* **is being aware through the senses.** Provide an example to demonstrate meaning. **Our** *perception* **of a kitten comes from seeing (and perhaps touching) it.**

Add the other vocabulary words.

Discuss the meaning of each word as it relates to perception, using the glossary as needed. (See p. 2 in this Teacher's Guide for definitions.)

Concept and Language Goals

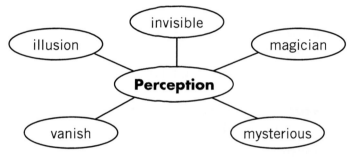

Model the multisyllabic word strategy.

Display each word. Say it as you display it.

Use Tested Vocabulary Cards. Follow this routine for each word:

Think aloud.

- **Look for Meaningful Parts** **Do you recognize any parts of this word? What do these parts mean? Use the parts to read the word.** As you introduce each word, be sure students notice the following: *in-* ("not"), *visible, magic, mystery.*

- **Model** **I see** *in* **at the beginning of** *invisible*. **I know** *in* **can mean "not." I also recognize the word** *visible*. **I know** *visible* **means "able to be seen." So I think** *invisible* **must mean "not visible, or not able to be seen."** Point out the Latin root *vis* ("see") in *invisible*. Discuss other words with this root. (*visible, vision, visor*)

Point to *vanish.*

- **Chunk Words with No Recognizable Parts** Model how to chunk the word *vanish*. **I see a chunk at the beginning of the word:** *van*. **I see a part at the end of the word:** *ish*. **I say each chunk slowly:** *van ish*. **I say the chunks fast to make a whole word:** *vanish*. **Is it a real word? Yes, I know the word** *vanish.*

- Have students practice reading each word.

Preview.

Read p. 6 with students.

Do you see any of the words we just learned on this page? Together with students, read the sentences on p. 6 describing each selection. Talk about how the vocabulary words might be used in the selections.

MORE PRACTICE

Deepen understanding of *perception.*

Have students demonstrate understanding by answering questions. **When you see something from a distance, can your** *perception* **be wrong? Why? Can you believe everything you** *perceive*, **or see? Give an example.**

ACTIVITY 2 Read a Passage

Develop Concepts "Mystery Spots," pp. 8–9

To Do	To Say	*10–15 minutes*

Practice strategic prereading.

See Routine Card 2.

Discuss Genre Read the title on p. 8 and have students look at the illustrations on pp. 8–9. Model determining genre.

Think aloud.

The photographs are a clue that this is nonfiction. They look like photos of real places. I think this article will tell me what "mystery spots" are.

Scaffold instruction.

Review text structure.

Ask Questions What questions do you ask yourself to help you understand nonfiction? (What did I learn? What is this mainly about?) **As you read this article, ask these questions and look for the answers.**

Guide comprehension.

Read pp. 8–9 aloud.

Read Read the article as students follow along. Then read it a second time, having students join in. If necessary, stop at the end of each paragraph to check comprehension. Ask questions to promote discussion and develop the concept.

Develop language and concepts.

- **What is a mystery spot?**

- **What happens at these mystery spots?**

- **Do you believe these things really happen, or are they illusions?**

- **What words on the concept web could help you describe a mystery spot?**

MORE PRACTICE

Have students reread "Mystery Spots." As they read, tell them to make a list of all the strange things that can happen in a mystery spot to share with family members tonight.

Reread for Fluency "Mystery Spots," p. 9

To Do	To Say	*5 minutes*

CORRECTIVE FEEDBACK

Monitor oral reading.

Read p. 9 aloud. Reread the page three or four times so your reading gets better each time. Give feedback on students' oral reading, using the *if . . . then* statements on Routine Card 4. Model fluent reading if necessary. You may want to have students read along with the DVD-ROM.

ACTIVITY 3 Write

Response to Literature

To Do	To Say	*5 minutes*

Prompt journal writing.

Write on the board or a transparency: *Can you always believe what you see?*

Take out your journals. This week we are reading about perception. Our question for this week is: *Can you always believe what you see?* Write an answer to this question based on what you read today. Have students write about the topic, using what they read and their own experiences.

Homework   Practice Book, p. 61, Vocabulary

ACTIVITY 1 Word Work

Phonics Compound Words

	To Do	**To Say**	
			5–10 minutes

Teach compound words.

Write on the board or a transparency: *How long can he hold his breath underwater?*

Remember, when you read a long word, look for meaningful parts. What parts do you see in this word? Frame *under* and *water.*

This word is a compound word. Compound words are made of two smaller words. To read a compound word, find the two smaller words. Put them together to read the word. The two smaller words in this word are *under* and *water.* The word is *underwater.*

Scaffold instruction.

Develop word meaning.

Have students think and converse. If you're *underwater,* you must hold your breath. Why? What kinds of ships can travel *underwater?* Why do they do that?

Write *handcuffs.*

Here is another compound word. What are the two smaller words in this word? (*hand* and *cuffs*) Guide students in blending the word parts into the whole word. Develop word meaning by pointing to the handcuffs pictured on p. 13. Why do the police use handcuffs? How do handcuffs work?

CORRECTIVE FEEDBACK

Write each practice word.

Have students practice reading these compound words. Correct any words students miss and have them reread the list.

cannot   something   tabletop   sometimes   watercolor

MORE PRACTICE

Write more practice words.

Have students practice reading these compound words.

anything   stovetop   waterfall   underground   handmade

Amazing Words Vocabulary

	To Do	**To Say**	
			5 minutes

Review vocabulary.

Review the homework.

Ask students to go over answers and share their writing from Practice Book p. 61. See Routine Card 1 for the multisyllabic word routine.

Deepen understanding of *illusion.*

Remember, an *illusion* is something that appears to be different from what it actually is. When you put a stick in the water, it sometimes looks as if it bends. Why is this an *illusion?* What else is an example of an *illusion?* Why?

ACTIVITY 2 Comprehension

Sequence

	To Do	**To Say**	
			5 minutes

Scaffold instruction.

Introduce sequence.

Today you will read about a real person, Harry Houdini. When you read about a person's life, it's important to keep track of the sequence, or order, of events, because it may help you understand the person. Words like *first, next,* and *finally* give you clues to the sequence.

Model the skill.

For example, if I read that *at first* this person was terribly shy, but *later* she became a famous public speaker, I need to pay attention to the sequence to help me understand how this person changed.

Distribute Graphic Organizer 5.

As you read "Harry Houdini Escapes," look for words that help you track the sequence of events in Houdini's life. Add these words to your graphic organizer. See Routine Card 7.

ACTIVITY **3** Read a Passage

Read for Comprehension "Harry Houdini Escapes," pp. 10–12

10–15 minutes

	To Do	To Say
Scaffold instruction.	Monitor student engagement.	**Read** Have students read pp. 10–12. Stop at the end of each page to ask questions. Students who can read on their own can do so without stopping. After reading, ask questions to promote discussion.
	See Routine Cards 2 and 3.	**On p. 11, what examples of illusions are given?** (a rabbit coming out of an empty hat, an elephant disappearing)
		On p. 12, what words help you follow the sequence? *(at first, over the years)* **What did Houdini do to improve his act?** (He corrected his grammar, exercised to get faster, and practiced holding his breath underwater.)
	Model using context for word meaning.	Read aloud the last two sentences on p. 10 and all of p. 11. Explain how the second sentence on p. 11 provides a clue to the meaning of *illusion* by giving a definition, and the rest of the paragraph gives examples of illusions.
		What do you think the rest of the article will be about? (Answers will vary. The title suggests it will describe one of Houdini's escapes.)
Model summarizing.	Think aloud.	**Summarize** **What were the first three pages mainly about? What did you learn about Harry Houdini?** Think aloud to model summarizing. **I learned a lot of details about Houdini, such as that he could make an elephant disappear. But the main thing I learned was that Houdini was a great magician who could create illusions.**
Develop language and concepts.	Ask questions.	• **Why do you think Harry Houdini became so famous?** • **What does the quote at the beginning of the article mean?**
MORE PRACTICE	Have students reread p. 12, paragraph 1.	**Reread** Tell students to draw a picture that shows what Houdini might have looked like when he first began performing as a magician.

Reread for Fluency "Harry Houdini Escapes," pp. 10–11

5 minutes

	To Do	To Say
MORE PRACTICE **CORRECTIVE FEEDBACK**	Pair students. Monitor paired reading.	Students read aloud pp. 10–11, switching readers at the end of the first page. Have partners reread; now the other partner begins. For optimal fluency, students should reread three or four times. Give feedback, using the *if . . . then* statements on Routine Card 4. You may want to have students read along with the DVD-ROM.

ACTIVITY **4** Write

Response to Literature

5 minutes

	To Do	To Say
Prompt writing.	Writing elements: support	**The article says that being a magician is "hard work." What have you learned so far about Houdini that shows he worked hard to be a good magician? Use details from the article to support your ideas.**
Homework		Practice Book, p. 62, Compound Words

ACTIVITY 1 Word Work

Phonics Compound Words

	To Do	To Say
Review compound words.	Review the homework. Discuss the compound word on p. 14.	Ask students to share answers from Practice Book p. 62. Point out *gentlemen* on p. 14. **Remember, look for meaningful parts when reading a long word. What are the two smaller words in this word?** *(gentle, men)* Guide students in blending the word parts into the word. Then point to *Frenchman* on p. 19, paragraph 2. **What parts do you see in this word? Use the parts to read the word. How is it like *gentleman?*** (It also ends in *man.*) Ask students to think of other words that end in *man* or *men. (firemen, workmen, Englishman)*
MORE PRACTICE	Model spelling compound words.	**Spell and Write** Write *hand* and *cuffs.* **How do we combine these words to make *handcuffs?*** Have a volunteer write *handcuffs.* Remind students that a compound word is made up of two smaller words. Continue with *gentle* and *man.*

Amazing Words Vocabulary

	To Do	To Say
Build vocabulary. **Lead cumulative review.**	Deepen understanding of *vanish* and *invisible.*	Read aloud the two paragraphs on p. 10. **The author gives a clue to the meaning of *vanish.* Can you find a synonym for *vanish* in the first paragraph?** *(disappear)* We learned another word this week that is related to *vanish.* Write *vanish* and *invisible.* **Say a sentence using *vanish* and *invisible.* Would you like to be *invisible?* Why?** Use the Tested Vocabulary Cards to review words from previous weeks.

ACTIVITY 2 Comprehension

Sequence

	To Do	To Say
Scaffold instruction.	Review sequence.	**An author gives you clues to the sequence. Look for dates, phrases like *for two minutes,* and words such as *first, next, finally,* and so on. As you read "Harry Houdini Escapes," look for the sequence of events.**
Guide practice.	Use Graphic Organizer 5.	**Listen as I read p. 13. The author tells about events that happened at different times. What words help you understand the sequence?** *(1908, tonight)* **Add these words to your graphic organizer. What happened before? What is happening now? Words like *it is a night in 1908* tell about what is happening "now" (in 1908). Words like *has escaped* tell things Houdini did before 1908.** See Routine Card 7.
MORE PRACTICE	Have students preview pp. 13–17.	**Read the captions and look at the photos on pp. 13–17. What do you think this section will be about?** (a Houdini act and how it was performed) **Why do you think so?** Think aloud to model using captions and illustrations to predict.
	Think aloud.	**The captions make me think the article will describe Houdini performing a trick. From the pictures I think Houdini will escape from a can full of water.**
Homework		Practice Book, p. 62, Compound Words

ACTIVITY 3 Read a Passage

Read for Comprehension "Harry Houdini Escapes," pp. 13–17

	To Do	To Say	*10–15 minutes*

Scaffold instruction.

To Do: Monitor student engagement.

See Routine Cards 2 and 3.

To Say: **Read** Have students read pp. 13–17. Stop at the end of each page to ask questions. Students who can read on their own can do so without stopping. After reading, ask questions to promote discussion.

How does Houdini try to convince the audience that his trick is not an illusion? (He pounds on the milk can and shows it has no secret openings. A helper stands by with an ax.)

How long does Houdini appear to stay locked in the milk can? (two minutes) **Is he really in the milk can that long? Explain.** (No. He gets out of the can quickly and then waits behind the curtain awhile.)

Review the phonics skill.

To Do: Point out *handcuffed* on p. 15, paragraph 2.

To Say: Remind students they learned the compound word *handcuffs.* The word is used here as a verb. Demonstrate framing the smaller words *hand* and *cuffed.* Have students blend the parts to read the compound word. See Routine Card 1.

Assess comprehension.

To Do: Monitor understanding.

To Say: **After Reading** Have students discuss the What Do You Think? question. Prompt them to use sequence words in telling how Houdini performs the trick. Listen as they talk to assess comprehension.

To Do: Summarize.

To Say: **What is this mainly about? What did you learn?** Work with students to summarize the selection.

MORE PRACTICE

To Do: Have students reread p. 17.

To Say: **Reread** As they read, tell students to note sequence words. *(first, next, finally)* Have students add these words to their graphic organizer. After they read, have them retell how the trick is done using sequence words.

Reread for Fluency "Harry Houdini Escapes," p. 15

	To Do	To Say	*5 minutes*

CORRECTIVE FEEDBACK

To Do: Monitor oral reading.

To Say: Read p. 15 aloud. Reread the page three or four times so your reading gets better each time. Give feedback on students' oral reading, using the *if . . . then* statements on Routine Card 4. Model fluent reading if necessary. You may want to have students read along with the DVD-ROM.

 ACTIVITY 4 Write

Response to Literature

	To Do	To Say	*5 minutes*

MORE PRACTICE

To Do: Prompt writing.

To Say: **What did Houdini do after he escaped to make people think the milk can trick was difficult? Use sequence words such as *first* and *then* to show the order of events.**

Homework Practice Book, p. 63, Sequence

ACTIVITY 1 Word Work

Amazing Words Vocabulary

	To Do	**To Say**	*5–10 minutes*
Extend word knowledge.	Write on the board or a transparency: *Harry Houdini was a great magician.*	Use the word *magician* to extend word knowledge. **Remember we read this word earlier this week. We looked for meaningful parts, and we noticed the word *magic*. Today I want you to notice the suffix -ian. We can use this suffix to read other words.**	
Teach suffix -ian. **Scaffold instruction.**		**The suffix -ian means "someone who is skilled in." So a magician is someone who is skilled in magic. Can you think of other words ending in -ian? (musician, politician, mathematician, electrician) Write words as students name them and some of your own. Talk about the meanings of the words. Point out that *c* is pronounced /sh/ when followed by -ian. Have students practice saying /shən/ as you write *cian* and then practice pronouncing all the words.**	
	Develop word meaning.	**Are a magician's tricks really magic or can they be explained?**	
MORE PRACTICE	Deepen understanding of *magician* and *illusion*.	Have individual students or partners use the two words *magician* and *illusion* in a sentence. (For example: A *magician* creates the *illusion* that she is practicing magic.) Share sentences. Ask: **How does a magician create illusions?**	

ACTIVITY 2 Comprehension

Skill and Strategy Practice

	To Do	**To Say**	*5 minutes*
Scaffold instruction.	Review sequence (homework).	Ask volunteers to read the passage and share answers from Practice Book p. 63. Remind students of the importance of following the sequence. **When you read a story, the sequence of events is often important. Often there are clue words to the order in which things happen. Look for these words. It may also help you to picture in your mind the events as they happen.**	
Practice strategic prereading.	See Routine Card 2.	**Discuss Genre** Read the title and the first paragraph on p. 18 in the Student Reader. Model determining genre.	
	Think aloud.	**I first thought this might be fiction because of the illustrations. When I read the first paragraph, I knew it was fiction because of the rabbit narrator.**	
	Review story structure.	**Ask Questions** **What questions do you ask yourself to help you understand a fictional story?** (What is the problem or goal? How is the problem solved or the goal reached?) **As you read this story, ask these questions and look for the answers.**	

ACTIVITY 3 Read a Passage

Read for Comprehension "Inside a Top Hat," pp. 18–25

	To Do	To Say	*10–15 minutes*
Scaffold instruction.	Monitor student engagement.	**Read** Have students read pp. 18–25 on their own and then discuss. For students who need more help, stop at the end of each page to discuss. After reading, ask questions.	
	See Routine Card 3.	**Who is telling this story?** (Puff, a white rabbit) **Who are the main characters?** (the rabbit and Marva the Mysterious)	
		What is the setting? Where is the rabbit? (inside a top hat, on a stage)	
		What is the rabbit's goal? (to successfully complete the trick and amaze the audience)	
		How does the rabbit get pulled out of the hat? (The rabbit is in a box hidden under a table, below the top hat. The magician reaches into the hat, opens the false bottom, and pulls the rabbit out of the box.)	
	LOOK AT POINT OF VIEW	**Explain whether you think the story would be as interesting if Marva had told it.** (The rabbit's point of view makes it more interesting because you feel you are right there inside the hat during the trick.)	
Assess comprehension.	Monitor understanding.	**After Reading** Have students discuss the What Do You Think? question. Prompt them to use sequence words in telling what steps the magician takes to prepare. Listen as they talk to assess comprehension.	
MORE PRACTICE		**Reread** Have students reread pp. 23–24 and then explain the trick to a partner.	

Reread for Fluency "Inside a Top Hat," pp. 21–24

	To Do	To Say	*5–10 minutes*
CORRECTIVE FEEDBACK	Pair students. Monitor paired reading.	Students read aloud pp. 21–24, switching readers at the end of each page. Have partners reread; now the other partner begins. For optimal fluency, students should reread three or four times. Give feedback, using Routine Card 4. You may want to have students read along with the DVD-ROM.	
MORE PRACTICE	**READERS' THEATER**	Work with a group of three students to adapt pp. 21–24 as a radio play. Have students rehearse reading the parts, with one student being Puff, one a narrator, and one Marva.	

ACTIVITY 4 Write

Response to Literature

	To Do	To Say	*5 minutes*
Prompt narrative writing.	Review pp. 22–24. Writing elements: organization, conventions	**Tell how Marva performs the hat trick. Start with the sentence "First, Marva shows people that the hat is empty." Include other sequence words such as then and last to show the order of events. Use complete sentences to express your ideas.**	

Read a Passage

Read Together *"Disappearing Act!"* pp. 26–29

To Do	To Say
	10 minutes

Scaffold instruction.

Review sequence.

Have students preview pp. 26–29. **This article tells how to do a magic trick. When you read how to do something, the sequence of steps is very important. If you don't do the trick in the right sequence, it won't work. In this article, the author uses big numbers to help you see the sequence, or order, of the steps.**

See Routine Card 3.

Read Read the article as students follow along. Then read it a second time, having students join in on the script. After reading, ask questions.

The introduction says "The secret is to make the audience look where you want them to look." How do you do that? (by looking in a certain direction yourself or pointing)

In steps 2 and 3, why is it important to look only at the quarter? (It encourages the audience to look at the quarter, rather than at what you're doing with the pencil.)

In step 7, you open your fist and the quarter is gone. Why? How do you create the illusion that the quarter has disappeared? (In step 5, you dropped the quarter into your pocket. When you hold out a fist, there is no quarter in it, but the audience doesn't know this.)

Assess comprehension.

Monitor listening comprehension.

Summarize Have one student explain how to do the trick while the others assist.

Build Concepts

Amazing Words Vocabulary

To Do	To Say
	5–10 minutes

Review concept and vocabulary.

Display the concept web you began on Day 1.

This week's question is *Can you always believe what you see?* How do this week's words relate to the question? (Have students answer the question, using some of the vocabulary they learned this week.)

Ask students to add more words to the concept web. Have students explain how each word relates to perception. Monitor students' understanding of vocabulary as they discuss the web. See Routine Card 5.

MORE PRACTICE

Write *magician, perception,* and *illusion* on the board.

Have students relate *magician, perception,* and *illusion.* **Give me an example of an *illusion* created by a magician. Is an *illusion* a true or false *perception?* Why? How does a *magician* use *perception* to help create an *illusion?***

ACTIVITY 3 | Write

Response to Literature "4 You 2 Do," p. 30

To Do	To Say	
		5–10 minutes

Guide response activities.

To Do
Discuss the directions on p. 30. Tell students to choose one activity to complete. See Routine Card 8.

To Say

Word Play Have students complete the first part on their own and then meet with a partner to share word lists and make sentences.

Making Connections Discuss the question in a group. (Houdini created the illusion that he had escaped from inside a locked milk can. Marva created the illusion that a rabbit appeared in an empty top hat.)

On Paper Have students brainstorm some answers to the prompt before they write. Have them write on their own. Students can use Practice Book p. 64 to structure their written responses, or you can send the Practice Book page home for them to complete later.

MORE PRACTICE

If you have more time, direct students to complete all the activities.

ACTIVITY 4 | Assessment Options

Passage Reading

To Do	To Say	
		10–15 minutes

To Do
See Routine Card 6.

Check fluency.
Take a two-minute timed sample of each student's oral reading.

Check comprehension.

To Say

While some students are doing Activity 3, determine which students you want to assess this week and choose from these options.

Fluency Have a student read for two minutes from "Inside a Top Hat." Record the number of correct words read per minute. See p. 184 for monitoring fluency. Be sure each student is assessed at least every other week.

Have students graph their progress on the Fluency Progress Chart, p. 185.

Retelling Have students reread "Inside a Top Hat" and retell it. Prompt students if necessary. See p. 186 for monitoring retelling.

If you have time, assess every student.

Homework   Practice Book, p. 64, Writing

Unit 4 Week 2 *Wild Things*

 Why do animals act that way?

Objectives *This week students will...*

Vocabulary
- build concepts and vocabulary: *communication, instinct, protect, relationships, response, sense, young*

Phonics
- read the sound long *i* spelled *igh, ie,* final *y*
- apply knowledge of word structure to decode multisyllabic words when reading

Text Comprehension
- use compare and contrast to improve comprehension
- write in response to literature
- make connections across text

Fluency
- practice fluency with oral rereading

Word Work *This week's phonics focus is . . .*

Long *i* Spelled *igh, ie,* Final *y*

Amazing Words Concept/Amazing Words *Tested Vocabulary*

The week's vocabulary is related to the concept of wild things, or animal behavior.
The first appearance of each word in the Student Reader is noted below.

communication	giving news or information (p. 40)
instinct	a way of acting that an animal is born with, not learned (p. 38)
protect	to keep someone or something safe from harm or danger; defend (p. 34)
relationships	connections between people, groups, and other things (p. 46)
response	reaction by a living thing to some change in its surroundings (p. 44)
sense	to feel, to be aware of; to understand (p. 41)
young	children of humans and animals; offspring (p. 36)

Student Reader Unit 4 *This week students will read the following selections.*

Daily Lesson Plan

	ACTIVITIES	MATERIALS
Day 1	**Build Concepts** Weekly Concept: Wild Things Vocabulary: *communication, instinct, protect, relationships, response, sense, young* **Read a Passage** "Amazing Homes," pp. 34–35 Comprehension: Use Strategies Reread for Fluency **Write** Response to Literature	Student Reader: Unit 4 Routine Cards 2, 4, 5 Tested Vocabulary Cards Student journals Practice Book, p. 65, Vocabulary Student Reader DVD-ROM
Day 2	**Word Work** Phonics: Long *i* Spelled *igh, ie,* Final *y* Vocabulary: Deepen word meaning **Comprehension** Compare and Contrast **Read a Passage** "Keeping Baby Safe," pp. 36–39 Reread for Fluency **Write** Response to Literature	Student Reader: Unit 4 Practice Book, p. 65, Vocabulary Graphic Organizer 4 Routine Cards 1, 2, 3, 4, 7 Practice Book, p. 66, Long *i* Spelled *igh, ie,* Final *y* Student Reader DVD-ROM
Day 3	**Word Work** Phonics: Long *i* Spelled *igh, ie,* Final *y* Vocabulary: Deepen word meaning **Comprehension** Compare and Contrast **Read a Passage** "Keeping Baby Safe," pp. 40–43 Reread for Fluency **Write** Response to Literature	Practice Book, p. 66, Long *i* Spelled *igh, ie,* Final *y* Tested Vocabulary Cards Student Reader: Unit 4 Graphic Organizer 4 Routine Cards 2, 3, 4, 7 Practice Book, p. 67, Compare and Contrast Student Reader DVD-ROM
Day 4	**Word Work** Vocabulary: Extend word knowledge **Comprehension** Skill and Strategy Practice **Read a Passage** "Black Feather and the Ravens," pp. 44–51 Reread for Fluency **Write** Response to Literature	Practice Book, p. 67, Compare and Contrast Student Reader: Unit 4 Routine Cards 2, 3, 4 Student Reader DVD-ROM
Day 5	**Read a Passage** "Animal Expressions," pp. 52–55 Comprehension: Compare and Contrast; Listening **Build Concepts** Vocabulary **Write** Response to Literature: "4 You 2 Do," p. 56 **Assessment Options** Fluency Comprehension	Student Reader: Unit 4 Routine Cards 3, 5, 6, 8 Fluency Progress Chart, p. 185 Practice Book, p. 68, Writing

See pp. xvi–xvii for how *My Sidewalks* integrates instructional practices for ELL.

ACTIVITY 1 Build Concepts

Amazing Words **Vocabulary**

	To Do	**To Say**	*10–15 minutes*

Develop oral vocabulary.

See Routine Card 6 and p. 199.

Introduce the Concept/Amazing Words with an oral routine prior to displaying them in print. Page 199 in this Teacher's Guide provides specific guidelines for introducing each word.

Develop word meaning.

See Routine Card 5. Discuss pp. 33–34.

Have students read p. 33 and then look at the pictures on p. 34. **What do you see?** (a beaver building its lodge) **How could you relate the word** *behavior* **to this animal's home?** (Example: The type of home an animal builds depends on the animal's *behavior,* or actions.)

Scaffold instruction.

Create a concept web.

In the center of a web, write *Animal Behavior.* **This week's concept is** *wild things,* **or** *animal behavior. Behavior* **is a way of acting. Many animals are known for certain behaviors. What common animal behaviors have you observed?** (Examples: Cats lick themselves clean; dogs turn in circles before lying down; roosters crow at daybreak.) **The more we know of** *animal behavior,* **the more we can understand things in nature.**

Add the other vocabulary words.

Concept and Language Goals

Discuss the meaning of each word as it relates to animal behavior. (See p. 14 of this Teacher's Guide for definitions.)

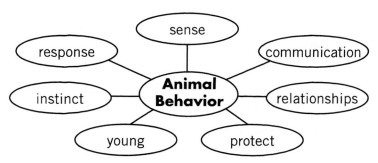

Model the multisyllabic word strategy.

Display each word. Say it as you display it.

Use Tested Vocabulary Cards. Follow this routine for each word:

- **Look for Meaningful Parts** Do you recognize any parts of this word? What do these parts mean? Use the parts to read the word. As you introduce each word, be sure students notice the following: *communicate* and *relation.*

Think aloud.

- **Model** I see the word *relation* at the beginning of *relationships.* I know *relations* can mean "people who are in the same family" or "connections between people or groups." I also know that the suffix *-ship* means "the condition of being something." So *relationships* must mean "connections or conditions of being connected."

Point to *protect.*

- **Chunk Words with No Recognizable Parts** Model how to chunk the word *protect:* I see a chunk at the beginning of the word: *pro.* I see a part at the end of the word: *tect.* I say each chunk slowly: *pro tect.* I say the chunks fast to make a whole word: *protect.* Is it a real word? Yes, I know the word *protect.*

- Have students practice reading each word.

Preview.

Read p. 32 with students.

Do you see any of the words we just learned on these pages? Together with students, read the sentences on p. 32 describing each selection. Talk about how the vocabulary words might be used in the selections.

MORE PRACTICE

Deepen understanding of *instinct.*

Have students demonstrate understanding by answering questions. **What animal behaviors do you think are** *instincts?* **What human behaviors might be** *instincts?* **Give an example of each. Explain your thinking.**

ACTIVITY 2 Read a Passage

Develop Concepts "Amazing Homes," pp. 34–35

To Do	To Say	

10–15 minutes

Practice strategic prereading.

See Routine Card 2.

Think aloud.

Discuss Genre Read the title on pp. 34–35 and have students look at the illustrations. Model determining genre.

The photographs are a clue that this may be nonfiction. They look like photos of real animals and places. I think this article will tell about the "amazing homes" that certain animals live in.

Scaffold instruction.

Review text structure.

Ask Questions What questions do you ask yourself to help you understand nonfiction? (What did I learn? What is this mainly about?) As you read this article, ask these questions and look for the answers.

Guide comprehension.

Read pp. 34–35 aloud.

Read the article as students follow along. Then read it a second time, having students join in. If necessary, stop at the end of each paragraph to check comprehension. Ask questions to promote discussion and develop the concept.

Develop language and concepts.

- What is amazing about building a home in the middle of a pond?
- What might harm a beaver lodge?
- How does a hermit crab's stomach affect its choice of a home?
- What protects a hermit crab's home?
- What words on the concept web could help you describe an amazing home?

MORE PRACTICE

Have students reread "Amazing Homes." As they read, tell them to make a list of questions they would like to ask about beaver and hermit crab homes. They can discuss these questions with family members tonight.

Reread for Fluency "Amazing Homes," pp. 34–35

To Do	To Say	

5 minutes

CORRECTIVE FEEDBACK

Monitor oral reading.

Read p. 34 aloud. Reread the page three or four times so your reading gets better each time. Give feedback on students' oral reading, using the *if . . . then* statements on Routine Card 4. Model fluent reading if necessary. You may want to have students read along with the DVD-ROM.

ACTIVITY 3 Write

Response to Literature

To Do	To Say	

5 minutes

Prompt journal writing.

Write on the board or a transparency: *Why do animals act that way?*

Take out your journals. This week we are reading about animal behavior. Our question for this week is: *Why do animals act that way?* Write an answer to this question based on what you read today. Have students write about the topic, using what they read and their own experiences.

Homework

Practice Book, p. 65, Vocabulary

ACTIVITY 1 | Word Work

Phonics Long *i* Spelled *igh, ie,* Final *y*

	To Do	**To Say**	*5–10 minutes*

Teach long *i* spelled *igh, ie,* final *y*.

Write on the board or a transparency: *Why might you lie down?*

Read the sentence. Listen for the vowel sounds. How many words contain the sound long *i*? (3) How is the sound long *i* spelled in those words? *(y, igh, ie)* When *ie* or *igh* appear together, these letters usually stand for the sound long *i*. The letter *y* at the end of a word or syllable stands for either long *i* (as in *cry*) or long *e* (as in *baby*).

Scaffold instruction.

Write *frightened* and *python*.

Develop word meaning.

Would you feel like this if one of these came by? Let's read the words together. Remember to look for meaningful parts when you read a long word. Do you see any parts you know in these words? (Students may notice *fright* in *frightened*.) If you don't see any meaningful parts, you can look for chunks. Think about how you pronounce the vowel in each chunk. Model reading the chunks *py* and *thon* in *python*. Clarify that although the word *python* does not end in *y*, its first syllable does. Then help students read the chunks *fright* and *ened* in *frightened*.

CORRECTIVE FEEDBACK

Write each practice word.

Have students practice reading these long *i* words. Correct any words students miss and have them reread the list.

sighing	nighttime	fighting	crying	hydrant	fireflies	skylight

MORE PRACTICE

Write more practice words.

Have students practice reading these additional words with long *i*.

higher	brightest	lullaby	shyness	dragonfly	replied	terrified

Vocabulary

	To Do	**To Say**	*5 minutes*

Review vocabulary.

Review the homework.

Ask students to go over answers and share their writing from Practice Book, p. 65. See Routine Card 1 for the multisyllabic word routine.

Deepen understanding of *protect*.

Remember, to *protect* means "to keep safe from harm or danger." Think about how the homes of the beaver and hermit crab *protect* them. What behaviors do you know that animals use to *protect* themselves?

ACTIVITY 2 | Comprehension

Compare and Contrast

	To Do	**To Say**	*5 minutes*

Scaffold instruction.

Introduce compare and contrast.

Today you will read about how animal parents keep their young safe. You already know that humans and animals have many similar behaviors. As you read, look for ways to compare and contrast animal behaviors with human behaviors. The compare and contrast strategy helps you make sense of the text and link it to what you already know. Look for clue words, such as *both, like, similar, but, however, unlike.*

Model the skill.

For example, if I read *both care for their young*, I know that here is something humans and animals do that is alike.

Distribute Graphic Organizer 4.

As you read "Keeping Baby Safe," look for ways that animals and humans are alike and different. Record likenesses and differences and words that signal them *(both, but)* on your graphic organizer. See Routine Card 7.

ACTIVITY **3** ## Read a Passage

Read for Comprehension "Keeping Baby Safe," pp. 36–39

To Do	To Say	
		5–10 minutes

Scaffold instruction.

Monitor student engagement.

Read Have students read pp. 36–39. Stop at the end of each page to ask questions. Students who can read on their own can do so without stopping. After reading, ask questions to promote discussion.

See Routine Cards 2 and 3.

On p. 36, what examples show behaviors that animals and humans share? (Both protect, care for, and communicate with their young.)

On p. 39, what is the main contrast given between human and animal parents? (Most animals lack arms, so they must move their young in other ways.)

Point out *everywhere* and *sometimes* on p. 38.

Remember, when you read a long word, look for meaningful parts. What parts do you see in *everywhere*? Frame *every* and *where*. **This word is a compound word. To read a compound word, find the two smaller words. Put them together to read and understand the word.** Have students practice reading *sometimes*.

What behaviors of parents and their young do you think you will learn about? (parents working together, children recognizing parents, traveling)

Model summarizing.

Think aloud.

Summarize **What were the first four pages mainly about? What did you learn about animal behavior?** Think aloud to model summarizing. **I learned certain things that penguin, swan, and lion parents do to care for their young. But the main thing I learned was that both animal and human parents have similar caring instincts.**

Develop language and concepts.

Ask questions.

- **In what ways do instincts help animal parents keep their young safe? In what ways do instincts help the young survive?**
- **Why is it hard to keep animal babies safe?**

MORE PRACTICE

Have students reread p. 39.

Reread After students read, brainstorm to come up with situations that might cause a mother lion to move her cubs as described here.

Reread for Fluency "Keeping Baby Safe," pp. 36–37

To Do	To Say	
		5 minutes

MORE PRACTICE

CORRECTIVE FEEDBACK

Pair students. Listen and give feedback.

Students read aloud pp. 36–37, switching readers at the end of the first page. Have partners reread; now the other partner begins. For optimal fluency, students should reread three or four times. Give feedback, using the *if . . . then* statements on Routine Card 4. You may want to have students read along with the DVD-ROM.

 ACTIVITY **4** ## Write

Response to Literature

To Do	To Say	
		5 minutes

Prompt writing.

Writing elements: support

The article says that animals and humans protect and care for their young. What have you learned so far about the ways that animals protect and care for their young? Include specific examples from the article to support your response.

Homework

Practice Book, p. 66, Long *i* Spelled *igh, ie*, Final *y*

ACTIVITY 1 Word Work

Phonics Long *i* Spelled *igh, ie*, Final *y*

	To Do	To Say	
			5 minutes

Review long *i* spelled *igh, ie*, final *y*.

Review the homework. Discuss long *i* words on p. 40.

Ask students to share answers from Practice Book p. 66.

Point out *cries* on p. 40. **What vowel sound do you hear in this word?** (long *i*) **How is it spelled?** *(ie)* Point out *crying*. **How is the long *i* spelled?** *(y)*

Ask students to think of other words that end in *y* and have the sound long *i*. *(shy, dry, fly, deny, try, July, satisfy)*

MORE PRACTICE

Model spelling words with the long *i* vowel sound.

Spell and Write Write *right, tie*, and *by*. Say *right*. **What vowel sound do you hear? What letters spell that vowel sound?** Underline *igh*. Continue with *tie (ie)* and *by (y)*. **Look for long *i* words and tell what letters spell the long *i* sound.**

Amazing Words Vocabulary

	To Do	To Say	
			5 minutes

Build vocabulary.

Lead cumulative review.

Deepen understanding of *communication* and *sense*.

Point out *communication* on p. 40. **The author gives a clue to the meaning of *communication* by making a comparison. What does *communication* mean here?** (the exchange of information between parents and their young) **We learned another word this week that is related to *communication*.** Point out *sense* on p. 41. **How do parents know when there is danger? How do they communicate what they sense?**

Use the Tested Vocabulary Cards to review words from previous weeks.

ACTIVITY 2 Comprehension

Compare and Contrast

	To Do	To Say	
			5–10 minutes

Scaffold instruction.

Review compare and contrast.

Remind students that authors compare and contrast examples to help readers better understand the ideas they want to convey. **An author helps you understand new ideas by comparing them with things you already know. The author of this article compares and contrasts how animal parents care for their young with how human parents do this. As you read the second part of "Keeping Baby Safe," look for comparisons and contrasts. Write them on your graphic organizer.**

Guide practice.

Use Graphic Organizer 4.

Listen as I read p. 40. I want you to picture human and animal parents and their young. Think of likenesses and differences. Read p. 40. Then ask: **What parents did the author compare?** (humans and raccoons) **What do both kinds of young do?** (cry out) **How do both kinds of parents respond?** (with comforting sounds) **How are the responses different?** (Humans speak; raccoons purr.) See Routine Card 7.

MORE PRACTICE

Have students preview pp. 40–43.

Read the headings and look at the photos on pp. 40–43. What do you think this section will cover? (more ways animals protect their young; when the young go out on their own) **Why do you think so?** Think aloud to model using headings and illustrations to predict.

Think aloud.

These headings make me think the article will tell how animals communicate with their young and send their young out on their own. From the pictures, I think the author will use contrasting examples with different kinds of animals.

Read a Passage

Read for Comprehension "Keeping Baby Safe," pp. 40–43

10–15 minutes

	To Do	**To Say**
Scaffold instruction.	Monitor student engagement. See Routine Cards 2 and 3.	**Read** Have students read pp. 40–43 on their own and then discuss. For students who need more help, stop at the end of each page to discuss. After reading, ask questions to promote discussion. **How do animals sense danger?** (Their instinct tells them when trouble is near.) **In what ways do clownfish families differ from bear and human families?** (Clownfish babies are born knowing all they need to survive. The parents let them go; bears and humans spend time raising their young.)
Review the phonics skill.	Point out *fry* on p. 43, paragraph 2.	Remind students they learned the sound long *i* spelled *y*. The word *fry*, which contains this sound, is a noun as used here. Students may know the verb *fry* as a cooking term.
Assess comprehension.	Monitor understanding. Summarize.	**After Reading** Have students discuss the What Do You Think? question. Prompt them to compare likenesses in telling about two animals caring for their young. Listen as they talk to assess comprehension. **What is this mainly about? What did you learn?** Work with students to summarize the selection.
MORE PRACTICE	Have students reread p. 43.	**Reread** As they read, tell students to contrast the roles the mother and father clownfish have in bringing young clownfish to life. After they read, have students identify a behavior of clownfish parents that is most unlike the behavior of human parents.

Reread for Fluency "Keeping Baby Safe," p. 40

5 minutes

	To Do	**To Say**
CORRECTIVE FEEDBACK	Pair students. Monitor paired reading.	Students read aloud p. 40, switching readers at the end of each paragraph. Have partners reread; now the other partner begins. For optimal fluency, students should reread three or four times. Give feedback, using the *if . . . then* statements on Routine Card 4. You may want to have students read along with the DVD-ROM.

 Write

Response to Literature

5 minutes

	To Do	**To Say**
MORE PRACTICE	Prompt writing.	**Describe some of the ways that animals communicate with their young without using words? Use vivid words and complete sentences to express your ideas.**
Homework		Practice Book, p. 67, Compare and Contrast

ACTIVITY 1 Word Work

Amazing Words Vocabulary

	To Do	To Say	5–10 minutes

Extend word knowledge. | Write on the board or a transparency: *communication*. | Use the word *communication* to extend word knowledge. **Remember we read this word earlier in the week. We chunked it to decode it, and we noticed familiar parts, such as *tion*. Today I want you to look at other words related to *communication*.**

Read related forms. | Write *communicate, communicator, communicating* | **Look at these related words. Let's read them together.** Talk about the meaning and usage of each word. **Can you give me a sentence for each word?** Write representative sentences on the board.

Scaffold instruction. | Develop word meaning. | **How does body language help you *communicate* without words?** Answers will vary. Have students demonstrate gestures that convey meaning without the use of words or sounds.

MORE PRACTICE | Deepen understanding of *relationships* and *communication*. | Have individual students or partners use the two words *communication* and *relationships* in a sentence. (Example: Good *communication* helps us have better *relationships* with others.) Share sentences. Ask: **In what ways can *relationships* develop between humans and animals?**

ACTIVITY 2 Comprehension

Skill and Strategy Practice

	To Do	To Say	5 minutes

Scaffold instruction. | Review compare and contrast (homework). | Ask volunteers to read the passage and share answers from Practice Book p. 67. Remind students of the value of comparing and contrasting to strengthen understanding. **When you read a story, you can compare and contrast how characters behave. You can also compare and contrast how you might behave in similar situations. Think about similarities and differences as you read today's selection. They will help you understand how relationships develop in the story.**

Practice strategic prereading. | See Routine Card 2. | **Discuss Genre** Read the title, the paragraph on p. 44, and the first paragraph on p. 45 in the Student Reader. Model determining genre.

| Think aloud. | **I first thought this might be fiction because of the illustrations. When I read the first two paragraphs, I knew it was fiction because of the "once-upon-a-time" setting, the description of the title character, and the talking animals. But more than that, I can tell from the sign the raven has in its beak that this is a legend. Now I know that it is an old story that was told and retold over the years.**

| Review story structure. | **Ask Questions** **What questions do you ask yourself to help you understand a legend?** (As in most fictional stories: What is the problem or goal? How is the problem solved or the goal reached?) **As you read this story, ask these questions and look for the answers.**

22 DAY 4 Wild Things

ACTIVITY 3 Read a Passage

Read for Comprehension "Black Feather and the Ravens," pp. 44–51

	To Do	To Say	*10–15 minutes*

Scaffold instruction.

To Do: Monitor student engagement.

See Routine Card 3.

To Say: **Read** Have students read pp. 44–51 on their own and then discuss. For students who need more help, stop at the end of each page to discuss. After reading, ask questions.

Who is the main character in this story? (a man named Black Feather)

What early clue confirms that this story is not realistic? (Ravens and a human speak together.)

What is Black Feather's goal? (to learn more about the ravens) **Why is this a problem?** (Ravens and humans are different creatures; they live and behave differently; Black Feather's neighbors think he is odd.)

Describe how the relationship between Black Feather and the ravens changes. (Black Feather learns more about the ravens. Eventually, they learn to accept and adapt to each other's ways.)

LOOK AT A LEGEND

A legend is a story passed on by being told and retold orally. Some legends have lessons. What lesson does Black Feather learn? (Understanding those different from us can lead to acceptance on everyone's part.)

Assess comprehension.

To Do: Monitor understanding.

To Say: **After Reading** Have students discuss the What Do You Think? question. Prompt them to compare and contrast raven and human behaviors using words such as *too* and *but*. Listen as they talk to assess comprehension.

MORE PRACTICE

Reread Have students reread pp. 50–51 and then explain how they know that the problems between Black Feather and the ravens are solved.

Reread for Fluency "Black Feather and the Ravens," pp. 48–49

	To Do	To Say	*5–10 minutes*

CORRECTIVE FEEDBACK

To Do: Pair students. Monitor paired reading.

To Say: Students read aloud pp. 48–49, switching readers at the end of each paragraph. Have partners reread; now the other partner begins. For optimal fluency, students should reread three or four times. Give feedback, using Routine Card 4. You may want to have students read along with the DVD-ROM.

MORE PRACTICE

READERS' THEATER

Work with a group of three or four students to adapt pp. 48–49 as a scene. Have students rehearse reading the parts, with one student being the narrator; another, Black Feather; and the rest, ravens.

ACTIVITY 4 Write

Response to Literature

	To Do	To Say	*5 minutes*

Prompt expository writing.

To Do: Writing elements: support

To Say: **Explain why the ravens drop a walnut on Black Feather's head, peck him, and call him names.** (Students should include specific information from the selection to support their ideas.)

ACTIVITY 1 Read a Passage

Read Together "Animal Expressions," pp. 52–55

| | **To Do** | **To Say** | *10 minutes* |

10 minutes

Scaffold instruction.

Review compare and contrast.

Have students preview pp. 52–55. **This article explains expressions based on actual animal behaviors. You will learn a scientific fact behind each expression. Each expression compares behaviors of animals to those of people. Some of these expressions use the words *like* or *as* to make comparisons.**

Preview the article.

Read the eight expressions with students. Have students indicate which ones they have heard before and which ones are unfamiliar to them.

See Routine Card 3.

Read Read the article as students follow along. Then read it a second time, having students join in to read each expression and its explanation. After reading, ask questions.

Look at p. 53. What *instinct* does a horse lack? What *instinct* do lion groups follow when they feed? (Horses lack the instinct to stop eating. Male lions feed first; then the females eat.)

How is a map like a bird's-eye view of a place? (It is a flat picture of how a place would look from high above.)

When have you been an early bird? How did it help?

Assess comprehension.

Monitor listening comprehension.

Summarize Have students summarize some of the most interesting animal behaviors they learned about in this week's readings.

ACTIVITY 2 Build Concepts

Amazing Words Vocabulary

| | **To Do** | **To Say** | *5–10 minutes* |

5–10 minutes

Review concept and vocabulary.

Display the concept web you began on Day 1.

This week's question is: *Why do animals act that way?* How do this week's words relate to the question? (Have students answer the question, using some of the vocabulary they learned this week.)

Ask students to add more words to the concept web. Have students explain how each word relates to animal behavior. Monitor students' understanding of vocabulary as they discuss the web. See Routine Card 5.

MORE PRACTICE

Write *response, young,* and *relationships* on the board.

Have students relate *response, young,* and *relationships.* **Parents of all kinds build *relationships* with their *young* by using certain *responses* over and over again. Why? Give an example of a parent's *response* to danger in birds, lions, and humans. How do *responses* like these build the *relationships* between parents and their *young?* What kinds of *responses* are you used to in your *relationship* with a good friend?**

ACTIVITY **3** Write

Response to Literature "4 You 2 Do," p. 56

| To Do | To Say | *10–15 minutes* |

Guide response activities.

To Do: Discuss the directions on p. 56. Tell students to choose one activity to complete. See Routine Card 8.

To Say:

Word Play Have students start on their own and then meet with a partner to share word lists.

Making Connections Discuss the question in a group. (Understanding animals helps you understand some of your own behaviors; it makes you see how and why animals act as they do; it might make you less afraid of some animals.)

On Paper Brainstorm some characters, problems, or lessons with the group before students write. Tell students that instead of writing a complete folk tale, they need only describe a main character, tell about a problem and how it is resolved, and perhaps tell about the lesson learned. Have them write on their own. Students can use Practice Book p. 68 to structure their written responses, or you can send the Practice Book page home for them to complete later.

MORE PRACTICE

If you have more time, direct students to complete all the activities. Students who wrote about a legend or folk tale may wish to flesh out their writings by telling the whole story.

ACTIVITY **4** Assessment Options

Passage Reading

| To Do | To Say | *10–15 minutes* |

To Do: See Routine Card 6.

To Say: While some students are doing Activity 3, determine which students you want to assess this week and choose from these options.

Check fluency.

To Do: Take a two-minute timed sample of each student's oral reading.

Fluency Have a student read for two minutes from "Keeping Baby Safe." Record the number of correct words read per minute. See p. 184 for monitoring fluency. Be sure each student is assessed at least every other week.

Have students graph their progress on the Fluency Progress Chart, p. 185.

Check comprehension.

Retelling Have students reread "Keeping Baby Safe" and retell it. Prompt students if necessary. See p. 186 for monitoring retelling.

If you have time, assess every student.

Homework   Practice Book, p. 68, Writing

Unit 4 Week 3 *Secret Codes*

 Why do we need secret codes?

Objectives *This week students will...*

Vocabulary
- build concepts and vocabulary: *conceals, creative, exchange, interprets, transmit, visible*

Phonics
- read consonant + *le* syllables (open and closed)
- apply knowledge of word structure to decode multisyllabic words when reading

Text Comprehension
- use compare and contrast to improve comprehension
- write in response to literature
- make connections across texts

Fluency
- practice fluency with oral rereading

Word Work *This week's phonics focus is . . .*

Consonant + *le* Syllables

Amazing Words Concept/Amazing Words *Tested Vocabulary*

The week's vocabulary is related to the concept of secret codes.
The first appearance of each word in the Student Reader is noted below.

conceals	hides (p. 62)
creative	being able to think of new things or ideas (p. 62)
exchange	to give and take things of the same kind (p. 60)
interprets	understands (p. 60)
transmit	to send out signals (p. 62)
visible	able to be seen (p. 61)

Student Reader Unit 4 *This week students will read the following selections.*

Daily Lesson Plan

	ACTIVITIES	MATERIALS
Day 1	**Build Concepts** Weekly Concept: Secret Codes Vocabulary: *conceals, creative, exchange, interprets, transmit, visible* **Read a Passage** "Sports Signals," pp. 60–63 Comprehension: Use Strategies Reread for Fluency **Write** Response to Literature	Student Reader: Unit 4 Routine Cards 2, 4, 5 Tested Vocabulary Cards Student journals Practice Book, p. 69, Vocabulary Student Reader DVD-ROM
Day 2	**Word Work** Phonics: Consonant + *le* Syllables Vocabulary: Deepen word meaning **Comprehension** Compare and Contrast **Read a Passage** "Codes for Kids," pp. 64–67 Reread for Fluency **Write** Response to Literature	Student Reader: Unit 4 Practice Book, p. 69, Vocabulary Graphic Organizer 3 Routine Cards 1, 2, 3, 4, 7 Practice Book, p. 70, Consonant + *le* Syllables Student Reader DVD-ROM

Day 3	**Word Work** Phonics: Consonant + *le* Syllables
	Vocabulary: Deepen word meaning
	
	Comprehension Compare and Contrast
	
	Read a Passage "Codes for Kids," pp. 68–71
	Reread for Fluency
	
	Write Response to Literature
		Practice Book, p. 70, Consonant + *le*
		  Syllables
		Tested Vocabulary Cards
		Student Reader: Unit 4
		Graphic Organizer 3
		Routine Cards 2, 3, 4, 7
		Practice Book, p. 71, Compare and
		  Contrast
		Student Reader DVD-ROM

Day 4	**Word Work** Vocabulary: Extend word knowledge **Comprehension** Skill and Strategy Practice **Read a Passage** "A Case of Cat and Mouse," pp. 72–79 Reread for Fluency **Write** Response to Literature	Practice Book, p. 71, Compare and Contrast Student Reader: Unit 4 Routine Cards 2, 3, 4 Student Reader DVD-ROM
Day 5	**Read a Passage** "Leonardo's Secret Code," pp. 80–81 Comprehension: Compare and Contrast; Listening **Build Concepts** Vocabulary **Write** Response to Literature: "4 You 2 Do," p. 82 **Assessment Options** Fluency Comprehension	Student Reader: Unit 4 Routine Cards 3, 5, 6, 8 Fluency Progress Chart, p. 185 Practice Book, p. 72, Writing

See pp. xvi–xvii for ways *My Sidewalks* integrates instructional practices for ELL.

ACTIVITY 1 | Build Concepts

Amazing Words Vocabulary

	To Do	**To Say**
Develop oral vocabulary.	See Routine Card 6 and p. 200.	Introduce the Concept/Amazing Words with an oral routine prior to displaying them in print. Page 200 in this Teacher's Guide provides specific guidelines for introducing each word.
Develop word meaning.	See Routine Card 5. Discuss pp. 59–63.	Have students read p. 59 and then look at the pictures on pp. 60–63. **What do you notice?** (athletes, some using sports signals) **Can you use the words *secret codes* to describe what you see?** (The signals players use during a game are like *secret codes*.)
Scaffold instruction.	Create a concept web.	In the center of a web, write *Secret Codes*. **This week's concept is *secret codes*. *Secret codes* are private signals people can use to communicate with each other.** Provide an example to demonstrate meaning. Hold your pinky and thumb as if you are talking on a telephone. **If I hold my hand like this, I am using a *secret code* to communicate, "Call me."**
	Add the other vocabulary words.	Discuss the meaning of each word as it relates to secret codes, using the glossary as needed. (See p. 26 in this Teacher's Guide for definitions.)
	Concept and Language Goals	

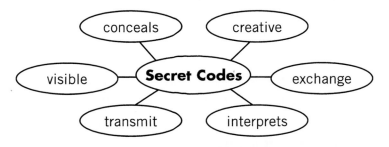

Model the multisyllabic word strategy.	Display each word. Say it as you display it.	Use the Tested Vocabulary Cards. Follow this routine for each word:
		• **Look for Meaningful Parts** Do you recognize any parts of this word? What do the parts mean? Use the parts to read the word. Be sure students notice the following: *conceal, create, change, interpret.*
	Point to *visible*.	• **Chunk Words with No Recognizable Parts** Model how to chunk the word *visible* to read it.
	Think aloud.	• **Model** I see a chunk at the beginning of the word: *vis.* I see a chunk in the middle: *i* and one at the end of the word: *ble.* I say each chunk slowly: *vis i ble.* I say the chunks fast to make a whole word: *visible.* Is it a real word? Yes, I know the word *visible.*
		• Have students practice reading each word.
Preview.	Read p. 58 with students.	**Do you see any words we just learned on this page?** Together with students, read the sentences on p. 58 describing each selection. Talk about how the vocabulary words might be used in the selections.
MORE PRACTICE	Deepen understanding of *secret codes*.	Have students demonstrate understanding by answering questions. **If I put my finger to my lips, I am using a *secret code*. What does that *secret code* mean?** (hush) **What other *secret codes* do we use in this classroom? Give examples.**

ACTIVITY 2   Read a Passage

Develop Concepts "Sports Signals," pp. 60–63

	To Do	**To Say**	*10–15 minutes*

Practice strategic prereading.

See Routine Card 2.

Think aloud.

Discuss Genre Read the title on p. 60 and look at the pictures on pp. 60–63. Model determining genre.

The photographs are a clue that this is nonfiction. They look like pictures of real people playing sports. I think this article will tell me about these athletes and the signals they use.

Scaffold instruction.

Teach text structure.

Ask Questions What questions do you ask yourself to help you understand nonfiction? (What did I learn? What is this mainly about?) **As you read the article, ask these questions and look for the answers.**

Guide comprehension.

Read pp. 60–63.

Read Read the article as students follow along. Then read it a second time, having students join in. If necessary, stop at the end of each page to check comprehension. Ask questions to promote discussion and develop the concept.

Develop language and concepts.

- **On p. 60, what secret code does the baseball coach use with the batter?**
- **How does the secret code help the batter?**
- **What are some secret codes used in football? in volleyball? in basketball?**
- **Why do players and coaches use secret codes?**

MORE PRACTICE

Have students reread "Sports Signals." As they read, ask them to list each of the secret codes mentioned in the article. Have them share the list with family members and ask which secret codes they have used or seen someone use.

Reread for Fluency "Sports Signals," p. 61

	To Do	**To Say**	*5 minutes*

CORRECTIVE FEEDBACK

Monitor oral reading.

Read p. 61 aloud. Reread the page three or four times so your reading gets better each time. Give feedback on students' oral reading, using the *if . . . then* statements on Routine Card 4. Model fluent reading if necessary. You may want to have students read along with the DVD-ROM.

ACTIVITY 3   Write

Response to Literature

	To Do	**To Say**	*5 minutes*

Prompt journal writing.

Write on the board or a transparency: *Why do we need secret codes?*

Take out your journals. This week we are reading about secret codes. Our question for the week is: *Why do we need secret codes?* **Have you ever used a secret code or tried to invent your own? Write an answer to this question based on what you read today.** Have students write about the topic, using what they read and their own experiences.

Homework   Practice Book, p. 69, Vocabulary

ACTIVITY 1 Word Work

Phonics Consonant + *le* Syllables

	To Do	**To Say**	*5–10 minutes*
Teach consonant + *le* syllables.	Write on the board or a transparency: *Inventors may <u>stumble</u> upon a discovery.*	Read the sentence. How many parts are in the word *stumble*? (2) What does the last part of the word end in? *(le)* Frame the two parts. If the last part or syllable of a word ends in -*le* preceded by a consonant, that consonant usually begins the last syllable.	
Scaffold instruction.	Write the word *bubble*.	Let's look at the word *bubble* together. Does the last syllable end in -*le*? (yes) What consonant comes before the *le*? *(b)* So we know that the letter *b* begins the last syllable in *bubble*. Now look at the first syllable in *bubble*. If the first syllable ends with a vowel, it is open; if the first syllable ends with a consonant, it is closed. The open syllable has a long vowel sound; the closed syllable has a short vowel sound.

Is the first syllable in *bubble* open or closed? (closed) Is the first syllable in *table* open or closed? (open) | |
| **CORRECTIVE FEEDBACK** | Write each practice word. | Have students practice reading these words that end in a consonant + *le*. Help them identify the first syllable as open or closed. Correct any words students miss and have them reread the list. Discuss the meaning of each word.

ripple   crackle   stable   giggle   noble   cradle   uncle | |
| **MORE PRACTICE** | Write more practice words. | Have students practice reading these words and identify their meaning.

middle   cable   tumble   babble   bugle   single   twinkle | |

Vocabulary

	To Do	**To Say**	*5 minutes*
Review vocabulary.	Review the homework.	Ask students to go over answers and share their writing from Practice Book p. 69. See Routine Card 1 for the multisyllabic word routine.	
	Deepen understanding of *visible*.	Remember, *visible* means "able to be seen." A coach makes sure his hand signals are *visible* to the whole team. Why would a coach's signals need to be *visible* to everyone on the team? What can a coach do to keep his signals from being *visible*?	

ACTIVITY 2 Comprehension

Compare and Contrast

	To Do	**To Say**	*5 minutes*
Scaffold instruction.	Introduce compare and contrast.	Today you will read about secret codes that you can use. As you read, compare and contrast the different codes.	
	Model the skill.	For example, if I read about two different secret codes that both involve unscrambling mixed-up words, I see that these two codes are similar.	
	Distribute Graphic Organizer 3.	As you read "Codes for Kids," look for ways to compare and contrast the secret codes. Add these ideas to your graphic organizer. See Routine Card 7.	

ACTIVITY 3 Read a Passage

Read for Comprehension "Codes for Kids," pp. 64–67

	To Do	To Say	5–10 minutes

Scaffold instruction.

Monitor student engagement.

See Routine Cards 2 and 3.

Read Have students read pp. 64–67. Stop at the end of each page to ask questions. Students who can read on their own can do so without stopping. After reading, ask questions to promote discussion.

What is one of the easiest secret codes to make? (a code in which all the words are written backward)

On p. 65, what does the message say? (Call off meeting tonight.)

What is the secret message shown on the route cipher? (Tina, look under the back porch.)

What do you think the rest of the article will be about? (Answers will vary. The title and pictures suggest it will be about more secret codes kids will enjoy.)

Model summarizing.

Think aloud.

Summarize What were the first four pages mainly about? What did you learn? Think aloud to model summarizing. I learned about different secret codes and how to make them. You can write all the words backward, you can use a special mask to hide a message in other words, you can make a secret route, and you can use a ruler as a key.

Develop language and concepts.

Ask questions.

• **How does the mask work to make a secret code?**

• **Why does someone need to know the key to read a secret code that was made with a ruler?**

MORE PRACTICE

Have students reread p. 66.

Reread After they reread this page, have students write a sentence explaining how to make a key that unscrambles letters in a message.

Reread for Fluency "Codes for Kids," pp. 66–67

	To Do	To Say	5 minutes

MORE PRACTICE

CORRECTIVE FEEDBACK

Pair students. Monitor paired reading.

Students read aloud pp. 66–67, switching readers at the end of each page. Have partners reread; now the other partner begins. For optimal fluency, students should reread three or four times. Give feedback, using the *if . . . then* statements on Routine Card 4. You may want to have students read along with the DVD-ROM.

ACTIVITY 4 Write

Response to Literature

	To Do	To Say	5 minutes

Prompt writing.

Writing elements: support

The article tells about secret codes for kids and how to make them. Use details from the selection to explain how one of the codes works.

Homework Practice Book, p. 70, Consonant + *le* Syllables

ACTIVITY 1 | Word Work

Phonics Consonant + *le* Syllables

	To Do	**To Say**	5 minutes

Review consonant + le syllables.

Review the homework. Discuss *simple* and *puzzle*.

Ask students to share answers from Practice Book p. 70.

Point out the word *simple* on p. 65. **Remember to look for parts to help you read a long word. How many parts are in this word?** (2) **How does the second syllable end?** (with a consonant + *le*) Ask students to identify the first syllable in *simple* as open or closed and the vowel sound as short or long.

Then point to *puzzle* on p. 66. **How many parts are in this word?** (2) **What are they? Use the parts to read the word. How is it like *simple*?** (It also ends in a consonant + *le*.) Ask students to think of other words that end in a consonant + *le*. (Examples: *cycle, sniffle, shuffle, stifle, gentle, stumble, rifle*)

MORE PRACTICE

Model spelling words with consonant + *le*.

Spell and Write Write *puzzle*. Say *puzzle* with me and listen to the ending. What letters spell the ending sounds? Underline *le*. The word ends with a consonant and *le*. Repeat with *bubble*. Ask students to name words with consonant + *le*.

 ### Vocabulary

	To Do	**To Say**	5 minutes

Build vocabulary.

Lead cumulative review.

Deepen understanding of *conceals* and *interprets*.

Read aloud p. 69. **What *conceals* the message in this secret code?** (other letters) **A person who *interprets* this message uses a ruler. How would someone use a ruler to *interpret* the message?** (Put a ruler under the letters and read only the letters above the inch and half-inch marks on the ruler.)

Use the Tested Vocabulary Cards to review words from previous weeks.

ACTIVITY 2 | Comprehension

Compare and Contrast

	To Do	**To Say**	5–10 minutes

Scaffold instruction.

Review compare and contrast.

Remind students that comparing and contrasting can help make information and ideas more clear. **This article is about secret codes. As you read the next part of "Codes for Kids," look for the similarities and differences among the codes.**

Guide practice.

Use Graphic Organizer 3.

Listen as I read p. 70. Compare and contrast a picture code to other secret codes the author described. Read p. 70. How is a picture code similar to the other codes? (It conceals a secret message.) **How is a picture code different?** (Unlike the other codes, which use arrangements of letters or words, a picture code uses pictures.) **Add these similarities and differences to your graphic organizer.** See Routine Card 7.

MORE PRACTICE

Have students preview pp. 68–71.

Think aloud.

Read the captions and look at the photos on pp. 68–71. What do you think this section will be about? (more secret codes) **Why do you think so?**

The pictures make me think that the article will describe additional secret codes that kids can make. I can tell that we'll read about ways to make more codes.

ACTIVITY 3 Read a Passage

Read for Comprehension "Codes for Kids," pp. 68–71

	To Do	**To Say**	*10–15 minutes*

Scaffold instruction.

Monitor student engagement.

Read Have students read pp. 68–71 on their own. Stop at the end of each page to ask questions. Students who can read on their own can do so without stopping. After reading, ask questions to promote discussion.

See Routine Cards 2 and 3.

On pp. 68–69, what does the message say? (Rex has our book.)

How can you use pictures to write in secret code? (In your message, you can substitute pictures for words. Only the people who know what the pictures stand for will understand the message.)

How is Morse code different from the other codes in this article? (Morse code is not written, and it is not a secret code.)

Decode multisyllabic words.

Point out *understand* on p. 71.

Remind students to look for meaningful parts when reading long words. **This is a compound word. What are the two smaller words that make it up?** *(under* and *stand)* **Use these meaningful parts to read the word.** Guide students in blending the word parts into the word.

Assess comprehension.

Monitor understanding.

After Reading Have students discuss the What Do You Think? question. Prompt them to find as many similarities and differences as they can when responding. Listen as they talk to assess comprehension.

Summarize.

What is this mainly about? What did you learn? Work with students to summarize the selection.

MORE PRACTICE

Have students reread p. 69.

Reread As they read, have students compare the code that uses a mask to the code that uses a ruler. After they reread, have them share ideas for their own inventions.

Reread for Fluency "Codes for Kids," p. 70

	To Do	**To Say**	*5 minutes*

CORRECTIVE FEEDBACK

Monitor oral reading.

Read p. 70 aloud. Reread the page three or four times so your reading gets better each time. Give feedback on students' oral reading, using the *if . . . then* statements on Routine Card 4. Model fluent reading if necessary. You may want to have students read along with the DVD-ROM.

ACTIVITY 4 Write

Response to Literature

	To Do	**To Say**	*5 minutes*

Prompt writing.

Do you think it's easy to make a secret code? Why or why not? Support your opinion with details. Use complete sentences to express your thoughts.

Homework Practice Book, p. 71, Compare and Contrast

ACTIVITY 1 | Word Work

Amazing Words Vocabulary

To Do	To Say		5–10 minutes

Extend word knowledge.

Teach words related to creative.

Scaffold instruction.

Write on the board or a transparency: *Creative kids can invent secret codes.*

Use the word *creative* to extend word knowledge. **Remember, we read this word earlier this week. We looked for meaningful parts, and we noticed that** *creative* **comes from the word** *create,* **which means "to make something that has not been made before." The word** *create* **is a verb, and the word** *creative* **is an adjective used to describe someone who has the power to create. Can you think of other adjectives that end in** *-ive***?** (Examples: *descriptive, expensive, informative, expressive, sensitive, effective*) Write words as students name them and add some of your own. Talk about the meanings of the words. Point out that each one can describe a noun based on the same root. Help students read the word together.

Develop word meaning.

What are some other ways kids can be *creative***? What can you do to be** *creative***?**

MORE PRACTICE

Deepen understanding of *creative* and *transmit.*

Have individual students or partners use the two words *creative* and *transmit* in a sentence. (Example: It takes a *creative* person to *transmit* a secret message.) Share sentences. Ask: **What are some** *creative* **ways to** *transmit* **a message?**

ACTIVITY 2 | Comprehension

Skill and Strategy Practice

To Do	To Say		5 minutes

Scaffold instruction.

Review compare and contrast (homework).

Ask volunteers to read the passage and share answers from Practice Book p. 71. Remind students of the importance of comparing and contrasting information so as to understand better what they read. **When you read a story or an article, look for the ways that details, characters, and events are alike and different. Comparing and contrasting may help you identify the main idea or theme of a story or article.**

Practice strategic prereading.

See Routine Card 2.

Discuss Genre Read the title and text on p. 72 in the Student Reader. Model determining genre.

Think aloud.

I first thought this might be fiction because of the illustrations. When I read the first page, I knew it was fiction because of the dialogue.

Review story structure.

Ask Questions What questions do you ask yourself to help you understand a fictional story? (What is the problem or goal? How is the problem solved or the goal reached?) **As you read this story, ask these questions and look for the answers.**

ACTIVITY **3** ## Read a Passage

Read for Comprehension "A Case of Cat and Mouse," pp. 72–79

	To Do	To Say	

10–15 minutes

Scaffold instruction.

Monitor student engagement.

See Routine Card 3.

Read Have students read pp. 72–79 on their own and then discuss. For students who need more help, stop at the end of each page to discuss. After reading, ask questions.

Who is telling this story? (a narrator) **Who are the main characters?** (Donna, Zack, Mrs. Bittle, Jason)

What is the setting? (the neighborhood around Mrs. Bittle's house)

What is the problem? (Donna and Zack think Mrs. Bittle might be a spy.)

What happens when Donna and Zack watch Mrs. Bittle's house? (They see the window shade move up and down and think it's a spy signal. Then they see her talking on the phone and think she's talking to her spy boss.)

How do Donna and Zack solve the problem? (They speak with Jason and Mrs. Bittle.)

LOOK AT AUTHOR'S CRAFT

What is funny about how the story ends? (The kids find out that Mrs. Bittle's brother is coming to visit and that she hopes he can fix her broken window shade.)

Assess comprehension.

Monitor understanding.

After Reading Have students discuss the What Do You Think? question. Invite them to use Graphic Organizer 3 to compare the actions that make Mrs. Bittle seem like an ordinary neighbor with the actions that make her seem like a spy.

MORE PRACTICE

Reread Have students reread p. 79 and then describe how Donna, Zack, and Jason figure out that Mrs. Bittle is not a spy.

Reread for Fluency "A Case of Cat and Mouse," pp. 72–74

	To Do	To Say	

5–10 minutes

CORRECTIVE FEEDBACK

Pair students. Monitor paired reading.

Students read aloud pp. 72–74, switching readers at the end of each page. Have partners reread; now the other partner begins. For optimal fluency, students should reread three or four times. Give feedback, using the *if . . . then* statements on Routine Card 4. Model fluent reading if necessary. You may want to have students read along with the DVD-ROM.

MORE PRACTICE

READERS' THEATER

Work with a group of three students to adapt pp. 72–74 as a radio play. Have students rehearse reading the parts of the narrator, Donna, and Zack.

ACTIVITY **4** ## Write

Response to Literature

	To Do	To Say	

5 minutes

Prompt descriptive writing.

Writing elements: focus, organization

Compare and contrast how Donna and Zack feel about Mrs. Bittle at the beginning of the story with how they feel about her at the end. Give examples to support the similarities and differences you find. Use words such as *alike* and *unlike* to show similarities and differences.

ACTIVITY 1 | Read a Passage

Read Together "Leonardo's Secret Code," pp. 80–81

	To Do	To Say	
			10 minutes

Scaffold instruction.

To Do: Review compare and contrast.

To Say: Have students preview pp. 80–81. **This article tells about a famous artist and inventor, Leonardo da Vinci, and the secret mirror code he used. Finding similarities between the mirror code and the other codes we read about this week can help you understand what you have learned. As you read the article, compare the mirror code to another secret code. How are the two codes similar? How are the two codes different?**

To Do: See Routine Card 3.

To Say: **Read** Read the article as students follow along. Then read it a second time, having students join in on the text. After reading, have students try writing a sentence in mirror code. Then ask questions.

What is a mirror code and why did Leonardo da Vinci use it? (It is backwards writing, which can be read only by holding the page up to a mirror. He didn't want his ideas to be stolen.)

How is the mirror code similar to the other secret codes you read about? (Example: All of the codes are designed to confuse readers.)

What is a difference between the mirror code and another code? (Example: Different tools are needed to interpret the codes. To interpret the mirror code, you need a mirror. To interpret a route cipher code, you need a route box.)

Assess comprehension.

To Do: Monitor listening comprehension.

To Say: **Summarize** Have students discuss how this selection relates to the unit theme of *Secret Codes*. Listen as they talk to assess comprehension.

ACTIVITY 2 | Build Concepts

Amazing Words Vocabulary

	To Do	To Say	
			5–10 minutes

Review concept and vocabulary.

To Do: Concept and Language Goals

Display the concept web you began on Day 1.

To Say: **This week's question is *Why do we need secret codes?* How do this week's words relate to the question?** (Have students answer the question, using some of the vocabulary they learned this week.)

Ask students to add more words to the concept web. Have students explain how each word relates to the concept of why we need secret codes. Monitor students' understanding of vocabulary as they discuss the web. See Routine Card 5.

MORE PRACTICE

To Do: Write *creative, interprets,* and *visible* on the board.

To Say: Have students relate *creative, interprets,* and *visible*. **A person who likes writing codes *interprets creative* codes easily. If the code is *visible,* almost anyone can figure out how to crack it.** Give students the following instructions. **On the board, write a *creative* message in code. Make sure it is *visible* to the whole class. Ask the class to *interpret* your message.**

ACTIVITY 3 Write

Response to Literature "4 You 2 Do," p. 82

To Do   **To Say**   *10–15 minutes*

Guide response activities.

Discuss the directions on p. 82. Tell students to choose one activity to complete. See Routine Card 8.

Word Play Have students reverse the order of the letters in the words on their own or working with a partner. If necessary, you might offer clues by giving the first letter in each word. *(i, c, v, t, c, e)*

Making Connections Discuss the question in a group. (Possible answer: The team could make the wrong play.)

On Paper Have students brainstorm their secret message and then decide what kind of code they want to use. Have them write on their own. Students can use Practice Book p. 72 to structure their written responses, or you can send the Practice Book page home for them to complete later.

MORE PRACTICE

If you have more time, direct students to complete all the activities.

ACTIVITY 4 Assessment Options

Passage Reading

To Do   **To Say**   *10–15 minutes*

See Routine Card 6.

While some students are doing Activity 3, determine which students you want to assess this week and choose from these options.

Check fluency.

Take a two-minute timed sample of each student's oral reading.

Fluency Have students read for two minutes from "A Case of Cat and Mouse." Record the number of correct words read per minute. See p. 184 for monitoring fluency. Be sure each student is assessed at least every other week.

Have students graph their progress on the Fluency Progress Chart, p. 185.

Check comprehension.

Retelling Have students reread "A Case of Cat and Mouse" and retell it. Prompt students if necessary. See p. 186 for monitoring retelling.

If you have time, assess every student.

Homework   Practice Book, p. 72, Writing

Unit 4 Week 4 *Communication*

 How can we communicate in different ways?

Objectives *This week students will...*

Vocabulary
- build concepts and vocabulary: *combine, conversation, dialect, phrase, region, shouts, symbols*

Phonics
- read diphthongs *ou, ow* /ou/
- apply knowledge of word structure to decode multisyllabic words when reading

Text Comprehension
- use main idea to improve comprehension
- write in response to literature
- make connections across text

Fluency
- practice fluency with oral rereading

Word Work *This week's phonics focus is . . .*

Diphthongs *ou, ow* /ou/

Amazing Words Concept/Amazing Words *Tested Vocabulary*

The week's vocabulary is related to the concept of communication.
The first appearance of each word in the Student Reader is noted below.

combine	to join two or more things together (p. 96)
conversation	friendly talk between two or more people (p. 92)
dialect	a form of language that is spoken by a group of people from the same community or area (p. 98)
phrase	a short group of words that expresses a familiar idea (p. 102)
region	any place, space, or area (p. 98)
shouts	calls or yells loudly (p. 98)
symbols	things that stand for or mean the same thing as some other things (p. 96)

Student Reader Unit 4 *This week students will read the following selections.*

86	**Communication**	Expository Nonfiction
90	**Sending the Message**	Expository Nonfiction
98	**Trading Phrases**	Expository Nonfiction
106	**Do You Speak English?**	Expository Nonfiction
108	**4 You 2 Do**	Activity Page

Daily Lesson Plan

	ACTIVITIES	MATERIALS
Day 1	**Build Concepts** Weekly Concept: Communication Vocabulary: *combine, conversation, dialect, phrase, region, shouts, symbols* **Read a Passage** "Communication," pp. 86–89 Comprehension: Use Strategies Reread for Fluency **Write** Response to Literature	Student Reader: Unit 4 Routine Cards 2, 4, 5 Tested Vocabulary Cards Student journals Practice Book, p. 73, Vocabulary Student Reader DVD-ROM
Day 2	**Word Work** Phonics: Diphthongs *ou, ow* /ou/ Vocabulary: Deepen word meaning **Comprehension** Main Idea **Read a Passage** "Sending the Message," pp. 90–93 Reread for Fluency **Write** Response to Literature	Student Reader: Unit 4 Practice Book, p. 73, Vocabulary Routine Cards 1, 2, 3, 4, 7 Graphic Organizer 1 Practice Book, p. 74, Diphthongs *ou, ow* /ou/ Student Reader DVD-ROM
Day 3	**Word Work** Phonics: Diphthongs *ou, ow* /ou/ Vocabulary: Deepen word meaning **Comprehension** Main Idea **Read a Passage** "Sending the Message," pp. 94–97 Reread for Fluency **Write** Response to Literature	Practice Book, p. 74, Diphthongs *ou, ow* /ou/ Tested Vocabulary Cards Student Reader: Unit 4 Graphic Organizer 1 Routine Cards 1, 2, 3, 4, 7 Practice Book, p. 75, Main Idea and Details Student Reader DVD-ROM
Day 4	**Word Work** Vocabulary: Extend word knowledge **Comprehension** Skill and Strategy Practice **Read a Passage** "Trading Phrases," pp. 98–105 Reread for Fluency **Write** Response to Literature	Practice Book, p. 75, Main Idea and Details Student Reader: Unit 4 Routine Cards 2, 3, 4 Student Reader DVD-ROM
Day 5	**Read a Passage** "Do You Speak English?" pp. 106–107 Comprehension: Main Idea; Listening **Build Concepts** Vocabulary **Write** Response to Literature: "4 You 2 Do," p. 108 **Assessment Options** Fluency Comprehension	Student Reader: Unit 4 Routine Cards 3, 5, 6, 8 Fluency Progress Chart, p. 185 Practice Book, p. 76, Writing

See pp. xvi–xvii for how *My Sidewalks* integrates instructional practices for ELL.

Build Concepts

Vocabulary

To Do	To Say	

Develop oral vocabulary.

See Routine Card 6 and p. 201.

Introduce the Concept/Amazing Words with an oral routine prior to displaying them in print. Page 201 in this Teacher's Guide provides specific guidelines for introducing each word.

Develop word meaning.

See Routine Card 5. Discuss pp. 85–89.

Have students read p. 85 and then look at the pictures on pp. 86–89. **What might a drum have in common with a cell phone?** (Both might be used to send messages.) **How can you use the word *communication* to describe the objects in these pictures?** (Example: There are many different forms of *communication*.)

Scaffold instruction.

Create a concept web.

In the center of a web, write *Communication*. **This week's concept is *communication*. Communication is how people give or exchange news or information.** Provide an example to demonstrate meaning. **We have many different forms of communication these days, including cell phones, e-mail, and telephones.**

Add the other vocabulary words.

Concept and Language Goals

Discuss the meaning of each word as it relates to communication, using the glossary as needed. (See p. 38 of this Teacher's Guide for definitions.)

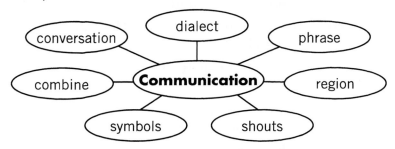

Model the multisyllabic word strategy.

Display each word. Say it as you display it.

Use the Tested Vocabulary Cards. Follow this routine for each word:

- **Look for Meaningful Parts** **Do you recognize any parts of this word? What do these parts mean? Use the parts to read the word.** As you introduce each word, call students' attention to these specific graphemes: *tion* /shən/; *phr* /fr/; and *gion* /jən/.

Think aloud.

- **Model** Model using the multisyllabic word strategy with *conversation*. **I recognize the word *converse*. I know *converse* means "to talk together." And I know the suffix *-ation*; it's pronounced /ā shən/, and it means "act or result of." So I think *conversation* must mean "the act of talking between people."**

- **Chunk Words with No Recognizable Parts** Model how to chunk the word *symbol:* **I see a chunk at the beginning of the word: *sym*. I see a part at the end of the word: *bol*. I say each chunk slowly: *sym bol*. I say the chunks fast to make a whole word: *symbol*. Is it a real word? Yes, I know the word *symbol*.**

- Have students practice reading each word.

Preview.

Read p. 84 with students.

Do you see any of the words we just learned on this page? Together with students, read the sentences on p. 84 describing each selection. Talk about how the vocabulary words might be used in the selections.

MORE PRACTICE

Deepen understanding of *communication*.

Have students demonstrate understanding by answering questions. **Why have different forms of communication changed over the years? How would you communicate with your friends if you couldn't use a telephone, cell phone, or e-mail? Give an example.**

ACTIVITY 2 Read a Passage

Develop Concepts "Communication," pp. 86–89

	To Do	To Say	
			10–15 minutes

Practice strategic prereading.

See Routine Card 2.

Think aloud.

Discuss Genre Read the title and have students look at the illustrations on pp. 86–89. Model determining genre.

The photographs are a clue that this is nonfiction. They look like photos of real objects and people. I think that this article will be about devices people use to communicate.

Scaffold instruction.

Review text structure.

Ask Questions What questions do you ask yourself to help you understand nonfiction? (What did I learn? What is this mainly about?) As you read this article, ask these questions and look for the answers.

Guide comprehension.

Read pp. 86–89 aloud.

Read Read the article as students follow along. Then read it a second time, having students join in. If necessary, stop at the end of each paragraph to check comprehension. Ask questions to promote discussion and develop the concept.

Develop language and concepts.

- **What were some of the problems people had sending messages in the past?**
- **How have satellites helped people communicate?**
- **What are the benefits of being able to communicate with people quickly?**
- **What words on the concept web could help you describe communication?**

MORE PRACTICE

Have students reread "Communication." As they read, tell them to make a list of all the ways people used to communicate in the past. Have them share their lists with family members tonight.

Reread for Fluency "Communication," p. 87

	To Do	To Say	
			5 minutes

CORRECTIVE FEEDBACK

Monitor oral reading.

Read p. 87 aloud. Reread the page three or four times so your reading gets better each time. Give feedback on students' oral reading, using the *if . . . then* statements on Routine Card 4. Model fluent reading if necessary. You may want to have students read along with the DVD-ROM.

ACTIVITY 3 Write

Response to Literature

	To Do	To Say	
			5 minutes

Prompt journal writing.

Write on the board or a transparency: *How can we communicate in different ways?*

Take out your journals. This week we are reading about communication. Our question for this week is: *How can we communicate in different ways?* Write an answer to this question based on what you read today. Have students write about the topic, using what they read and their own experiences.

Homework

Practice Book, p. 73, Vocabulary

ACTIVITY 1 · Word Work

Phonics Diphthongs *ou, ow* /ou/

	To Do	**To Say**	*5–10 minutes*
Teach diphthongs *ou, ow* /ou/.	Write on the board or a transparency: *After a game, my team clowns around.*	Read these two words aloud. What vowel sound do the letters *ow* in *clowns* make? (/ou/). What vowel sound do the letters *ou* in *around* make? (/ou/). Sometimes *ow* and *ou* stand for a diphthong. A diphthong is a single vowel sound, represented by two letters. The single vowel sound you hear resembles a glide from one sound to another. Each vowel contributes to the sound, /ou/, that you hear.	
Scaffold instruction.	Write *thousand* and *frowning*.	Let's read these two words together. Remember to look for meaningful parts in long words. Do you see any parts you know in these words? (Students may notice *frown* in *frowning*.) If you don't see any meaningful parts, you can look for chunks. Think about the vowel sound you hear in each chunk. Model reading the chunks *thou* and *sand* in *thousand* and then the chunks *frown* and *-ing* in *frowning*. What single vowel sound do you hear in each word? (/ou/). What two letters is the vowel sound represented by in each word? (*ou* in *thousand*; *ow* in *frowning*)	
CORRECTIVE FEEDBACK	Write each practice word.	Have students practice reading these words with the diphthong /ou/. Correct any words students miss and have them reread the list. countless surround towel grounded powerful township	
MORE PRACTICE	Write more practice words.	Have students practice reading these additional words with the /ou/ sound. foundation coward couches hourly allowance flowering	

Vocabulary

	To Do	**To Say**	*5 minutes*
Review vocabulary.	Review the homework.	Ask students to go over answers and share their writing from Practice Book p. 73. See Routine Card 1 for the multisyllabic word routine.	
	Deepen understanding of *conversation*.	Remember, *conversation* is friendly talk between two or more people. Can you have a *conversation* with someone without speaking out loud? How are conversations on the telephone different from face-to-face conversations?	

ACTIVITY 2 · Comprehension

Main Idea

	To Do	**To Say**	*5 minutes*
Scaffold instruction.	Introduce main idea.	Today you will read about changes in the ways that people communicate with each other. It's important to identify the main, or most important, idea about the topic of this article, so that you can understand how communication has changed. The title and the headings may contain clues that help you identify the main idea.	
	Model the skill.	From the title and headings, I can tell that the article contains information about both old and new methods of communicating. So I know that the main idea won't just be about communication long ago.	
	Distribute Graphic Organizer 1.	As you read "Sending the Message," identify the main idea of the article and three supporting details and record them on your graphic organizer. See Routine Card 7.	

ACTIVITY 3 Read a Passage

Read for Comprehension "Sending the Message," pp. 90–93

To Do	To Say	*10–15 minutes*

Scaffold instruction.

Monitor student engagement.

Read Have students read pp. 90–93. Stop at the end of each page to ask questions. Students who can read on their own can do so without stopping. After reading, ask questions to promote discussion.

See Routine Cards 2 and 3.

How did sending a telegram differ from sending a letter? (A telegram was more expensive to send but was delivered faster.)

Why doesn't Sarah call her grandmother? (In 1900 few people had phones.)

How have telephones changed since 1915? (no longer need an operator to make a call; clearer conversations; can call from almost anywhere using a cell phone)

Point out *telegram* and *telegraph* on p. 91.

Point out the prefix *tele-* at the beginning of each word. Ask students to share other words that begin with *tele-*. (*telephone, television, telescope*) Then ask what other words they know that end in *-gram* or *-graph*. (*diagram, program, phonograph, paragraph, autograph, monogram*)

Model summarizing.

Think aloud.

Summarize What were the first four pages mainly about? What did you learn about the ways that communication has changed? Think aloud to model summarizing. **I learned about the ways that people used to send messages to each other, such as writing letters or sending telegrams, and the first telephones. But the main thing I learned was how much easier and faster it is to communicate with people now than it was a hundred years ago.**

Develop language and concepts.

Ask questions.

- **Do you think people are better off now that they have cell phones? Why?**
- **Do you think there were benefits in communicating by letter? Explain.**

MORE PRACTICE

Have students reread p. 92.

Reread After they read, ask students to role-play an imaginary conversation between a telephone caller and an operator.

Reread for Fluency "Sending the Message," pp. 90–91

To Do	To Say	*5 minutes*

MORE PRACTICE

CORRECTIVE FEEDBACK

Pair students. Monitor paired reading.

Students read aloud pp. 90–91, switching readers at the end of the first page. Have partners reread; now the other partner begins. For optimal fluency, students should reread three or four times. Give feedback, using the *if . . . then* statements on Routine Card 4. You may want to have students read along with the DVD-ROM.

 ACTIVITY 4 Write

Response to Literature

To Do	To Say	*5 minutes*

Prompt writing.

Writing elements: support

What have you learned so far that answers this week's question: *How can we communicate in different ways?* Use examples from the text to support your answer.

Homework

Practice Book, p. 74, Diphthongs *ou, ow* /ou/

ACTIVITY **1** Word Work

Phonics Diphthongs *ou, ow* /ou/

5 minutes

	To Do	To Say
Review diphthongs *ou, ow* /ou/.	Review the homework. Discuss the word *without* on p. 93 in the Student Reader.	Ask students to share answers from Practice Book p. 74. Point out *without* on p. 93, paragraph 1. **Remember, look for meaningful parts when you read a long word. What are the two smaller words in this compound word?** *(with and out)* **Which part of the word has the vowel sound /ou/?** *(out)* Then point to *download* on p. 93, paragraph 2. **What parts do you see in this word?** *(down and load)* **Use the parts to read the word. Which part of the word has the vowel sound /ou/?** *(down)* **What other compound words can you think of that have *down* in them?** (Examples: *downstairs, downtown, touchdown, breakdown*)
MORE PRACTICE	Model words with diphthongs *ou* and *ow*.	**Spell and Write** Write *sound* and *down*. Say *sound*. **What vowel sound do you hear in this word? What letters spell that vowel sound?** Underline *ou*. Continue with *down* (*ow*). **Look for words with *ou* or *ow* that have the same vowel sound.**

Amazing Words Vocabulary

5 minutes

	To Do	To Say
Build vocabulary. **Lead cumulative review.**	Deepen understanding of *combine* and *symbols*.	Read aloud p. 96. **How else might you *combine symbols* to communicate? What other *symbols* do you see every day?** Use the Tested Vocabulary Cards to review words from previous weeks.

ACTIVITY **2** Comprehension

Main Idea

5–10 minutes

	To Do	To Say
Scaffold instruction.	Review main idea.	Remind students that the main idea is the most important idea about the topic of a paragraph, passage, or article. Titles and headings can sometimes provide clues for finding the main idea. **As you continue reading "Sending the Message," try to identify the main idea of the article.**
Guide practice.	Use Graphic Organizer 1.	**Listen as I read the first paragraph on p. 94. Try to identify the most important information in that paragraph.** Read p. 94, paragraph 1. Then ask: **What is the main idea?** (Early computers were very big but did only simple jobs.) See Routine Card 7.
MORE PRACTICE	Have students preview pp. 94–97. Think aloud.	**Read the captions and look at the illustrations on pp. 94–97. What do you think this section will be about?** (how computers have changed) **Why do you think so?** **The captions make me think that this section will describe the first computers and how they've improved over the years. From the pictures I can see that this section will talk about how computers have gotten smaller and smaller.**

ACTIVITY 3 # Read a Passage

Read for Comprehension "Sending the Message," pp. 94–97

	To Do	To Say	
			10–15 minutes

Scaffold instruction.

Monitor student engagement.

See Routine Cards 2 and 3.

Read Have students read pp. 94–97. Stop at the end of each page to ask questions. Students who can read on their own can do so without stopping. After reading, ask questions to promote discussion.

What is a computer network? (a way to connect separate computers so they can "talk" to each other)

What was the biggest difference between the first computers and the first personal computers? (PCs could fit on a desk.)

What are some of the things people can do on the World Wide Web? (get information, shop, and communicate)

Decode multisyllabic words.

Point out *emoticons* on p. 96.

Remember, look for meaningful parts when you read a long word. Do you recognize any parts of this word? Model using the multisyllabic word strategy. See Routine Card 1. *I see* emot *at the beginning of the word. I know the word* emotion, *which means "strong feelings," so I think the word has to do with feelings. I see* icon *at the end of the word. I know that an icon is a symbol that you see on a computer screen. I think the word* emoticon *might mean "a symbol that tells how you feel."*

Assess comprehension.

Monitor understanding.

After Reading Have students discuss the What Do You Think? question. Prompt them to identify the main idea of the article as they discuss the ways that communication has changed. Listen as they talk to assess comprehension.

Summarize.

What is this mainly about? What did you learn? Work with students to summarize the selection.

MORE PRACTICE

Have students reread p. 97.

Reread As they read, have students translate the symbols in Sarah's e-mail (see p. 96). After they read, have them discuss how they think communication will change in the coming years.

Reread for Fluency "Sending the Message," p. 94

	To Do	To Say	
			5 minutes

CORRECTIVE FEEDBACK

Monitor oral reading.

Read p. 94 aloud. Reread the page three or four times so your reading gets better each time. Give feedback on students' oral reading, using the *if . . . then* statements on Routine Card 4. Model fluent reading if necessary. You may want to have students read along with the DVD-ROM.

ACTIVITY 4 # Write

Response to Literature

	To Do	To Say	
			5 minutes

MORE PRACTICE

Prompt writing.

What details from the article support the idea that methods of communication have changed dramatically over the last 100 years? Use details from the selection to support your ideas.

Homework

Practice Book, p. 75, Main Idea and Details

ACTIVITY 1 Word Work

Amazing Words **Vocabulary**

To Do	To Say	5–10 minutes

Extend word knowledge.

Teach antonyms for regional.

Scaffold instruction.

Write on the board or a transparency: *region* and *regional.*

Use the word *region* to extend word knowledge. **We read this word earlier in the week. What does region mean?** (any place, space, or area) **Today we'll explore a related word, regional, and try to find an antonym.** *Regional* **is an adjective that describes something that is "of or in a particular region." Now try to think of a word that means the opposite of** *regional.* **If we ask about** *regional* **climate, we're asking about the climate in one particular part of the world. What would be the opposite of** *regional* **climate?** Guide students toward understanding that the opposite of something that is of one particular region is something that is of many or all regions: *widespread, global, universal.* **The word** *globe* **means "the world," so** *global* **describes anything involving the whole world.**

Develop word meaning.

Is it easier to identify things such as weather or languages that are *regional* **or** *global?* **Why?**

MORE PRACTICE

Deepen understanding of *region* and *dialect.*

Have individual students or partners use the words *region* and *dialect* together in a sentence. (For example: People from other *regions* have a hard time understanding our *dialect.*) Share sentences. Ask: **What can we learn about our past from studying different dialects?**

ACTIVITY 2 Comprehension

Skill and Strategy Practice

To Do	To Say	5 minutes

Scaffold instruction.

Review main idea (homework).

Ask volunteers to read the passage and share answers from Practice Book p. 75. Remind students of the importance of finding the main idea and supporting details to understand a passage better. **When you read an article, you can better understand it if you think about the main idea of each paragraph or section. Remember that titles and headings may offer clues about the main idea.**

Practice strategic prereading.

See Routine Card 2.

Discuss Genre Read the title on p. 98 in the Student Reader and look at the illustrations on pp. 98–105. Read p. 98 aloud. Model determining genre.

Think aloud.

I thought this might be nonfiction because of the photographs of real people and places and the map. When I read the first page, I knew it was nonfiction because of the information about different regions.

Review text structure.

Ask Questions **What questions do you ask yourself to help you understand nonfiction?** (What is this mainly about? What did I learn?) **As you read this article, ask these questions and look for the answers.**

ACTIVITY 3 · Read a Passage

Read for Comprehension "Trading Phrases," pp. 98–105

	To Do	To Say
		10–15 minutes

Scaffold instruction.

To Do: Monitor student engagement.

See Routine Card 3.

Read Have students read pp. 98–105 on their own and then discuss. For students who need more help, stop at the end of each page to discuss. After reading, ask questions.

On p. 98, what makes the conversation confusing? (People are using different words for the same items.)

How can words be clues to local history? (They can tell you something about the people who used to live in a place.)

Why don't local words and phrases die out? (People keep their old words and pick up new ones when they move.)

What can the names of foods and drinks tell us about some people? (what part of the country they're from)

Assess comprehension.

Monitor understanding.

After Reading Have students discuss the What Do You Think? question. Prompt them to identify the main idea of the article as they consider why some foods have more than one name. Listen as they talk to assess comprehension.

MORE PRACTICE

Reread Have students reread p. 104. Ask them to use the word *combine* to explain some of the reasons why our language keeps changing.

Reread for Fluency "Trading Phrases," pp. 98–99

	To Do	To Say
		5–10 minutes

CORRECTIVE FEEDBACK

Pair students. Monitor paired reading.

Students read aloud pp. 98–99, switching readers at the end of each page. Have partners reread; now the other partner begins. For optimal fluency, students should reread three or four times. Give feedback, using Routine Card 4. You may want to have students read along with the DVD-ROM.

MORE PRACTICE

READERS' THEATER

Work with a group of students to adapt pp. 98–100 for a Readers' Theater presentation. Help students decide how to divide the lines to suggest different characters from different areas. Encourage them to find character voices and to read their lines with expression and humor.

ACTIVITY 4 · Write

Response to Literature

	To Do	To Say
		5 minutes

Prompt expository writing.

Writing elements: focus, support

What is the main idea, or most important idea, of "Trading Phrases"? Provide at least three details from the article to support your answer.

ACTIVITY 1   Read a Passage

Read Together *"Do You Speak English?"* pp. 106–107

10 minutes

	To Do	**To Say**
Scaffold instruction.	Review main idea.	Have students preview pp. 106–107. **This article tells about the differences between two kinds of English: American English and British English. The main idea, or most important idea, of the article is that people in these two countries often use different words to talk about the same things.**
	See Routine Card 3.	**Read** Read the article as students follow along. Then read it a second time, having students join in on the text. After reading, ask questions.
		What language do both Americans and British people speak? (English)
		Why might British English sound like a foreign language to an American? (The British use different words and phrases for some things.)
Assess comprehension.	Monitor listening comprehension.	**Summarize** Have students quiz each other on the different British words and phrases they learned from the chart on p. 107, as well as on the regional words and phrases they learned from "Trading Phrases." Listen as they talk to assess comprehension.

ACTIVITY 2   Build Concepts

Amazing Words Vocabulary

5–10 minutes

	To Do	**To Say**
Review concept and vocabulary.	Display the concept web you began on Day 1.	**This week's question is *How can we communicate in different ways?* How do this week's words relate to the question?** (Have students answer the question, using some of the vocabulary they learned this week.)
		Ask students to add more words to the concept web. Have students explain how each word relates to communication. See Routine Card 5.
MORE PRACTICE	Write *dialect, region,* and *conversation* on the board.	Have students relate *dialect, region,* and *conversation.* **A word expert might say that it's tricky to have a *conversation* with people who speak different *dialects* or who are from different *regions.* Why? Give an example of a *conversation* that two people from two different *regions* might have. Is your speech influenced at all by the *region* of the country you're from? Explain.**

ACTIVITY 3 | Write

Response to Literature "4 You 2 Do," p. 108

To Do **To Say** *10–15 minutes*

Guide response activities.

Discuss the directions on p. 108. Tell students to choose one activity to complete. See Routine Card 8.

Word Play Invite students to review the word list on p. 85 to help them solve this puzzle.

Making Connections Discuss the question in a group. (Different languages or dialects can make it hard for people to communicate; access to phones or computers may be limited; people might be busy and lack time.)

On Paper Have students brainstorm some answers to the prompt before they write. Have them write on their own. Students can use Practice Book p. 76 to structure their written responses, or you can send the Practice Book page home for them to complete later.

MORE PRACTICE

If you have more time, direct students to complete all the activities.

ACTIVITY 4 | Assessment Options

Passage Reading

To Do **To Say** *10–15 minutes*

See Routine Card 6.

While some students are doing Activity 3, determine which students you want to assess this week and choose from these options.

Check fluency.

Take a two-minute timed sample of each student's oral reading.

Fluency Have a student read for two minutes from "Sending the Message." Record the number of correct words read per minute. See p. 184 for monitoring fluency. Be sure each student is assessed at least every other week.

Have students graph their progress on the Fluency Progress Chart, p. 185.

Check comprehension.

Retelling Have students reread "Sending the Message" and retell it. Prompt students if necessary. See p. 186 for monitoring retelling.

If you have time, assess every student.

Homework

Practice Book, p. 76, Writing

Unit 4 Week 5 *Finding Clues*

How do we solve a mystery?

Objectives *This week students will...*

Vocabulary
- build concepts and vocabulary: *convince, curious, diver, evidence, explorer, investigate, scrutiny*

Phonics
- read suffixes *-er, -or, -ish, -ous*
- apply knowledge of word structure to decode multisyllabic words when reading

Text Comprehension
- draw conclusions to improve comprehension
- write in response to literature
- make connections across text

Fluency
- practice fluency with oral rereading

Word Work *This week's phonics focus is . . .*

Suffixes *-er, -or, -ish, -ous*

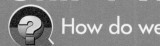 **Concept/Amazing Words** *Tested Vocabulary*

The week's vocabulary is related to the concept of finding clues.
The first appearance of each word in the Student Reader is noted below.

convince	to make someone believe something (p. 125)
curious	eager to know something (p. 126)
diver	someone who works under water wearing special equipment (p. 120)
evidence	anything that shows what happened; facts (p. 116)
explorer	someone who travels to unknown places to discover new things (p. 117)
investigate	to examine something in order to find out more about it (p. 127)
scrutiny	close study or careful inspection (p. 119)

Student Reader Unit 4 *This week students will read the following selections.*

Daily Lesson Plan

	ACTIVITIES	MATERIALS
Day 1	**Build Concepts** Weekly Concept: Finding Clues Vocabulary: *convince, curious, diver, evidence, explorer, investigate, scrutiny* **Read a Passage** "Dinosaur Hunters," pp. 112–115 Comprehension: Use Strategies Reread for Fluency **Write** Response to Literature	Student Reader: Unit 4 Routine Cards 2, 4, 5 Tested Vocabulary Cards Student journals Practice Book, p. 77, Vocabulary Student Reader DVD-ROM
Day 2	**Word Work** Phonics: Suffixes *-er, -or, -ish, -ous* Vocabulary: Deepen word meaning **Comprehension** Draw Conclusions **Read a Passage** "Monster Mysteries: Bigfoot and Nessie," pp. 116–119 Reread for Fluency **Write** Response to Literature	Student Reader: Unit 4 Practice Book, p. 77, Vocabulary Graphic Organizer 2 Routine Cards 1, 2, 3, 4, 7 Practice Book, p. 78, Suffixes *-er, -or, -ish, -ous* Student Reader DVD-ROM
Day 3	**Word Work** Phonics: Suffixes *-er, -or, -ish, -ous* Vocabulary: Deepen word meaning **Comprehension** Draw Conclusions **Read a Passage** "Monster Mysteries: Bigfoot and Nessie," pp. 120–123 Reread for Fluency **Write** Response to Literature	Practice Book, p. 78, Suffixes *-er, -or, -ish, -ous* Tested Vocabulary Cards Student Reader: Unit 4 Graphic Organizer 2 Routine Cards 1, 2, 3, 4, 7 Practice Book, p. 79, Draw Conclusions Student Reader DVD-ROM
Day 4	**Word Work** Vocabulary: Extend word knowledge **Comprehension** Skill and Strategy Practice **Read a Passage** "The Creature on Pine Tree Lane," pp. 124–131 Reread for Fluency **Write** Response to Literature	Practice Book, p. 79, Draw Conclusions Student Reader: Unit 4 Routine Cards 2, 3, 4 Student Reader DVD-ROM
Day 5	**Read a Passage** "The Bermuda Triangle Mystery," pp. 132–133 Comprehension: Draw Conclusions; Listening **Build Concepts** Vocabulary **Write** Response to Literature: "4 You 2 Do," p. 134 **Assessment Options** Fluency, Comprehension End-of-Unit Test	Student Reader: Unit 4 Routine Cards 3, 5, 8 Practice Book, p. 80, Writing Assessment Book, p. 60

See pp. xvi–xvii for how *My Sidewalks* integrates instructional practices for ELL.

Build Concepts

Amazing Words **Vocabulary**

| **To Do** | **To Say** | *10–15 minutes* |

Develop oral vocabulary.

See Routine Card 6 and p. 202.

Introduce the Concept/Amazing Words with an oral routine prior to displaying them in print. Page 202 in this Teacher's Guide provides specific guidelines for introducing each word.

Develop word meaning.

See Routine Card 5. Discuss pp. 111–115.

Have students read p. 111 and then look at the pictures on pp. 112–115. **What do you see?** (scientists uncovering dinosaur bones and footprints) **Can you use the word** *evidence* **to describe what you see in these pictures?** (Example: Bones and footprints are *evidence* that dinosaurs lived on our planet long ago.)

Scaffold instruction.

Create a concept web.

In the center of a web, write *Finding Clues.* **This week's concept is** *finding clues.* *Clues* **are signs or hints that help solve a mystery or problem.** Provide an example to demonstrate meaning. *Clues* **such as how hot or cold it is outside can tell you what time of year it is.**

Add the other vocabulary words.

Concept and Language Goals

Discuss the meaning of each word as it relates to finding clues, using the glossary as needed. (See p. 50 of this Teacher's Guide for definitions.)

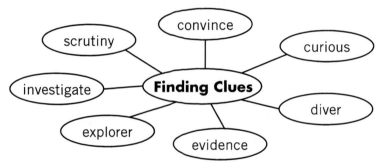

Model the multisyllabic word strategy.

Display each word. Say it as you display it.

Use the Tested Vocabulary Cards. Follow this routine for each word:

- **Look for Meaningful Parts** **Do you recognize any parts of this word? What do these parts mean? Use the parts to read the word.** As you introduce each word, be sure students notice the following: *-ous* in *curious* and *-er* in *diver* and *explorer.*

Think aloud.

- **Model** **I recognize the word** *explore* **at the beginning of** *explorer.* **I know that** *explore* **means "to travel to unknown places to discover new things." I see the suffix** *-er* **at the end of** *explorer.* **I know that a suffix like** *-er* **can change a verb into a noun, so I think an** *explorer* **must be "a person who travels to unknown places to discover new things."**

- **Chunk Words with No Recognizable Parts** Model how to chunk the word *convince:* **I see a chunk at the beginning of the word:** *con.* **I see a part at the end of the word:** *vince.* **I say each chunk slowly:** *con vince.* **I say the chunks fast to make a whole word:** *convince.* **Is it a real word? Yes, I know the word** *convince.*

- Have students practice reading each word.

Preview.

Read p. 110 with students.

Do you see any of the words we just learned on this page? Together with students, read the sentences on p. 110 describing each selection. Talk about how the vocabulary words might be used in the selections.

MORE PRACTICE

Deepen understanding of *clues.*

Have students demonstrate understanding by answering questions. **What are some** *clues* **that you might use to tell what time of day it is without looking at a clock, or to tell what the weather is like without reading a weather report? How can your five senses help you find** *clues?*

ACTIVITY 2 Read a Passage

Develop Concepts "Dinosaur Hunters," pp. 112–115

5–10 minutes

	To Do	**To Say**
Practice strategic prereading.	See Routine Card 2.	**Discuss Genre** Read the title and have students look at the illustrations on pp. 112–115. Model determining genre.
	Think aloud.	The photographs are a clue that this is nonfiction. They look like photos of real people and real dinosaur fossils. I think that this article will tell me about dinosaurs and the people who study them.
Scaffold instruction.	Review text structure.	**Ask Questions** What questions do you ask yourself to help you understand nonfiction? (What did I learn? What is this mainly about?) As you read this article, ask these questions and look for the answers.
Guide comprehension.	Read pp. 112–115 aloud.	**Read** Read the article as students follow along. Then read it a second time, having students join in. If necessary, stop at the end of each paragraph to check comprehension. Ask questions to promote discussion and develop the concept.
Develop language and concepts.		• What is the job of a paleontologist?
		• What makes dinosaur clues difficult to find?
		• What key questions do dinosaur hunters hope to answer about dinosaurs?
		• What words on the concept web could help you describe dinosaur hunting?

MORE PRACTICE   Have students reread "Dinosaur Hunters." As they read, tell them to make a list of four key questions dinosaur hunters hope to answer. They can share these questions with family members tonight.

Reread for Fluency "Dinosaur Hunters," p. 113

5 minutes

	To Do	**To Say**
CORRECTIVE FEEDBACK	Monitor oral reading.	Read p. 113 aloud. Reread the page three or four times so your reading gets better each time. Give feedback on students' oral reading, using the *if . . . then* statements on Routine Card 4. Model fluent reading if necessary. You may want to have students read along with the DVD-ROM.

ACTIVITY 3 Write

Response to Literature

	To Do	**To Say**
Prompt journal writing.	Write on the board or a transparency: *How do we solve a mystery?*	Take out your journals. This week we are reading about finding clues. Our question for the week is: *How do we solve a mystery?* Write an answer to this question based on what you read today. Have students write about the topic, using what they read and their own experiences.
Homework		Practice Book, p. 77, Vocabulary

ACTIVITY 1 — Word Work

Phonics Suffixes -er, -or, -ish, -ous

	To Do	**To Say**	*5–10 minutes*
Teach suffixes -er, -or, -ish, -ous.	Write on the board or a transparency: *diver, director.*	Remember that a suffix is a group of letters added to the end of a word that can change the word's meaning by changing its part of speech. What part of speech is *dive*? (a verb) Add *-er* to *dive*. What part of speech is *diver*? (a noun) If you add the suffix *-er* or *-or* to a word, it changes the word's meaning to "someone who makes or does something." What does *director* mean? (someone who directs)	
Scaffold instruction.	Write *childish* and *curious.*	*Selfish* ends with the suffix *-ish*, and *curious* ends with the suffix *-ous*. The suffix *-ish* means "like or somewhat." How would a *childish* person behave? (like a child) The suffix *-ous* means "full of." How would a curious person behave? (full of curiosity or the desire to know something)	
	Develop word meaning.	Have students think and converse. What kinds of jobs might a *curious* person be well-suited for? Can being *curious* help you solve problems? How?	
CORRECTIVE FEEDBACK	Write each practice word.	Have students practice reading these words that use the suffixes *-er, -or, -ish,* and *-ous*. Correct any words students miss and have them reread the list.	
		officer reporter senator editor foolish impish joyous dangerous	
MORE PRACTICE	Write more practice words.	Have students practice reading these additional words with the suffixes:	
		biker builder collector inventor sheepish selfish venomous nervous	

Amazing Words — Vocabulary

	To Do	**To Say**	*5 minutes*
Review vocabulary.	Review the homework.	Ask students to go over answers and share their writing from Practice Book p. 77. See Routine Card 1 for the multisyllabic word routine.	

ACTIVITY 2 — Comprehension

Draw Conclusions

	To Do	**To Say**	*5 minutes*
Scaffold instruction.	Introduce drawing conclusions.	Today you will read about mysterious monsters. When you read nonfiction, it's important to draw conclusions based upon the information in the article, as well as your own experience.	
	Model the skill.	For example, if I read that a mysterious creature like Bigfoot might really exist, I need to search the article for facts and think about my own experience, to decide whether or not those claims are true.	
	Distribute Graphic Organizer 2.	As you read "Monster Mysteries: Bigfoot and Nessie," ask yourself the following questions: What assumptions am I making? What assumptions is the author making? Am I generalizing? What can I conclude that the author doesn't say directly? Record the facts and details that support your conclusions on your graphic organizer. See Routine Card 7.	

ACTIVITY 3 Read a Passage

Read for Comprehension "Monster Mysteries: Bigfoot and Nessie," pp. 116–119

| | | *10–15 minutes* |

To Do **To Say**

Scaffold instruction.

Monitor student engagement.

Read Have students read pp. 116–119. Stop at the end of each page to ask questions. Students who can read on their own can do so without stopping. After reading, ask questions to promote discussion.

See Routine Cards 2 and 3.

What evidence supports the idea that Bigfoot exists? (An explorer found large footprints that he claimed were Bigfoot's. Another man filmed Bigfoot and made plaster casts of his footprints. Researchers found a body print of Bigfoot.)

What are some reasons for doubting that Bigfoot is real? (Some footprints and pictures are fakes. No one has ever found any bones or captured Bigfoot.)

Model using context for word meaning.

Read aloud the second paragraph on p. 119. Explain how the examples in sentences 2 and 3 provide clues to the meaning of *convinced*. **Do these people believe that Bigfoot is real?**

Model summarizing.

Think aloud.

Summarize What were the first four pages mainly about? What did you learn about these mysterious monsters? Think aloud to model summarizing. **I learned about evidence that Bigfoot exists, such as stories, sightings, and footprints. But the main thing I learned was that most scientists still don't believe Bigfoot is real, because no one has ever captured Bigfoot or found any Bigfoot bones.**

Develop language and concepts.

Ask questions.

• **Why do people want to believe that Bigfoot is real?**

• **What evidence, besides bones, might convince you that Bigfoot is real?**

MORE PRACTICE

Have students reread p. 119.

Reread After they read, have students draw pictures that show what Bigfoot might look like.

Reread for Fluency "Monster Mysteries: Bigfoot and Nessie," pp. 117–118

| | | *5 minutes* |

To Do **To Say**

MORE PRACTICE

CORRECTIVE FEEDBACK

Pair students. Monitor paired reading.

Students read aloud pp. 117–118, switching readers at the end of the first page. Have partners reread; now the other partner begins. For optimal fluency, students should reread three or four times. Give feedback, using the *if . . . then* statements on Routine Card 4. You may want to have students read along with the DVD-ROM.

ACTIVITY 4 Write

Response to Literature

| | | *5 minutes* |

To Do **To Say**

Prompt writing.

Writing elements: support

After reading pp. 116–119, **what conclusion did you draw about the existence of Bigfoot? Use details from the article as well as your own experience to support your conclusion.**

Homework

Practice Book, p. 78, Suffixes -er, -or, -ish, -ous

ACTIVITY 1 — Word Work

Phonics Suffixes *-er, -or, -ish, -ous*

5 minutes

	To Do	**To Say**
Review suffixes *-er, -or, -ish, -ous.* **Scaffold instruction.**	Review the homework. Discuss the words *Scottish* and *mysterious* on p. 120 in the Student Reader.	Ask students to share answers from Practice Book p. 78. Point out *Scottish*. The suffix *-ish* can mean "like or somewhat." It can also describe a member of a country. What country does a *Scottish* person belong to? (Scotland) Point to *mysterious*. Remember that the suffix *-ous* means "full of." What does *mysterious* mean? ("full of mystery") Ask students to search for nouns that can be changed into adjectives by adding *-ish* or *-ous*. (*Monster* can be changed into *monstrous.*)
MORE PRACTICE	Model spelling words with suffixes.	**Spell and Write** Write *skillful*. What suffix has been added to *skill?* Does the spelling of the base word change when the suffix is added? Continue with *careful* and *carefully* (point out the suffixes).

Amazing Words Vocabulary

5 minutes

	To Do	**To Say**
Build vocabulary. **Lead cumulative review.**	Deepen understanding of *scrutiny*.	Read aloud the last paragraph on p. 119. The author gives a clue to the meaning of *scrutiny* when he says that closer *scrutiny* revealed that the footprints were fakes. What synonym could you substitute for *scrutiny?* (investigation; examination) Why is it important for scientists to subject the evidence they find to close *scrutiny?* (to find information; to figure out whether something is real) Use the Tested Vocabulary Cards to review words from previous weeks.

ACTIVITY 2 — Comprehension

Draw Conclusions

5–10 minutes

	To Do	**To Say**
Scaffold instruction.	Review drawing conclusions.	Remind students to use the information they read in a passage, as well as their own experience, to draw conclusions. An author may not tell you what conclusions he or she has drawn about a subject. You may need to draw your own conclusions based on the information you gather, as well as your own experience.
Guide practice.	Use Graphic Organizer 2.	Listen as I read p. 120. The author is describing the Loch Ness monster. What conclusion do you think you'll be asked to draw? (whether or not the Loch Ness monster exists) What information do you think the article will give to help you draw a conclusion? As you read, add details that help you draw a conclusion to your graphic organizer. See Routine Card 7.
MORE PRACTICE	Have students preview pp. 120–123. Think aloud.	Read the captions and look at the photos on pp. 120–123. What do you think this section will be about? (evidence that the Loch Ness monster exists) Why do you think so? The captions make me think the article will talk about the ways that people have tried to find the Loch Ness monster. From the pictures, I think that people have tried many ways to prove that Nessie is real, like searching underwater or taking pictures.

ACTIVITY **3** # Read a Passage

Read for Comprehension "Monster Mysteries: Bigfoot and Nessie," pp. 120–123

	To Do	To Say	*10–15 minutes*
Scaffold instruction.	Monitor student engagement.	**Read** Have students read pp. 120–123. Stop at the end of each page to ask questions. Students who can read on their own can do so without stopping. After reading, ask questions to promote discussion.	
	See Routine Cards 2 and 3.	**How did things change after Duncan McDonald first reported seeing the Loch Ness monster?** (A road was built along the lake, and many people began to report seeing Nessie.)	
		What did Rines's and Operation Deepscan's sonar find in the lake? (large moving objects) **Why didn't this prove the Loch Ness monster's existence?** (The sonar findings could be explained by waves, gas, or schools of fish.)	
Decode multisyllabic words.	Point out *nicknamed* on p. 120, paragraph 1.	Remind students that a compound word is made up of two smaller words. **What two smaller words do you see in this word?** (*nick* and *named*) A *nickname* is a word used in place of someone's or something's real name. **Why do you think people *nicknamed* the Loch Ness monster "Nessie"?** See Routine Card 1.	
Assess comprehension.	Monitor understanding.	**After Reading** Have students discuss the What Do You Think? question. Prompt them to draw conclusions about what makes the stories of Bigfoot and the Loch Ness monster exciting. Listen as they talk to assess comprehension.	
	Summarize.	**What is this mainly about? What did you learn?** Work with students to summarize the selection.	
MORE PRACTICE	Have students reread p. 122.	**Reread** Have students imagine that they are researchers working on Operation Deepscan. After they read, have them list the possible conclusions that the researchers might have drawn at the end of the study.	

Reread for Fluency "Monster Mysteries: Bigfoot and Nessie," p. 123

	To Do	To Say	*5 minutes*
CORRECTIVE FEEDBACK	Monitor oral reading.	**Read p. 123 aloud. Reread the page three or four times so your reading gets better each time.** Give feedback on students' oral reading, using the *if . . . then* statements on Routine Card 4. Model fluent reading if necessary. You may want to have students read along with the DVD-ROM.	

ACTIVITY **4** # Write

Response to Literature

	To Do	To Say	*5 minutes*
MORE PRACTICE	Prompt writing.	**How are the mysteries of Bigfoot and Nessie similar? Use words that compare, such as *both* and *alike,* to show the similarities.**	
	Homework	Practice Book, p. 79, Draw Conclusions	

Word Work

Amazing Words **Vocabulary**

	To Do	**To Say**	*5–10 minutes*
Extend word knowledge.	Write on the board or a transparency: *investigator, investigation.*	Use the word *investigate* to extend word knowledge. **We read the word *investigate* earlier this week. It means "to examine something in order to find out more about it." Today I want you to notice how adding different suffixes to a word can change that word's meaning.**	
Teach suffixes *-or* and *-ion.*		**What endings have been added to *investigate*?** *(-or, -ion)* **Remember that the suffix *-or* means "one who makes or does something." So an *investigator* is "someone who investigates."**	
		The suffix *-ion* means "the act or result of something." What is an *investigation*? (the act of investigating)	
Scaffold instruction.	Develop word meaning.	**What kinds of people perform *investigations*?** (Examples: researchers, scientists, students, detectives) **What kinds of tools might an investigator use?** (Examples: cameras, sonar, microscopes, telescopes, reference materials)	
MORE PRACTICE	Deepen understanding of *investigator* and *evidence.*	Have individual students or partners use the two words *investigator* and *evidence* together in their own sentences. (For example: An *investigator* looks for *evidence* in order to figure out who committed a crime.) Share sentences. Ask: **What are some ways that an *investigator* might search for *evidence*?**	

Comprehension

Skill and Strategy Practice

	To Do	**To Say**	*5 minutes*
Scaffold instruction.	Review draw conclusions (homework).	Ask volunteers to read the passage and share answers from Practice Book p. 79. Remind students of the importance of drawing conclusions based on the details and information they read, along with their own experience. **Look for details and information that help you draw conclusions about what you read. You can also use your own experience to decide whether something makes sense. For example, if you read that a scientist wears a heavy coat and hat and gloves while working outdoors, you can conclude that he is working in a cold climate.**	
Practice strategic prereading.	See Routine Card 2.	**Discuss Genre** Read the title on p. 124 in the Student Reader. Read page 124 aloud. Model determining genre.	
	Think aloud.	**I first thought this might be fiction because of the funny title. When I read the first page, I knew it was fiction because of the way the characters speak to each other and because of the wild noise that Sue describes.**	
	Review story structure.	**Ask Questions** **What questions do you ask yourself to help you understand a mystery story?** (What is the problem or goal? How is the problem solved or the goal reached?) **As you read this story, ask these questions and look for the answers.**	

ACTIVITY 3 Read a Passage

Read for Comprehension "The Creature on Pine Tree Lane," pp. 124–131

To Do	To Say	*10–15 minutes*

Scaffold instruction.

Monitor student engagement.

See Routine Card 3.

Read Have students read pp. 124–131 on their own and then discuss. For students who need more help, stop at the end of each page to discuss. After reading, ask questions.

What is the first clue that something strange is happening in Jason's backyard? (Sue hears a wild noise and trashcans crashing.)

What does Jason do when he hears the strange noises in the middle of the night? (He goes outside to investigate.)

What does the evidence reveal? (The strange creature is a raccoon.)

How do they capture the creature? (Animal Control captures it in a cage.)

Assess comprehension.

Monitor understanding.

After Reading Have students discuss the What Do You Think? question. Prompt them to name the clues that helped them draw a conclusion. Listen as they talk to assess comprehension.

MORE PRACTICE

Reread Have students reread p. 126. Ask them to guess what conclusion Jason might have drawn about what was hitting the fence before he discovered the trashcan knocking against the gate.

Reread for Fluency "The Creature on Pine Tree Lane," pp. 127–129

To Do	To Say	*5–10 minutes*

CORRECTIVE FEEDBACK

Pair students. Monitor paired reading.

Students read aloud pp. 127–129, switching readers at the end of each page. Have partners reread; now the other partner begins. For optimal fluency, students should reread three or four times. Give feedback, using Routine Card 4. You may want to have students read along with the DVD-ROM.

MORE PRACTICE

READERS' THEATER

Work with a group of four students to adapt pp. 127–129 for Readers' Theater. Have students rehearse reading the parts of Sue, Steve, Jason, and a narrator. Discuss with them what should be cut or added to make the narration read smoothly and make good sense.

ACTIVITY 4 Write

Response to Literature

To Do	To Say	*5 minutes*

Prompt descriptive writing.

Writing elements: organization

Look back at "The Creature on Pine Tree Lane." Describe each of the clues that the three friends find and what conclusions they draw from the clues. Use transitional words and phrases to connect your ideas.

ACTIVITY 1 Read a Passage

Read Together "The Bermuda Triangle Mystery," pp. 132–133

10 minutes

	To Do	To Say
Scaffold instruction.	Review drawing conclusions.	Have students preview pp. 132–133. **This article describes an area of water known as the Bermuda Triangle. Although evidence suggests that this area is not unusual, many people still believe it is a mysterious place. As you read about the Bermuda Triangle, use the information in the article, as well as your own experience, to draw conclusions about its existence.**
	See Routine Card 3.	**Read** Read the article as students follow along. Then read it a second time, having students join in on the text. After reading, ask questions.
		Why did people begin believing that the Bermuda Triangle is a mysterious place? (A reporter wrote an article claiming that many planes and ships had disappeared there.)
		Does the author believe that the Triangle exists? How do you know? (No; the author says that most disappearances within the Triangle have explanations, such as human error or bad weather.)
		What does the U.S. Coast Guard say about the Bermuda Triangle? (There is nothing strange about the area.)
Assess comprehension.	Monitor listening comprehension.	**Summarize** Have students summarize the evidence that the author presents in the article. Listen as they talk to assess comprehension.

ACTIVITY 2 Build Concepts

Amazing Words Vocabulary

5–10 minutes

	To Do	To Say
Review concept and vocabulary	Display the concept web you began on Day 1.	**This week's question is *How do we solve a mystery?* How do this week's words relate to the question?** (Have students answer the question, using some of the vocabulary they learned this week.)
		Ask students to add more words to the concept web. Have students explain how each word relates to finding clues. See Routine Card 5.
MORE PRACTICE	Write *convinced* and *evidence* on the board.	Have students relate *convinced* and *evidence*. **Some people wait to be *convinced* until they see the *evidence* that something is real. But many people continue to believe in strange things, even though *evidence* suggests that these things don't exist. Why?**

ACTIVITY 3 | Write

Response to Literature "4 You 2 Do," p. 134

To Do	To Say	
		5–10 minutes

Guide response activities.

Discuss the directions on p. 134. Tell students to choose one activity to complete. See Routine Card 8.

Word Play Have students complete the first part on their own and then meet with a partner to share their synonyms for the other vocabulary words.

Making Connections Discuss the questions in a group. (Possible answers: The mystery of the creature on Pine Tree Lane is solved completely, and so was the mystery of the Bermuda Triangle. The mysteries of Bigfoot and Nessie have not been solved completely.)

On Paper Invite partners or small groups to brainstorm some ideas before students write their own legends. Have them write on their own. Students can use Practice Book p. 80 to structure their written responses, or you can send the Practice Book page home for them to complete later.

MORE PRACTICE

Extend the writing.

If you have more time, direct students to complete all the activities.

ACTIVITY 4 | Assessment Options

End-of-Unit Test

To Do	To Say	
		10–15 minutes

Assess fluency and comprehension.

Use Assessment Book, p. 60.

Options for end-of-unit assessment are available in the Assessment Book, p. 60.

Homework

Practice Book, p. 80, Writing

Unit 5 Week 1 *Emergencies*

 What can we do in emergencies?

Objectives *This week students will...*

Vocabulary
- build concepts and vocabulary: *dangerous, destroyed, exciting, hazards, hero, profession*

Phonics
- read words with vowel combinations: diphthongs *oi, oy*
- apply knowledge of word structure to decode multisyllabic words when reading

Text Comprehension
- compare and contrast to improve comprehension
- write in response to literature
- make connections across texts

Fluency
- practice fluency with oral rereading

Word Work *This week's phonics focus is . . .*

Diphthongs *oi, oy*

Amazing Words Concept/Amazing Words *Tested Vocabulary*

The week's vocabulary is related to the concept of emergencies.
The first appearance of each word in the Student Reader is noted below.

dangerous	not safe (p. 9)
destroyed	damaged something very badly; ruined (p. 14)
exciting	thrilling; causing strong, lively feelings (p. 12)
hazards	things that may cause damage or injury (p. 11)
hero	someone admired for his or her bravery (p. 8)
profession	an occupation that requires special training and study (p. 15)

Student Reader Unit 5 *This week students will read the following selections.*

Daily Lesson Plan

	ACTIVITIES	MATERIALS
Day 1	**Build Concepts** Weekly Concept: Emergencies Vocabulary: *dangerous, destroyed, exciting, hazards, hero, profession* **Read a Passage** "Quick Thinking," pp. 8–11 Comprehension: Use Strategies Reread for Fluency **Write** Response to Literature	Student Reader: Unit 5 Routine Cards 2, 4, 5 Tested Vocabulary Cards Student journals Practice Book, p. 81, Vocabulary Student Reader DVD-ROM
Day 2	**Word Work** Phonics: Words with vowel combinations: Diphthongs *oi, oy* Vocabulary: Deepen word meaning **Comprehension** Compare and Contrast **Read a Passage** "Heroes Who Help," pp. 12–15 Reread for Fluency **Write** Response to Literature	Student Reader: Unit 5 Practice Book, p. 81, Vocabulary Graphic Organizer 3 Routine Cards 1, 2, 3, 4, 7 Practice Book, p. 82, Diphthongs *oi, oy* Student Reader DVD-ROM
Day 3	**Word Work** Phonics: Words with vowel combinations: Diphthongs *oi, oy* Vocabulary: Deepen word meaning **Comprehension** Compare and Contrast **Read a Passage** "Heroes Who Help," pp. 16–19 Reread for Fluency **Write** Response to Literature	Practice Book, p. 82, Diphthongs *oi, oy* Tested Vocabulary Cards Student Reader: Unit 5 Graphic Organizer 3 Routine Cards 1, 2, 3, 4, 7 Practice Book, p. 83, Compare and Contrast Student Reader DVD-ROM
Day 4	**Word Work** Vocabulary: Extend word knowledge **Comprehension** Skill and Strategy Practice **Read a Passage** "Calling New Smokejumpers," pp. 20–27 Reread for Fluency **Write** Response to Literature	Practice Book, p. 83, Compare and Contrast Student Reader: Unit 5 Routine Cards 2, 3, 4 Student Reader DVD-ROM
Day 5	**Read a Passage** "Wildfires!," pp. 28–29 Comprehension: Compare and Contrast; Listening **Build Concepts** Vocabulary **Write** Response to Literature: "4 You 2 Do," p. 30 **Assessment Options** Fluency Comprehension	Student Reader: Unit 5 Routine Cards 3, 5, 6, 8 Fluency Progress Chart, p. 185 Practice Book, p. 84, Writing

See pp. xvi–xvii for how *My Sidewalks* integrates instructional practices for ELL.

Amazing Words **Vocabulary**

| To Do | To Say | *10–15 minutes* |

Develop oral vocabulary.

See Routine Card 6 and p. 203.

Introduce the Concept/Amazing Words with an oral routine prior to displaying them in print. Page 203 in this Teacher's Guide provides specific guidelines for introducing each word.

Develop word meaning.

See Routine Card 5. Discuss pp. 7–11.

Have students read p. 7 and then look at the pictures on pp. 8–11. **What kinds of workers do you see?** (firefighter, police officer, paramedic, someone who answers 911 calls) **Can you use the word** *emergencies* **to describe what you see on p. 9?** (These people can help during *emergencies*.)

Scaffold instruction.

Create a concept web.

In the center of a web, write *Emergencies*. **This week's concept is** *emergencies*. **Emergencies are times when people need to do something right away to fix serious problems.** Provide an example to demonstrate meaning. **Fires and car accidents are examples of emergencies.**

Add the other vocabulary words.

Concept and Language Goals

Discuss the meaning of each word as it relates to emergencies, using the glossary as needed. (See p. 62 in this Teacher's Guide for definitions.)

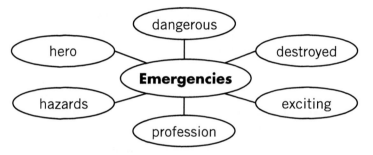

Model the multisyllabic word strategy.

Display each word. Say it as you display it.

Use the Tested Vocabulary Cards. Follow this routine for each word:

- **Look for Meaningful Parts** **Do you recognize any parts of this word? What do these parts mean? Use the parts to read the word.** Be sure students notice the following: *danger, destroy, excite.*

Think aloud.

- **Model** **I recognize the word** *danger* **at the beginning of** *dangerous*. **I know that** *danger* **means "something that may cause harm." I also see the suffix** *-ous* **at the end of the word. I know that** *-ous* **at the end of a word means "full of." So** *dangerous* **must mean "full of harm."** Discuss other words with this base word: *dangerously, endanger.*

Point to *hazards.*

- **Chunk Words with No Recognizable Parts** Model how to chunk the word *hazards*. **I see a chunk at the beginning of the word:** *haz*. **I see another chunk at the end of the word:** *ards*. **I say each chunk slowly:** *haz ards*. **I say the chunks fast to make a whole word:** *haz ards*. **Is it a real word? Yes, I've heard the word** *hazards*.

- Have students practice reading each word.

Preview.

Read p. 6 with students.

Do you see any words we just learned on this page? Together with students, read the sentences on p. 6 describing each selection. Talk about how the vocabulary words might be used in the selections.

MORE PRACTICE

Deepen understanding of *emergencies.*

Have students demonstrate understanding by answering questions. **What kinds of** *emergencies* **do rescue workers respond to? Give examples. Why must rescue workers handle emergencies quickly?**

ACTIVITY 2 Read a Passage

Develop Concepts "Quick Thinking," pp. 8–11

| To Do | To Say | *10–15 minutes* |

Practice strategic prereading.

See Routine Card 2.

Discuss Genre Read the title on p. 8 and look at the pictures on pp. 8–11. Model determining genre.

Think aloud.

The photographs are a clue that this is nonfiction. I see pictures of real people. I think this article will tell me about these people and how they can help in emergencies.

Scaffold instruction.

Review text structure.

Ask Questions What questions do you ask yourself to help you understand nonfiction? (What did I learn? What is this mainly about?) **As you read this article, ask these questions and look for answers.**

Guide comprehension.

Read pp. 8–11 aloud.

Read Read the article as students follow along. Then read it a second time, having students join in. If necessary, stop at the end of each page to check comprehension. Ask questions to promote discussion and develop the concept.

Develop language and concepts.

- **Why does the nine-year-old boy call 9-1-1?**
- **Why are rescue workers important to people in an emergency?**
- **How can people keep cleaning supplies from harming small children?**
- **What words on the concept web could help you describe emergencies?**

MORE PRACTICE

Have students reread "Quick Thinking." As they read, tell them to list ways they can help others in an emergency. They can share what they learned about emergencies with family members.

Reread for Fluency "Quick Thinking," p. 9

| To Do | To Say | *5 minutes* |

CORRECTIVE FEEDBACK

Monitor oral reading.

Read p. 9 aloud. Reread the page three or four times so your reading gets better each time. Give feedback on students' oral reading, using the *if . . . then* statements on Routine Card 4. Model fluent reading if necessary. You may want to have students read along with the DVD-ROM.

ACTIVITY 3 Write

Response to Literature

| To Do | To Say | *5 minutes* |

Prompt journal writing.

Write on the board or a transparency: *What can we do in emergencies?*

Take out your journals. This week we are reading about emergencies. Our question for the week is: *What can we do in emergencies?* Write an answer to this question based on what you read today. Have students write about the topic, using what they read and their own experiences.

Homework   Practice Book, p. 81, Vocabulary

ACTIVITY 1 Word Work

Phonics Diphthongs *oi, oy*

5–10 minutes

	To Do	**To Say**
Teach diphthongs *oi, oy*.	Write on the board or a transparency: *The <u>royal</u> yacht headed out to sea.*	Remember, when you read a long word, look for meaningful parts. What parts do you see in *royal*? *(roy al)* What vowel sound do you hear in the first syllable of *royal*? (/oi/) The first syllable in *royal* contains the diphthong *oy*, pronounced /oi/. A diphthong is a single vowel sound, represented by two letters, that resembles a glide from one sound to another. Sometimes *oy* and *oi* stand for a diphthong. In a diphthong each letter contributes to the sound you hear.
Scaffold instruction.	Develop word meaning.	Have students think and converse. Hundreds of years ago, *royalty* frequently traveled on ships. Why? What might a *royal* ship carry on board?
	Write *pointing*.	Here is another word with a diphthong. What parts do you see in the word? *(point, ing)* What sound do you hear in the first syllable? (/oi/) What letters contribute to the vowel sound? *(oi)* Guide students in blending the word parts into the whole word.
CORRECTIVE FEEDBACK	Write each practice word.	Have students practice reading these words with diphthongs *oi* and *oy*. Correct any words students miss and have them reread the list.
		broiler viewpoint moisture enjoying employer boyish
MORE PRACTICE	Write more practice words.	Have students practice reading these words.
		sirloin recoil noisiest annoying oysters disloyal

Amazing Words Vocabulary

5 minutes

	To Do	**To Say**
Review vocabulary.	Review the homework.	Ask students to go over answers and share their writing from Practice Book p. 81. See Routine Card 1 for the multisyllabic word routine.
	Deepen understanding of *hero*.	Remember, a *hero* is a person admired for his or her bravery. A person who saves someone from drowning is considered a *hero*. What other things might a hero do? Who is a hero in your family or community?

ACTIVITY 2 Comprehension

Compare and Contrast

5 minutes

	To Do	**To Say**
Scaffold instruction.	Introduce compare and contrast.	Today you will read about people who help in emergencies. When you read, you can discover the ways that two or more things are alike, and the ways that they are different. Finding similarities and differences is called comparing and contrasting. Comparing and contrasting can help you to better understand what you read.
	Model the skill.	For example, if I read about two heroes who helped save people's lives in a fire, but one hero put out the fire and the other took people to the hospital, I've found one way that the heroes are similar, and one way that they are different.
	Distribute Graphic Organizer 3.	As you read "Heroes Who Help," look for similarities and differences between the heroes. Add these details to your graphic organizer. See Routine Card 7.

ACTIVITY 3 Read a Passage

Read for Comprehension "Heroes Who Help," pp. 12–15

To Do	**To Say**	
		10–15 minutes

Scaffold instruction.

Monitor student engagement.

Read Have students read pp. 12–15. Stop at the end of each page to ask questions. Students who can read on their own may do so without stopping. After reading, ask questions to promote discussion.

See Routine Cards 2 and 3.

What do paramedics do? (They treat people who are injured.) **What tools do they use?** (ambulance, bandages, cold packs, splints, breathing masks, heart monitors)

How is a firefighter similar to a paramedic? (They both help people in emergencies; both complete many hours in training.)

Point out *destroyed* on p. 14.

First, I look for a base word. Here is the base word *destroy,* **and here is an ending, *-ed.* I know from the letters** *oy* **that the vowel sound is /oi/. So now I can say the whole word:** *destroyed.*

What do you think the rest of the article will be about? (Answers will vary. The title suggests it will tell more about people who are "heroes who help.")

Model summarizing

Think aloud.

Summarize What were these four pages mainly about? What did you learn about heroes who help? Think aloud to model summarizing. **I learned that paramedics and firefighters are heroes who help. I learned details about their jobs, like the kinds of emergencies they respond to, the training they need, and the tools they use. The main thing I learned is that they both help people in emergencies.**

Develop language and concepts.

Ask questions.

• **What do paramedics do in an emergency?**

• **How are firefighters heroes?**

MORE PRACTICE

Have students reread p. 13.

After they reread this page, have students write a sentence explaining what they learned.

Reread for Fluency "Heroes Who Help," pp. 14–15

To Do	**To Say**	
		5 minutes

MORE PRACTICE

CORRECTIVE FEEDBACK

Pair students. Monitor paired reading.

Students read aloud pp. 14–15, switching readers at the end of each page. Have partners reread; now the other partner begins. For optimal fluency, students should reread three or four times. Give feedback, using the *if . . . then* statements on Routine Card 4. You may want to have students read along with the DVD-ROM.

 ACTIVITY 4 Write

Response to Literature

To Do	**To Say**	
		5 minutes

Prompt writing.

Writing elements: support

The article says that the paramedics' work is exciting. Use details from the selection to describe the exciting part of a paramedic's job.

Homework

Practice Book, p. 82, Diphthongs *oi, oy*

ACTIVITY 1 — Word Work

Phonics Diphthongs *oi, oy*

5 minutes

	To Do	To Say
Review diphthongs *oi, oy*. **Scaffold instruction.**	Review the homework. Discuss *poisonous* on p. 11 in the Student Reader.	Ask students to share answers from Practice Book p. 82. Point out *poisonous* on p. 11, in the last item of the checklist. **Remember that *oy* and *oi* can stand for a diphthong. In a diphthong each letter contributes to the vowel sound you hear. What vowel sound do you hear in the first syllable of *poisonous*?** (/oi/) **What letters combine to make the diphthong?** *(oi)* Then point to *destroyed* on p. 14. **What vowel sound do you hear in the second syllable of *destroyed*?** (/oi/) **What letters combine to make the diphthong?** *(oy)* Ask students to think of other words that contain diphthongs *oy* and *oi*.
MORE PRACTICE	Model words with diphthongs *oi* and *oy*.	**Spell and Write** Write *join* and *boy*. Say *join*. **What vowel sound do you hear in this word? What letters spell that vowel sound?** Underline *oi*. Continue with *boy* (*oy*). **Do you know other words with *oi* or *oy* that have the same vowel sound as *join* and *boy*?** List responses on the board.

 ### Vocabulary

5 minutes

	To Do	To Say
Build vocabulary.	Deepen understanding of *professions*.	Read aloud the paragraph on p. 18. **Remember that *professions* are jobs that require special training. People in the lifeguard profession help others at pools and beaches. What are some other professions that help people? Where do they work?**

ACTIVITY 2 — Comprehension

Compare and Contrast

5–10 minutes

	To Do	To Say
Scaffold instruction.	Review compare and contrast.	Comparing and contrasting things can help you better understand a reading. Clue words, such as *like, also, unlike,* and *however,* may signal a comparison. Remember, not all comparisons are signaled by clue words.
Guide practice.	Use Graphic Organizer 3.	Listen as I read p. 16. I want you to notice that the author is describing the job of a lifeguard. Read p. 16. Then ask: **How are lifeguards like paramedics and fire fighters?** (They are all rescue workers.) **How are they different?** (Lifeguards work where the emergency happens.) **Add these details to your graphic organizer.** See Routine Card 7.
MORE PRACTICE	Have students preview pp. 16–19.	**Read the captions and look at the pictures on pp. 16–19. What do you think this section will be about?** (other kinds of rescue workers) **Why do you think so?** Think aloud to model using photographs and captions to predict.
	Think aloud.	I see several different kinds of workers. From the captions, I think the article will tell about lifeguards, rescue workers who teach about safety, and people who hand out food.

ACTIVITY 3 Read a Passage

Read for Comprehension "Heroes Who Help," pp. 16–19

To Do	To Say	
		10–15 minutes

Scaffold instruction.

Monitor student engagement.

Read Have students read pp. 16–19. Stop at the end of each page to ask questions. Students who can read on their own can do so without stopping. After reading, ask questions to promote discussion.

See Routine Cards 2 and 3.

What do lifeguards do? (rescue swimmers who are in trouble; warn about dangers in the water; enforce rules)

What are two ways lifeguards are like other rescue workers? (They help people in trouble; they use special equipment.)

How are rescue workers heroes every day? (They help us even when there is no emergency. They teach us how to stay safe and prevent emergencies.)

Review the multisyllabic word strategy.

Point out *professions* on p. 18.

Remember what you've learned about chunking a word into parts that you recognize. Ask a volunteer to divide *professions* into chunks *(pro fes sions)*. Have another volunteer pronounce the chunks. Point out the short *e* in *fes*. See Routine Card 1.

Assess comprehension.

Monitor understanding.

After Reading Have students discuss the What Do You Think? question. Prompt them to find similarities and differences among rescue worker jobs. Listen as they talk to assess comprehension.

Summarize.

What is this mainly about? What did you learn? Work with students to summarize the selection.

MORE PRACTICE

Have students reread p. 18.

Reread As they read, tell students to note the similarities and differences in how various types of rescue workers help others to prevent emergencies. Have students add these details to their graphic organizers.

Reread for Fluency "Heroes Who Help," p. 18–19

To Do	To Say	
		5 minutes

CORRECTIVE FEEDBACK

Monitor oral reading.

Read pp. 18–19 aloud. Reread the page three or four times so your reading gets better each time. Give feedback on students' oral reading, using the *if . . . then* statements on Routine Card 4. Model fluent reading if necessary. You may want to have students read along with the DVD-ROM.

 ACTIVITY 4 Write

Response to Literature

To Do	To Say	
		5 minutes

MORE PRACTICE

Prompt writing.

In what ways are paramedics, firefighters, and lifeguards heroes? Use details from the article to support your answer.

Homework   Practice Book, p. 83, Compare and Contrast

ACTIVITY **1** Word Work

 **Vocabulary**

	To Do	**To Say**	*5–10 minutes*
Extend word knowledge.	Write on the board or a transparency: *Our trip down the river was <u>exciting</u>.*	Use the word *exciting* to extend word knowledge. **Remember we read this word earlier this week and learned its meaning. Something that is** *exciting* **causes strong and lively feelings. Today I want you to find synonyms and antonyms for** *exciting.*	
Teach synonyms and antonyms for *exciting*.		**You know that synonyms are words that have the same or similar meanings. Antonyms are words that have opposite meanings. What are some synonyms for** *exciting*? *(thrilling, breathtaking, amazing, intense, inspiring, awesome)* Write words as students name them and add some of your own. **What are some antonyms for** *exciting*? *(boring, dull, tiresome, ordinary, calm, numbing)* Write words as students name them and add some of your own. Practice pronouncing all of the words.	
Scaffold instruction.	Develop word meaning.	**If you do something over and over, can it still be** *exciting*? **Why or why not?**	
MORE PRACTICE	Deepen understanding of *exciting* and *dangerous*.	Have individual students or partners use the two words *exciting* and *dangerous* together in sentences. (For example: The rafting trip was *dangerous*, but it was also *exciting*.) Share sentences. Ask: **Does an activity need to be** *dangerous* **in order to be** *exciting*? **Why or why not?**	

ACTIVITY **2** Comprehension

Skill and Strategy Practice

	To Do	**To Say**	*5 minutes*
Scaffold instruction.	Review compare and contrast (homework).	Ask volunteers to read the passage and share answers from Practice Book p. 83. Remind students of the importance of comparing and contrasting. **When you read fiction, you can compare characters, settings, and events. You can also compare one story to another, or to real life. As you read "Calling New Smokejumpers," look for similarities and differences that help you better understand the story.**	
Practice strategic prereading.	See Routine Card 2.	**Discuss Genre** Read the title and the first paragraph on p. 20. Model determining genre.	
	Think aloud.	**I first thought "Smokejumpers" might be fiction because of the pictures. When I read the first page, I knew it was fiction because of the description of how the main character feels.**	
	Review story structure.	**Ask Questions** **What questions do you ask yourself to help you understand a fictional story?** (What is the problem or goal? How is the problem solved or the goal reached?) **As you read this story, ask these questions and look for the answers.**	

ACTIVITY 3 Read a Passage

Read for Comprehension "Calling New Smokejumpers," pp. 20–27

10–15 minutes

	To Do	**To Say**
Scaffold instruction.	Monitor student engagement. See Routine Card 3.	**Read** Have students read pp. 20–27 on their own and then discuss. For students who need more help, stop at the end of each page to discuss. After reading, ask questions. **Who are the main characters in this story?** (Steve, Uncle Henry, and Jim Park) **Where does the story take place?** (a smokejumper's cabin in Montana) **What problem does Steve face?** (He is alone in the cabin and has to handle any calls that come in.) **What problem does Jim have?** (He's trapped in his house and a fire is approaching. He's alone with his dog.) **How does Steve help in the rescue?** (First he keeps Jim calm by staying on the phone with him; then he follows the step-by-step instructions Uncle Henry gives him.)
Assess comprehension.	Monitor understanding.	**After Reading** Have students discuss the What Do You Think? question. Prompt them to use words that signal comparisons to describe Steve's feelings at the beginning and the end of the story. Listen as they talk to assess comprehension.
MORE PRACTICE		**Reread** Have students reread pp. 24–27 and list the sequence of events the rescuers follow after Jim's call for help comes in.

Reread for Fluency "Calling New Smokejumpers," pp. 21–23

5–10 minutes

	To Do	**To Say**
CORRECTIVE FEEDBACK	Pair students. Monitor paired reading.	Students read aloud pp. 21–23, switching readers at the end of each paragraph. Have partners reread; now the other partner begins. For optimal fluency, students should reread three or four times. Give feedback, using Routine Card 4. You may want to have students read along with the DVD-ROM.
MORE PRACTICE	**READERS' THEATER**	Work with a group of students to adapt pp. 21–23 as a radio play. Have students rehearse reading the parts: narrator and operator, Steve, Jim, and Uncle Henry. Decide in advance whether students should read the speech tags ("Steve asked") or delete them.

ACTIVITY 4 Write

Response to Literature

5 minutes

	To Do	**To Say**
Prompt expository writing.	Review pp. 23–25. Writing elements: organization	Before Uncle Henry leaves with the other smokejumpers, he gives Steve clear instructions. Explain the sequence of the instructions, using words such as *first* and *then.*

ACTIVITY 1 — Read a Passage

Read Together "Wildfires!" pp. 28–29

10 minutes

	To Do	To Say
Scaffold instruction.	Review compare and contrast.	Have students preview pp. 28–29. **This article tells how wildfires can start, how to put them out, and how to prevent them. When you read about an emergency, you can compare and contrast how to handle the emergency with how to prevent it. As you read "Wildfires!" look for similarities and differences between fighting wildfires and preventing them.**
	See Routine Card 3.	**Read** Read the article as students follow along. Then read it a second time, having students join in on the text. After reading, ask questions.
		What three things does a fire need in order to burn? (fuel, air, and heat)
		What do firefighters drop to control the heat of a fire? (water)
		What do they drop to cut off a fire's air supply? (a soupy mixture called slurry)
		How does NASA help prevent wildfires before they start? (Satellite photographs show danger zones so firefighters know where to go before trouble begins.)
Assess comprehension.	Monitor listening comprehension.	**Summarize** Have one student explain how wildfires start and another student explain some of the methods used to fight wildfires.

ACTIVITY 2 — Build Concepts

Amazing Words Vocabulary

5–10 minutes

	To Do	To Say
Review concept and vocabulary.	**Concept and Language Goals**	**This week's question is *What can we do in emergencies*? How do this week's words relate to the question?** (Have students answer the question, using some of the vocabulary they learned this week.)
	Display the concept web you began on Day 1.	Ask students to add more words to the concept web. Have students explain how each word relates to emergencies. Monitor students' understanding of vocabulary as they discuss the web. See Routine Card 5.
MORE PRACTICE	Write *profession* and *hazards* on the board.	Have students relate *profession* and *hazards*. **Give an example of a *profession* where you would face one or more *hazards*. What are some *hazards* you would face? Why do people undertake *professions* that involve *hazards*?**

ACTIVITY **3** Write

Response to Literature "4 You 2 Do," p. 30

| To Do | To Say | 5–10 minutes |

Guide response activities.

Discuss the directions on p. 30.

Tell students to choose one activity to complete. See Routine Card 8.

Word Play Have students make words on their own and then meet with a partner to share word lists.

Making Connections Discuss the question in a group. (Sample answer: Yes, Steve would make a good paramedic because he has shown the ability to follow instructions, stay calm, and keep a person calm during an emergency situation.)

On Paper Have students brainstorm answers to the prompt before they write. Then have them write on their own. Students can use Practice Book p. 84 to structure their written responses, or you can send the Practice Book page home for them to complete later.

MORE PRACTICE

If you have more time, direct students to complete all the activities.

ACTIVITY **4** Assessment Options

Passage Reading

| To Do | To Say | 10–15 minutes |

See Routine Card 6.

While some students are doing Activity 3, determine which students you want to assess this week and choose from these options.

Check fluency.

Take a two-minute timed sample of each student's oral reading.

Check comprehension.

Fluency Have a student read for two minutes from "Calling New Smokejumpers." Record the number of correct words read per minute. See p. 184 for monitoring fluency. Be sure each student is assessed at least every other week.

Have students graph their progress on the Fluency Progress Chart, p. 185.

Retelling Have students reread "Calling New Smokejumpers" and retell it. Prompt students if necessary. See p. 186 for monitoring retelling.

If you have time, assess every student.

Homework

Practice Book, p. 84, Writing

Unit 5 Week 2 *Past Times*

 What surprises can the past hold for us?

Objectives *This week students will...*

Vocabulary
- build concepts and vocabulary: *ancient, civilization, society, statue, theater, traditions*

Phonics
- read words with common syllables *-ion, -tion, -sion, -ture*
- apply knowledge of word structure to decode multisyllabic words when reading

Text Comprehension
- compare and contrast to improve comprehension
- write in response to literature
- make connections across text

Fluency
- practice fluency with oral rereading

Word Work *This week's phonics focus is . . .*

Common Syllables *-ion, -tion, -sion, -ture*

Amazing Words Concept/Amazing Words *Tested Vocabulary*

The week's vocabulary is related to the concept of past times.
The first appearance of each word in the Student Reader is noted below.

ancient	belonging to times long past (p. 35)
civilization	a group of people who work together in many ways, such as building cities, creating laws, and making art (p. 34)
society	all the people; human beings living together as a group (p. 38)
statue	a figure made from stone, wood, or metal to look like a person or animal (p. 48)
theater	a place where people go to see movies or plays (p. 47)
traditions	the process of handing down beliefs, opinions, customs, and stories from parents to children (p. 38)

Student Reader Unit 5 *This week students will read the following selections.*

34	**Civilization**	Expository Nonfiction
38	**Ancient Builders**	Expository Nonfiction
46	**It's Still Standing!**	Realistic Fiction
54	**Forever Sleeping Under Rome**	Expository Nonfiction
56	**4 You 2 Do**	Activity Page

Daily Lesson Plan

	ACTIVITIES	MATERIALS
Day 1	**Build Concepts** Weekly Concept: Past Times Vocabulary: *ancient, civilization, society, statue, theater, traditions* **Read a Passage** "Civilization," pp. 34–37 Comprehension: Use Strategies Reread for Fluency **Write** Response to Literature	Student Reader: Unit 5 Routine Cards 2, 4, 5 Tested Vocabulary Cards Student journals Practice Book, p. 85, Vocabulary Student Reader DVD-ROM
Day 2	**Word Work** Phonics: Common Syllables *-ion, -tion, -sion, -ture* Vocabulary: Deepen word meaning **Comprehension** Compare and Contrast **Read a Passage** "Ancient Builders," pp. 38–41 Reread for Fluency **Write** Response to Literature	Student Reader: Unit 5 Practice Book, p. 85, Vocabulary Graphic Organizer 3 Routine Cards 1, 2, 3, 4, 7 Practice Book, p. 86, Common Syllables *-ion, -tion, -sion, -ture* Student Reader DVD-ROM

Day 3	**Word Work** Phonics: Common Syllables *-ion, -tion, -sion, -ture*
	Vocabulary: Deepen word meaning
	Comprehension Compare and Contrast
	Read a Passage "Ancient Builders," pp. 42–45
	Reread for Fluency
	Write Response to Literature
		Practice Book, p. 86, Common Syllables
		  -ion, -tion, -sion, -ture
		Tested Vocabulary Cards
		Student Reader: Unit 5
		Graphic Organizer 3
		Routine Cards 2, 3, 4, 7
		Practice Book, p. 87,
		  Compare and Contrast
		Student Reader DVD-ROM

Day 4	**Word Work** Vocabulary: Extend word knowledge **Comprehension** Skill and Strategy Practice **Read a Passage** "It's Still Standing!" pp. 46–53 Reread for Fluency **Write** Response to Literature	Practice Book, p. 87, Compare and Contrast Student Reader: Unit 5 Routine Cards 2, 3, 4 Student Reader DVD-ROM
Day 5	**Read a Passage** "Forever Sleeping Under Rome," pp. 54–55 Comprehension: Compare and Contrast; Listening **Build Concepts** Vocabulary **Write** Response to Literature: "4 You 2 Do," p. 56 **Assessment Options** Fluency Comprehension	Student Reader: Unit 5 Routine Cards 3, 5, 6, 8 Fluency Progress Chart, p. 185 Practice Book, p. 88, Writing

See pp. xvi–xvii for how *My Sidewalks* integrates instructional practices for ELL.

Build Concepts

Amazing Words **Vocabulary**

	To Do	**To Say**
Develop oral vocabulary.	See Routine Card 6 and p. 204.	Introduce the Concept/Amazing Words with an oral routine prior to displaying them in print. Page 204 in this Teacher's Guide provides specific guidelines for introducing each word.
Develop word meaning.	See Routine Card 5. Discuss pp. 33–37.	Have students read p. 33 and then look at the pictures on pp. 34–37. **What do you notice?** (different buildings, new and old, from different civilizations around the world) **Can you use the word** *civilization* **to describe any of these pictures?** (Example: Some ancient *civilizations* are known today by the kinds of buildings they created.)
Scaffold instruction.	Create a concept web.	In the center of a web, write *Past Times*. **This week's concept is** *past times.* **Learning about the past can help us better understand the present.** Provide an example to demonstrate meaning. **When we study past** *civilizations,* **we learn about how people lived, what was important to them, and the similarities and differences between their lifestyles and ours.**
	Add the other vocabulary words.	Discuss the meaning of each word as it relates to past times, using the glossary as needed. (See p. 74 in this Teacher's Guide for definitions.)
	Concept and Language Goals	

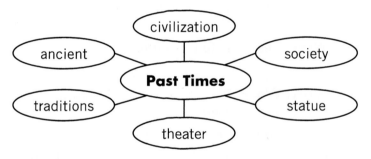

Model the multisyllabic word strategy.	Display each word. Say it as you display it.	Use the Tested Vocabulary Cards. Follow this routine for each word:
		• **Look for Meaningful Parts** **Do you recognize any parts of this word? What do these parts mean? Use the parts to read the word.** As you introduce each word, be sure students notice *civiliz(e).*
		• **Chunk Words with No Recognizable Parts** Model how to chunk the word *traditions* to read it.
	Think aloud.	• **Model** **I see a chunk at the beginning of the word:** *tra.* **I see a part in the middle:** *di.* **I see a part at the end of the word:** *tions.* **I say each chunk slowly:** *tra di tions.* **I say the chunks fast to make a whole word:** *traditions.* **Is it a real word? Yes, I know the word** *traditions.*
		• Have students practice reading each word.
Preview.	Read p. 32 with students.	**Do you see any of the words we just learned on this page?** Together with students, read the sentences on p. 32 describing each selection. Talk about how the concept words might be used in the selections.
MORE PRACTICE	Deepen understanding of *civilization.*	Have students demonstrate understanding by answering questions. **Which is an example of something you would find in most civilizations, a written language or a democratic government? Why? What kinds of things affect the way a civilization develops?**

ACTIVITY 2 Read a Passage

Develop Concepts "Civilization," pp. 34–37

To Do	To Say	
		10–15 minutes

Practice strategic prereading.

See Routine Card 2.

Discuss Genre Read the title on p. 34 and have students look at the illustrations on pp. 34–37. Model determining genre.

Think aloud.

The photographs are clues that this is nonfiction. They look like photos of real places. I think this article will tell me about different civilizations and how they grew.

Scaffold instruction.

Review text structure.

Ask Questions What questions do you ask yourself to help you understand nonfiction? (What did I learn? What is this mainly about?) **As you read this article, ask these questions and look for the answers.**

Guide comprehension.

Read pp. 34–37 aloud.

Read Read the article as students follow along. Then read it a second time, having students join in. If necessary, stop at the end of each paragraph to check comprehension. Ask questions to promote discussion and develop the concept.

Develop language and concepts.

- **What are the benefits of belonging to a civilization?**
- **Where did civilization begin?**
- **How have the ancient Egyptians influenced farmers today?**
- **What ancient civilizations have influenced our government? How?**
- **What words on the concept web could help you describe past civilizations?**

MORE PRACTICE

Have students reread "Civilization." As they read, tell them to make a list of the ways that we have been influenced by past civilizations. Invite students to share their lists with family members tonight.

Reread for Fluency "Civilization," p. 36

To Do	To Say	
		5 minutes

CORRECTIVE FEEDBACK

Monitor oral reading.

Read p. 36 aloud. Reread the page three or four times so your reading gets better each time. Give feedback on students' oral reading, using the *if . . . then* statements on Routine Card 4. Model fluent reading if necessary. You may want to have students read along with the DVD-ROM.

ACTIVITY 3 Write

Response to Literature

To Do	To Say	
		5 minutes

Prompt journal writing.

Write on the board or a transparency: *What surprises can the past hold for us?*

Take out your journals. This week we are reading about past times. Our question for this week is: *What surprises can the past hold for us?* Write an answer to this question based on what you read today. Have students write about the topic, using what they read and their own experiences.

Homework

Practice Book, p. 85, Vocabulary

ACTIVITY 1 — Word Work

Phonics Common Syllables *-ion, -tion, -sion, -ture*

	To Do	To Say	5–10 minutes
Teach common syllables -ion, -tion, -sion, -ture.	Write on the board or a transparency: *The members of a <u>civilization</u> usually practice a <u>religion</u>.*	Remember, when you read a long word, look for meaningful parts. **What part do you see in** *civilization?* *(civilize)* **How can we chunk** *civilization* **to read it?** *(civ il i za tion)* **What chunks do you see in** *religion?* *(re lig ion)* Guide students in blending the chunks into each whole word.	
		Syllables such as *ion, tion, sion,* and *ture* are often found in words. They are referred to as "common syllables." You can use these common syllables to read long words.	
Scaffold instruction.	Develop word meaning.	Have students think and converse. **Why is** *religion* **often an important part of a** *civilization?* **How does** *religion* **bring people together?**	
	Write *division* and *future.*	Here are two more words with common syllables. **What chunks do you see in** *division?* *(di vi sion)* **What chunks do you see in** *future?* *(fu ture)* Guide students in blending the chunks into each whole word.	
CORRECTIVE FEEDBACK	Write each practice word.	Have students practice reading words with *ion, tion, sion,* and *ture.* Correct any words students miss and have them reread the list.	
		fusion champion division admission pollution mature	
MORE PRACTICE	Write more practice words.	Have students practice reading words with *ion, tion, sion,* and *ture.*	
		companion creature station permission location lecture	

 ### Vocabulary

	To Do	To Say	5 minutes
Review vocabulary.	Review the homework.	Ask students to go over answers and share their writing from Practice Book p. 85. See Routine Card 1 for multisyllabic word routine.	
	Deepen understanding of *ancient.*	Remember, *ancient* things belong to times long past. The pyramids of Egypt are a popular tourist destination. **Why are the pyramids an example of something** *ancient?* **What else is an example of something** *ancient?* **Why?**	

ACTIVITY 2 — Comprehension

Compare and Contrast

	To Do	To Say	5 minutes
Scaffold instruction.	Introduce compare and contrast.	Today you will read about an ancient Native American civilization. When you read, you can compare the ways two or more things are alike and the ways they are different. Finding similarities and differences is called comparing and contrasting. Comparing and contrasting can help you understand better what you read.	
	Model the skill.	For example, if I read that one ancient civilization grew up near the Nile River and another grew up near the Tigris and Euphrates Rivers, I know the two civilizations are similar because they were both located near rivers.	
	Distribute Graphic Organizer 3.	As you read "Ancient Builders," look for similarities and differences among the different groups of Mound People. Add these details to your graphic organizer. See Routine Card 7.	

ACTIVITY **3**

Read a Passage

Read for Comprehension "Ancient Builders," pp. 38–41

To Do	To Say	

10–15 minutes

Scaffold instruction.

Monitor student engagement.

See Routine Cards 2 and 3.

Read Have students read pp. 38–41. Stop at the end of each page to ask questions. Students who can read on their own may do so without stopping. After reading, ask questions to promote discussion.

How did the Mound People get their name? (They built mounds of earth over the tombs of their greatest leaders.)

Why did the Mound People bury their leaders in this way? (to honor them)

What caused some mounds to get bigger over time? (New buildings and mounds were built on top of older buildings and mounds.)

What did the mounds in the northern Great Lakes look like? (They were often low and built in the shapes of different animals.)

What do you think the rest of the article will be about? (Answers will vary. The title suggests it will tell more about the tombs built by the ancient Mound People.)

Model summarizing.

Think aloud.

Summarize What were the first four pages mainly about? What did you learn about the Mound People? Think aloud to model summarizing. **I learned many details about the Mound People, such as that some mounds were as high as 100 feet. The main thing I learned is they built the mounds to honor their greatest leaders.**

Develop language and concepts.

Ask questions.

• **How did the Mound People build each mound?**

• **Why were the mounds difficult for later discoverers to see right away?**

MORE PRACTICE

Have students reread p. 40.

Reread Tell students to draw a picture that shows what the building of a new mound might look like.

Reread for Fluency "Ancient Builders," pp. 39–40

To Do	To Say	

5 minutes

MORE PRACTICE

CORRECTIVE FEEDBACK

Pair students. Monitor paired reading.

Students read aloud pp. 39–40, switching readers at each new paragraph. Have partners reread; now the other partner begins. For optimal fluency, students should reread three or four times. Give feedback, using the *if . . . then* statements on Routine Card 4. You may want to have students read along with the DVD-ROM.

 ACTIVITY **4**

Write

Response to Literature

To Do	To Say	

5 minutes

Prompt writing.

Writing elements: support

Compare and contrast the different groups of Mound People in "Ancient Builders." Include details from the article in your answer. Use words such as *both* and *unlike* to show similarities and differences.

Homework   Practice Book, p. 86, Common Syllables *-ion, -tion, -sion, -ture*

3

ACTIVITY **1** # Word Work

Phonics Common Syllables *-ion, -tion, -sion, -ture*

	To Do	To Say	*5 minutes*
Review common syllables *-ion, -tion, -sion, -ture.* **Scaffold instruction.**	Review the homework. Discuss *celebration* on p. 40 in the Student Reader.	Ask students to share answers from Practice Book p. 86. Point out *celebration* on p. 40, paragraph 2. **Remember, common syllables such as *-ion, -tion, -sion,* and *-ture* can be used to read long words. What chunks do you see in this word?** *(ce le bra tion)* Guide students in blending the chunks into the whole word. Then point to *architecture* on p. 45, paragraph 1. **What chunks do you see in this word?** *(ar chi tec ture)* **Use the chunks to read the word. Ask students to think of other words that end in *-ion, -tion, -sion,* and *-ture.***	
MORE PRACTICE	Model spelling words with common syllables.	**Spell and Write** Write *civilization, location,* and *tradition.* Say them. **What syllable is the same in these words?** Underline *tion.* Continue with *future (ture).* Have students look for words with the *-ture* or *-tion (-ion)* syllables.	

Amazing Words Vocabulary

	To Do	To Say	*5 minutes*
Build vocabulary. **Lead cumulative review.**	Deepen understanding of *society* and *traditions.*	Read aloud the second paragraph on p. 38. **The author says each group of Mound People formed its own *society* with its own *traditions.* Write *society* and *tradition.* Say a sentence using *society* and *traditions* together. How do *traditions* help to define a *society?* How does sharing common *traditions* help to hold a *society* together?** Use the Tested Vocabulary Cards to review words from previous weeks.	

ACTIVITY **2** # Comprehension

Compare and Contrast

	To Do	To Say	*5–10 minutes*
Scaffold instruction.	Review compare and contrast.	**Remember, comparing and contrasting things can help you better understand what you're reading. Look for similarities and differences as you read. Clue words, such as *like, also, unlike,* and *however,* may signal a comparison. Remember, not all comparisons are signaled by clue words.**	
Guide practice.	Use Graphic Organizer 3.	**Listen as I read p. 44. I want you to notice how the author compares the Mound People to another ancient civilization. Read p. 44. Then ask: What is one way some mounds were similar to ancient Aztec buildings?** (They both have four sloped sides.) **Add this detail to your graphic organizer.** See Routine Card 7.	
MORE PRACTICE	Have students preview pp. 42–45.	**Read the captions and look at the photographs on pp. 42–45. What do you think this section will be about?** (more about the architecture of the Mound People) **Why do you think so?** Think aloud to model using captions and illustrations to predict.	
	Think aloud.	**The captions and pictures make me think the article will be about the way the mounds looked and what we've learned about the architecture of the Mound People.**	

ACTIVITY 3 | Read a Passage

Read for Comprehension "Ancient Builders," pp. 42–45

To Do	To Say	
		10–15 minutes

Scaffold instruction.

Monitor student engagement.

Read Have students read pp. 42–45. Stop at the end of each page to ask questions. Students who can read on their own may do so without stopping. After reading, ask questions to promote discussion.

See Routine Cards 2 and 3.

On p. 42, why did some settlers plow down ancient mounds? (to prepare the land for farming)

What did a relative of Joseph Tomlinson use an ancient mound for? (He opened a museum in one and charged visitors to see it.)

In what way were the burial traditions of the Mound People similar to those of many other civilizations? (They buried their dead with jewelry and other artifacts.)

What have many states done to help future generations learn about the Mound People? (They have preserved the ancient mounds.)

Assess comprehension.

Monitor understanding.

After Reading Have students discuss the What Do You Think? question. Prompt them to find similarities and differences among the different groups of Mound People. Listen as they talk to assess comprehension.

Summarize.

What is this mainly about? What did you learn? Work with students to summarize the selection.

MORE PRACTICE

Have students reread p. 45.

Reread As they read, tell students to note some of the similarities between the Mound People and other ancient civilizations. Have students add these details to their graphic organizers.

Reread for Fluency "Ancient Builders," p. 45

To Do	To Say	
		5 minutes

CORRECTIVE FEEDBACK

Monitor oral reading.

Read p. 45 aloud. Reread the page three or four times so your reading gets better each time. Give feedback on students' oral reading, using the *if . . . then* statements on Routine Card 4. Model fluent reading if necessary. You may want to have students read along with the DVD-ROM.

ACTIVITY 4 | Write

Response to Literature

To Do	To Say	
		5 minutes

MORE PRACTICE

Prompt expository writing.

How do the burial traditions of the Mound People reflect their feelings toward their greatest leaders? Use details from the article to support your answer. Use complete sentences to express your ideas.

Homework

Practice Book, p. 87, Compare and Contrast

Word Work

 **Vocabulary**

	To Do	To Say	5–10 minutes

Extend word knowledge.

Teach the root word *civil*.

Scaffold instruction.

Write: *Many ancient civilizations have similar burial traditions.*

Develop word meaning.

Use the word *civilization* to extend word knowledge. **Remember we read this word earlier this week. We looked for meaningful parts, and we noticed the word *civilize*. The root word in *civilize* is *civil*. We can use this word to read other words.**

The word *civil* means "about the government, state, or nation." It also means "polite." Can you think of other words or phrases that contain the word *civil*? *(civilian, uncivilized, civil rights, civil defense, Civil War)* Write words and phrases as students name them and add some of your own. Talk about the meanings of the words and phrases and then practice pronouncing all of them.

How are the traditions of one *civilization* passed down to another?

MORE PRACTICE

Deepen understanding of *civilization* and *society*.

Have individual students or partners use the two words *civilization* and *society* together in sentences. (For example: Modern *society* still reflects some of the ancient traditions of other *civilizations*.) Share sentences. Ask: **What can we learn about a *civilization* by studying *society*? Why?**

Comprehension

Skill and Strategy Practice

	To Do	To Say	5 minutes

Scaffold instruction.

Review compare and contrast (homework).

Ask volunteers to read the passage and share answers from Practice Book p. 87. Remind students of the importance of comparing and contrasting. **When you read a story, comparing and contrasting settings, events, and characters can help you understand better what you read. You can also compare and contrast what happens in a story to something that happened in another story or in your own life.**

Practice strategic prereading.

See Routine Card 2.

Think aloud.

Review story structure.

Discuss Genre Read the title and p. 46 in the Student Reader. Model determining genre.

I first thought this might be fiction because of the illustrations. When I read the first page, I knew it was fiction because of the dialogue among the characters.

Ask Questions What questions do you ask yourself to help you understand a fictional story? (What is the problem or goal? How is the problem solved or the goal reached?) As you read this story, ask these questions and look for the answers.**

ACTIVITY **3** # Read a Passage

Read for Comprehension "It's Still Standing!" pp. 46–53

	To Do	**To Say**	*10–15 minutes*
Scaffold instruction.	Monitor student engagement.	**Read** Have students read pp. 46–53 on their own and then discuss. For students who need more help, stop at the end of each page to discuss. After reading, ask questions.	

Scaffold instruction.

Monitor student engagement.

See Routine Card 3.

Read Have students read pp. 46–53 on their own and then discuss. For students who need more help, stop at the end of each page to discuss. After reading, ask questions.

Who are the main characters in this story? (Chris, Katie, and Alex) **What is Chris describing for Katie and Alex?** (the places he visited in Greece)

What do all of the places and objects in Chris's photos have in common? (They're all ancient.)

What do the three friends begin to notice after they look at Chris's photos? (special details about their own town)

How do the friends' feelings about their town change by the end of the story? (They think maybe their town isn't so dull after all.)

Assess comprehension.

Monitor understanding.

After Reading Have students discuss the What Do You Think? question. Prompt them to compare the places in Chris's town to those in Greece. Listen as they talk to assess comprehension.

MORE PRACTICE

Reread Have students reread pp. 49–52 and describe the three places the friends notice on their way to the park.

	To Do	**To Say**	*5–10 minutes*

CORRECTIVE FEEDBACK

Pair students. Monitor paired reading.

Students read aloud pp. 51–53, switching readers after each paragraph. Have partners reread; now the other partner begins. For optimal fluency, students should reread three or four times. Give feedback, using Routine Card 4. You may want to have students read along with the DVD-ROM.

MORE PRACTICE

READERS' THEATER

Work with a group of four students to adapt pp. 49–52 as a Readers' Theater scene. Have students rehearse reading the parts, with one student as a narrator, one as Chris, one as Katie, and one as Alex. You may wish to omit speech tags ("said Katie") when reading parts.

ACTIVITY **4** # Write

Response to Literature

	To Do	**To Say**	*5 minutes*

Prompt expository writing.

Review pp. 50–53.

Writing elements: organization, support

What do Chris, Katie, and Alex learn about their town's past? Include details from the story in your answer. Use transitional words and phrases to connect your ideas.

ACTIVITY 1 — Read a Passage

Read Together "Forever Sleeping Under Rome," pp. 54–55

10 minutes

	To Do	To Say
Scaffold instruction.	Review compare and contrast. See Routine Card 3.	Have students preview pp. 54–55. **This article is about an ancient burial place in Italy. Comparing and contrasting two or more things can help you understand better what you read. As you read the article, look for similarities and differences between the Roman catacombs and other ancient burial places you've read about.** **Read** Read the article as students follow along. Then read it a second time, having students join in on the text. After reading, ask questions. **What are the Roman catacombs?** (a web of underground tunnels where people used to bury their family members) **Why did people bury their dead in the catacombs?** (as a way to honor them) **How did people decorate the tombs?** (by leaving artifacts and painting art on the walls) **Why were the catacombs forgotten?** (Romans began burying their dead in cemeteries instead.)
Assess comprehension.	Monitor listening comprehension.	**Summarize** Have students describe the similarities and differences among catacombs and other ancient burial places.

ACTIVITY 2 — Build Concepts

Amazing Words **Vocabulary**

5–10 minutes

	To Do	To Say
Review concept and vocabulary.	Display the concept web you began on Day 1.	**This week's question is *What surprises can the past hold for us?* How do this week's words relate to the question?** (Have students answer the question, using some of the vocabulary they learned this week.) Ask students to add more words to the concept web. Have students explain how each word relates to past times. Monitor students' understanding of vocabulary as they discuss the web. See Routine Card 5.
MORE PRACTICE	Write *theater* and *statue* on the board.	Have students relate *theater* and *statue.* **If the remains of an *ancient civilization* include *theaters* and *statues,* what does that tell you about that civilization? Why?**

ACTIVITY **3** | Write

Response to Literature "4 You 2 Do," p. 56

| To Do | To Say | *5–10 minutes* |

Guide response activities.

To Do: Discuss the directions on p. 56. Tell students to choose one activity to complete. See Routine Card 8.

To Say:

Word Play Have students unscramble the words on their own and then share their word lists with partners.

Making Connections Discuss the question in a group. (Answers may vary, but should include that the mounds and the statue publicly honor people of the past who have died and can be seen even to this day.)

On Paper Have students brainstorm some answers to the prompt before they write. Have them write on their own. Students can use Practice Book p. 88 to structure their written responses, or you can send the Practice Book page home for them to complete later.

MORE PRACTICE

If you have more time, direct students to complete all the activities.

ACTIVITY **4** | Assessment Options

Passage Reading

| To Do | To Say | *10–15 minutes* |

To Do: See Routine Card 6.

While some students are doing Activity 3, determine which students you want to assess this week and choose from these options.

Check fluency.

To Do: Take a two-minute timed sample of each student's oral reading.

Fluency Have a student read for two minutes from "Ancient Builders." Record the number of correct words read per minute. See p. 184 for monitoring fluency. Be sure each student is assessed at least every other week.

Have students graph their progress on the Fluency Progress Chart, p. 185.

Check comprehension.

Retelling Have students reread "Ancient Builders" and retell it. Prompt students if necessary. See p. 186 for monitoring retelling.

If you have time, assess every student.

Homework Practice Book, p. 88, Writing

Unit 5 Week 3 *Adventures and Heroes*

 How can adventures change us?

Objectives *This week students will...*

Vocabulary
- build concepts and vocabulary: *adventure, expeditions, forecasts, unfamiliar, wilderness*

Phonics
- read words that have syllables with vowel combinations: *oo, ew, ue*
- apply knowledge of word structure to decode multisyllabic words when reading

Text Comprehension
- use sequence to improve comprehension
- write in response to literature
- make connections across text

Fluency
- practice fluency with oral rereading

Word Work *This week's phonics focus is...*

Vowel Combinations *oo, ew, ue*

Amazing Words Concept/Amazing Words *Tested Vocabulary*

The week's vocabulary is related to the concept of adventures and heroes.
The first appearance of each word in the Student Reader is noted below.

adventure   an unusual or exciting experience (p. 60)

expeditions   long, well-planned trips for special purposes, such as exploration or scientific study (p. 62)

forecasts   statements of what is going to happen (p. 61)

unfamiliar   not well-known (p. 61)

wilderness   a wild place; a region with few or no people living in it (p. 60)

Student Reader Unit 5 *This week students will read the following selections.*

60	**Adventure on the Job**	Expository Nonfiction
64	**A Lesson in Adventure**	Expository Nonfiction
72	**Wits Versus Wilderness**	Realistic Fiction
80	**Sea Turtle Adventure**	Narrative Nonfiction
82	**4 You 2 Do**	Activity Page

Daily Lesson Plan

	ACTIVITIES	MATERIALS
Day 1	**Build Concepts** Weekly Concept: Adventures and Heroes Vocabulary: *adventure, expeditions, forecasts, unfamiliar, wilderness* **Read a Passage** "Adventure on the Job," pp. 60–63 Comprehension: Use Strategies Reread for Fluency **Write** Response to Literature	Student Reader: Unit 5 Routine Cards 2, 4, 5 Tested Vocabulary Cards Student journals Practice Book, p. 89, Vocabulary Student Reader DVD-ROM
Day 2	**Word Work** Phonics: Syllables with Vowel Combinations: *oo, ew, ue* Vocabulary: Deepen word meaning **Comprehension** Sequence **Read a Passage** "A Lesson in Adventure," pp. 64–67 Reread for Fluency **Write** Response to Literature	Student Reader: Unit 5 Practice Book, p. 89, Vocabulary Graphic Organizer 6 Routine Cards 1, 2, 3, 4, 7 Practice Book, p. 90, Vowels *oo, ew, ue* Student Reader DVD-ROM
Day 3	**Word Work** Phonics: Syllables with Vowel Combinations: *oo, ew, ue* Vocabulary: Deepen word meaning **Comprehension** Sequence **Read a Passage** "A Lesson in Adventure," pp. 68–71 Reread for Fluency **Write** Response to Literature	Practice Book, p. 90, Vowels *oo, ew, ue* Tested Vocabulary Cards Student Reader: Unit 5 Graphic Organizer 6 Routine Cards 2, 3, 4, 7 Practice Book, p. 91, Sequence Student Reader DVD-ROM
Day 4	**Word Work** Vocabulary: Extend word knowledge **Comprehension** Skill and Strategy Practice **Read a Passage** "Wits Versus Wilderness," pp. 72–79 Reread for Fluency **Write** Response to Literature	Practice Book, p. 91, Sequence Student Reader: Unit 5 Routine Cards 2, 3, 4 Student Reader DVD-ROM
Day 5	**Read a Passage** "Sea Turtle Adventure" pp. 80–81 Comprehension: Sequence; Listening **Build Concepts** Vocabulary **Write** Response to Literature: "4 You 2 Do," p. 82 **Assessment Options** Fluency Comprehension	Student Reader: Unit 5 Routine Cards 3, 5, 6, 8 Fluency Progress Chart, p. 185 Practice Book, p. 92, Writing

See pp. xvi–xvii for how *My Sidewalks* integrates instructional practices for ELL.

ACTIVITY 1 Build Concepts

Amazing Words Vocabulary

	To Do	To Say
Develop oral vocabulary.	See Routine Card 6 and p. 205.	Introduce the Concept/Amazing Words with an oral routine prior to displaying them in print. Page 205 in this Teacher's Guide provides specific guidelines for introducing each word.
Develop word meaning.	See Routine Card 5. Discuss pp. 59–63.	Have students read p. 59 and then look at the pictures on pp. 60–63. **What do you notice?** (people with cameras, people looking through lenses) **Can you use the word** *adventure* **to describe any of these pictures?** (Example: Working underwater in the sea would be an *adventure*.)
Scaffold instruction.	Create a concept web.	In the center of a web, write *Adventures and Heroes.* **This week's concept is** *adventures and heroes. Adventures* **are unusual or exciting experiences.** *Heroes* **are people admired for their bravery.** Provide examples to demonstrate meaning. **Mountain climbing and scuba diving can be** *adventures.* **Firefighters who rescue people from burning buildings are** *heroes.*
	Add the other vocabulary words. **Concept and Language Goals**	Discuss the meaning of each word as it relates to adventures and heroes, using the glossary as needed. (See p. 86 in this Teacher's Guide for definitions.)

Concept web: center reads "Adventures and Heroes" connected to adventure, wilderness, expeditions, unfamiliar, forecasts

	To Do	To Say
Model the multisyllabic word strategy.	Display each word. Say it as you display it.	Use the Tested Vocabulary Cards. Follow this routine for each word:
		• **Look for Meaningful Parts** Do you recognize any parts of this word? What do the parts mean? Use the parts to read the word. Be sure students notice the following: *familiar, wild.*
	Think aloud.	• **Model** I recognize the word *familiar* in *unfamiliar.* I know *familiar* means "well-known." I see the prefix *un-* at the beginning of the word. I know that *un-* means "not," so I think *unfamiliar* must mean "not well-known."
	Point to *adventure.*	• **Chunk Words with No Recognizable Parts** Model how to chunk the word *adventure.* I see a chunk at the beginning of the word: *ad.* I see a part in the middle: *ven.* I see a part at the end of the word: *ture.* I say each chunk slowly: *ad ven ture.* I say the chunks fast to make a whole word: *adventure.* Is it a real word? Yes, I know the word *adventure.*
		• Have students practice reading each word.
Preview.	Read p. 58 with students.	**Do you see any words we just learned on this page?** Together with students, read the sentences on p. 58 describing each selection. Talk about how the vocabulary words might be used in the selections.
MORE PRACTICE	Deepen understanding of *adventure.*	Have students demonstrate understanding by answering questions. **Which one is an** *adventure,* **trying a new food in a restaurant, or eating a peanut butter sandwich every day for lunch? Why? If something is an** *adventure,* **have you done it many times before, or is it a new experience? What makes an** *adventure* **exciting?**

ACTIVITY 2 Read a Passage

Develop Concepts "Adventure on the Job ," pp. 60–63

To Do	To Say	*10–15 minutes*

Practice strategic prereading.

See Routine Card 2.

Think aloud.

Discuss Genre Read the title and look at the pictures on pp. 60–61. Model determining genre.

The photographs are a clue that this is nonfiction. They look like photos of real people in real places. I think this article will tell me about jobs that involve adventure.

Scaffold instruction.

Teach text structure.

Ask Questions What questions do you ask yourself to help you understand nonfiction? (What did I learn? What is this mainly about?) As you read the article, ask these questions and look for the answers.

Guide comprehension.

Read pp. 60–63 aloud.

Read Read the article as students follow along. Then read it a second time, having students join in. If necessary, stop at the end of each paragraph to check comprehension. Ask questions to promote discussion and develop the concept.

Develop language and concepts.

- What kinds of things do photojournalists take pictures of?
- What makes chasing storms a dangerous job?
- Where do oceanographers do their work?
- How do crime scene investigators help solve mysteries?
- What words on the concept web could help you describe these jobs?

MORE PRACTICE

Have students reread "Adventure on the Job." As they read, tell them to list the four jobs described in this article to describe to family members tonight.

Reread for Fluency "Adventure on the Job," p. 63

To Do	To Say	*5 minutes*

CORRECTIVE FEEDBACK

Monitor oral reading.

Read p. 63 aloud. Reread the page three or four times so your reading gets better each time. Give feedback on students' oral reading, using the *if . . . then* statements on Routine Card 4. Model fluent reading if necessary. You may want to have students read along with the DVD-ROM.

ACTIVITY 3 Write

Response to Literature

To Do	To Say	*5 minutes*

Prompt journal writing.

Write on the board or a transparency: *How can adventures change us?*

Take out your journals. This week we are reading about adventures and heroes. Our question for this week is: *How can adventures change us?* Write an answer to this question based on what you read today. Have students write about the topic, using what they read and their own experiences.

Homework   Practice Book, p. 89, Vocabulary

ACTIVITY 1 Word Work

Phonics Syllables with Vowel Combinations: *oo, ew, ue*

	To Do	**To Say**	*5–10 minutes*

Teach syllables with vowel combinations: *oo, ew, ue*.

Scaffold instruction.

Write on the board or a transparency: *We sat on the <u>rooftop</u> to watch the sunset.*

Remember, when you read a long word, look for meaningful parts. What parts do you see in *rooftop*? Frame *roof* and *top*. What vowel sound do you hear in the first syllable? (/ü/) The letter pair *oo* makes the vowel sound /ü/ in *rooftop*.

Have students think and converse. You can see far into the distance from a *rooftop*. Why? What might you see from a *rooftop* in the city? How about in the country?

Develop word meaning.

The letter pairs *oo, ew,* and *ue* can all stand for the vowel sound /ü/. What parts do you see in *clueless*? *(clue less)* What vowel sound do you hear in the first syllable? (/ü/) What letter pair makes the sound /ü/? *(ue)* What parts do you see in *withdrew*? *(with drew)* What vowel sound do you hear in the second syllable? (/ü/) What letter pair makes the sound /ü/? *(ew)*

CORRECTIVE FEEDBACK

Write each practice word.

Have students practice reading words with vowel combinations *oo, ew,* and *ue*. Correct any words students miss and have them reread the list.

groom	foolish	withdrew	cashew	glue	avenue

MORE PRACTICE

Write more practice words.

Have students practice reading words with vowel combinations *oo, ew,* and *ue*.

bamboo	toolbox	renew	outgrew	blueberry	untrue

 **Vocabulary**

	To Do	**To Say**	*5 minutes*

Review vocabulary.

Review the homework.

Ask students to go over answers and share their writing from Practice Book p. 89. See Routine Card 1 for multisyllabic word routine.

Deepen understanding of *expeditions*.

Remember, *expeditions* are "long, well-planned trips for special purposes." A group of people tried for weeks to climb Mount Everest, in Asia. Why is this an *expedition*? What else are examples of *expeditions*? Why?

ACTIVITY 2 Comprehension

Sequence

	To Do	**To Say**	*5 minutes*

Scaffold instruction.

Introduce sequence.

Today you will read about a real organization called Outward Bound. It's often important to keep track of the sequence, or order of events, because it may help you understand what you're reading about. Words such as *first, next, then,* and *finally,* as well as dates and times, give you clues to the sequence.

Model the skill.

For example, if I read that the first and last steps in building a rope bridge are to tie ropes around two different trees, I need to pay attention to the sequence to help me understand the steps in between.

Distribute Graphic Organizer 6.

As you read "A Lesson in Adventure," look for words that help you track the sequence of events in different wilderness challenges. Add these sequence words to your graphic organizers. See Routine Card 7.

ACTIVITY 3 Read a Passage

Read for Comprehension "A Lesson in Adventure," pp. 64–67

To Do	To Say	5–10 minutes

Scaffold instruction. | Monitor student engagement. | **Read** Have students read pp. 64–67. Stop at the end of each page to ask questions. Students who can read on their own can do so without stopping. After reading, ask questions to promote discussion.

See Routine Cards 2 and 3. | **What is Outward Bound?** (a program that teaches students to face the challenges of the wilderness)

Where did the name "Outward Bound" come from? (from sailors leaving the safety of a port for hard work and adventure)

What does the motto "Leave No Trace" mean? (Students must keep their campgrounds clean and safe, leave behind no garbage, and put out all fires completely.)

What do you think the rest of the article will be about? (Answers will vary. The title suggests it will tell more about Outward Bound adventures.)

Model summarizing. | Think aloud. | **Summarize** What were the first four pages mainly about? What did you learn about wilderness adventures? Think aloud to model summarizing. I learned a lot of details about Outward Bound, such as that it began in England during World War II. The main thing I learned is that Outward Bound teaches young people survival skills and life lessons.

Develop language and concepts. | Ask questions. | • **What lessons do Outward Bound students learn by spending time together in the wilderness?**

• **How can overcoming challenges change your life?**

MORE PRACTICE | Have students reread p. 65. | **Reread** Tell students to draw a picture that shows what a person crossing a postman's bridge might look like.

Reread for Fluency "A Lesson in Adventure," pp. 66–67

To Do	To Say	5 minutes

MORE PRACTICE

CORRECTIVE FEEDBACK | Pair students. Monitor paired reading. | Students read aloud pp. 66–67, switching readers at each new paragraph. Have partners reread; now the other partner begins. For optimal fluency, students should reread three or four times. Give feedback, using the *if . . . then* statements on Routine Card 4. You may want to have students read along with the DVD-ROM.

 ACTIVITY 4 Write

Response to Literature

To Do	To Say	5 minutes

Prompt writing. | Writing elements: support, conventions | **In what ways do you think Outward Bound students are changed by their two-week wilderness adventures? Include information to support your ideas. Use correct spelling and punctuation to express your ideas.**

Homework | Practice Book, p. 90, Vowels *oo, ew, ue*

ACTIVITY **1** Word Work

Phonics Syllables with Vowel Combinations: *oo, ew, ue*

	To Do	**To Say**	5 minutes

Review syllables with vowel combintions: *oo, ew, ue*.

Scaffold instruction.

Review the homework. Discuss *blue* on p. 66.

Ask students to share answers from Practice Book p. 90.

Point out *blue* on p. 66, paragraph 1. **Remember, the letter pairs *oo, ew,* and *ue* all can stand for the vowel sound /ü/. What vowel sound do you hear in this word?** *(/ü/)* **What letter pair makes the vowel sound /ü/ in *blue*?** *(ue)* Guide students in pronouncing the word.

Then point to *soon* on p. 69, paragraph 2. **What vowel sound do you hear in *soon*?** *(/ü/)* **What letter pair makes the vowel sound /ü/ in *soon*?** *(oo)* Ask students to think of other words that have the vowel combinations *oo, ew,* or *ue* that make the sound /ü/.

MORE PRACTICE

Model spelling words with vowel combinations.

Spell and Write Write *news, clues,* and *soon*. Say *news*. **What vowel sound do you hear in this word? What letters spell that sound?** Underline *ew*. Continue with *clues* *(ue)* and *soon* *(oo)*. **Do you know other words with *ew, ue,* or *oo* that have the same sound as *news, clues,* and *soon*?** List responses on the board.

Amazing Words **Vocabulary**

	To Do	**To Say**	5 minutes

Build vocabulary.

Lead cumulative review.

Deepen understanding of *wilderness* and *adventure*.

Read aloud the first paragraph on p. 67. **Why is facing the challenges of the *wilderness* considered an *adventure*?** Write *wilderness* and *adventure*. **Say a sentence using *wilderness* and *adventure* together. What challenges would you be likely to face on a *wilderness adventure*? How would you respond to these challenges?**

Use the Tested Vocabulary Cards to review words from previous weeks.

ACTIVITY **2** Comprehension

Sequence

	To Do	**To Say**	5–10 minutes

Scaffold instruction.

Review sequence.

An author may give you clues to the sequence. Look for dates, times, phrases, and sequence words, such as *first, then, next, before, after,* or *at last*. As you read "A Lesson in Adventure," look for the sequence of events.

Guide practice.

Use Graphic Organizer 6.

Listen as I read the second paragraph on p. 69. Notice how the author describes how students changed during an Outward Bound experience. Read p. 69, paragraph 2. Ask: **How did the students feel when they were dropped off?** (They felt alone without their family and friends.) **What words help you understand the sequence?** *(At first, soon)* **Add these words to your graphic organizers.** See Routine Card 7.

MORE PRACTICE

Have students preview pp. 68–71.

Read the captions and look at the photographs on pp. 68–71. What do you think this section will be about? (more about Outward Bound adventures) **Why do you think so?** Think aloud to model using illustrations and captions to predict.

Think aloud.

The pictures and captions make me think the article will tell more about how Outward Bound teaches students to help each other and learn about themselves.

ACTIVITY **3** Read a Passage

Read for Comprehension "A Lesson in Adventure," pp. 68–71

	To Do	**To Say**

10–15 minutes

Scaffold instruction.

Monitor student engagement.

See Routine Cards 2 and 3.

Read Have students read pp. 68–71. Stop at the end of each page to ask questions. Students who can read on their own can do so without stopping. After reading, ask questions to promote discussion.

Why do Outward Bound students write about their daily expeditions? (Writing helps them uncover clues about themselves.)

What goals does Outward Bound have for its students? (to gain confidence, courage, and a better understanding of their strengths)

On p. 70, what did the students learn while on the island? (how to rock climb and live in the wilderness)

Model using context for word meaning.

Read aloud the first two sentences on p. 71. Discuss how the second sentence provides clues to the meaning of *programs.* **You can enjoy many activities with Outward Bound. The** *programs* **include rafting, hiking and boating.** *Programs* **must have something to do with activities.**

Assess comprehension.

Monitor understanding.

After Reading Have students discuss the What Do You Think? question. Prompt them to use sequence words in telling how to build a rope bridge. Listen as they talk to assess comprehension.

Summarize.

What is this mainly about? What did you learn? Work with students to summarize the selection.

MORE PRACTICE

Have students reread pp. 69–70.

Reread As they read, tell students to note the challenges students faced on the rock climbing and sailing expedition. After they read, have them describe what the students learned.

Reread for Fluency "A Lesson in Adventure," p. 71

	To Do	**To Say**

5 minutes

CORRECTIVE FEEDBACK

Monitor oral reading.

Read p. 71 aloud. Reread the page three or four times so your reading gets better each time. Give feedback on students' oral reading, using the *if . . . then* statements on Routine Card 4. Model fluent reading if necessary. You may want to have students read along with the DVD-ROM.

ACTIVITY **4** Write

Response to Literature

	To Do	**To Say**

5 minutes

MORE PRACTICE

Prompt expository writing.

Why is teamwork so important on Outward Bound challenges? Use details from the article to support your answer.

Homework   Practice Book, p. 91, Sequence

Word Work

Amazing Words Vocabulary

	To Do	**To Say**	*5 –10 minutes*
Extend word knowledge.	Write on the board or a transparency: *Last night, I heard different weather <u>forecasts</u> for today.*	Use the word *forecasts* to extend word knowledge. **Remember we read this word earlier this week and learned its meaning.** *Forecasts* are statements of what is going to happen. **Today I want you to notice the prefix** *fore-.* **We can use this prefix to read other words.**	
Teach the prefix *fore-*.		The prefix *fore-* means "front" or "before." A weather *forecast* tells what the weather is going to be like. **Can you think of other words that begin with** *fore-*? *(foresee, foresight, forefathers)* Write words as students name them and add some of your own. Talk about the meanings of the words, and then practice pronouncing them.	
Scaffold instruction.	Develop word meaning.	**How can weather** *forecasts* **help people plan their activities?**	
MORE PRACTICE	Deepen understanding of *forecasts* and *unfamiliar*.	Have individual students or partners use the two words *forecasts* and *unfamiliar* together in sentences. (For example: We were *unfamiliar* with the area, so we checked several different weather *forecasts*.) Share sentences. Ask: **If a place is** *unfamiliar*, **do you know it well? How can checking weather** *forecasts* **help you prepare for a trip to an** *unfamiliar* **place?**	

Comprehension

Skill and Strategy Practice

	To Do	**To Say**	*5 minutes*
Scaffold instruction.	Review sequence (homework).	Ask volunteers to read the passage and share answers from Practice Book p. 91. Remind students of the importance of following the sequence. **When you read about a process, the sequence of events is usually important. There might be clue words that tell you the order in which things happen. Look for these words. It may also help to picture in your mind the events as they happen or the steps as they are completed.**	
Practice strategic prereading.	See Routine Card 2.	**Discuss Genre** Read the title and the text on p. 72 in the Student Reader. Model determining genre.	
	Think aloud.	**I first thought this might be fiction because of the illustrations. When I read the first several paragraphs, I knew it was fiction because of the dialogue and the description of Sam.**	
	Review story structure.	**Ask Questions** What questions do you ask yourself to help you understand a fictional story? (What is the problem or goal? How is the problem solved or the goal reached?) **As you read this story, ask these questions and look for the answers.**	

ACTIVITY 3 Read a Passage

Read for Comprehension: "Wits Versus Wilderness," pp. 72–79

10–15 minutes

	To Do	To Say
Scaffold instruction.	Monitor student engagement. See Routine Card 3.	**Read** Have students read pp. 72–79 on their own and then discuss. For students who need more help, stop at the end of each page to discuss. After reading, ask questions. **Who are the main characters in this story?** (Sam and Uncle Henry) **Where does the story take place?** (in the Colorado wilderness) **What problem do Sam and Uncle Henry face?** (A bear chases them.) **How does Sam use his wits to solve the problem?** (First, he remembers what he has learned about black bears; then he tells Uncle Henry that they must make noise to scare the bear away.)
Assess comprehension.	Monitor understanding.	**After Reading** Have students discuss the What Do You Think? question. Prompt them to use sequence words to describe the steps Sam and his uncle take to protect themselves from the bear. Listen as they talk to assess comprehension.
MORE PRACTICE		**Reread** Have students reread pp. 75–78 and list the sequence of events Sam and his uncle follow after they see the bears.

Reread for Fluency "Wits Versus Wilderness," pp. 77–79

5–10 minutes

	To Do	To Say
CORRECTIVE FEEDBACK	Pair students. Monitor paired reading.	Students read aloud pp. 77–79, switching readers at the end of each page. Have partners reread; now the other partner begins. For optimal fluency, students should reread three or four times. Give feedback, using the *if . . . then* statements on Routine Card 4. Model fluent reading if necessary. You may want to have students read along with the DVD-ROM.
MORE PRACTICE	**READERS' THEATER**	Work with a group of students to adapt pp. 74–79 as a radio play. Have students rehearse reading the parts: narrator, Sam, and Uncle Henry. Decide in advance whether students should read the speech tags ("laughed Uncle Henry") or delete them.

ACTIVITY 4 Write

Response to Literature

5 minutes

	To Do	To Say
Prompt expository writing.	Review pp. 75–77. Writing elements: organization	Once Sam understands that they are in danger from the bear, he gives Uncle Henry clear instructions. Explain the sequence of the instructions, using words such as *first* and *then*.

ACTIVITY 1 — Read a Passage

Read Together "Sea Turtle Adventure" pp. 80–81

10 minutes

	To Do	**To Say**
Scaffold instruction.	Review sequence.	Have students preview pp. 80–81. **This article tells how a family rescued a group of baby sea turtles. When you read how something happened, the sequence of events or the steps in the process are important. Knowing the sequence can help you better understand Andie's sea turtle adventure.**
	See Routine Card 3.	**Read** Read the article as students follow along. Then read it a second time, having students join in on the text. After reading, ask questions.
		What do Andie and her mother do after they spot the baby sea turtles? (scoop them up and put them into buckets)
		What happens after Andie and her mom and brother release the turtles into the shallow water? (The turtles make a u-turn and head back to the shore.)
		Why are the baby sea turtles confused? (They mistake the lights on the shore for the light of the moon.)
		How does Andie's father help? (He shines a flashlight on the water. The baby turtles think it's the moon, so they swim toward the light and stay in the water.)
Assess comprehension.	Monitor listening comprehension.	**Summarize** Have students explain why Andie and her family were heroes.

ACTIVITY 2 — Build Concepts

 **Vocabulary**

5–10 minutes

	To Do	**To Say**
Review concept and vocabulary.	**Concept and Language Goals** Display the concept web you began on Day 1.	This week's question is *How can adventures change us?* **How do this week's words relate to the question?** (Have students answer the question, using some of the vocabulary they learned this week.)
		Ask students to add more words to the concept web. Have students explain how each word relates to the concept of adventures and heroes. Monitor students' understanding of vocabulary as they discuss the web. See Routine Card 5.
MORE PRACTICE	Write *wilderness* and *expeditions* on the board.	Have students relate *wilderness* and *expeditions*. **What problems might people have on *expeditions* in the *wilderness*? How can people survive *wilderness expeditions*? Why do people undertake *wilderness expeditions*?**

ACTIVITY 3 | Write

Response to Literature "4 You 2 Do," p. 82

To Do　　　**To Say**　　　　　　　　　　　　　　*10–15 minutes*

Guide response activities.

Discuss the directions on p. 82.

Tell students to choose one activity to complete. See Routine Card 8.

Word Play Have students work individually or in pairs to create slogans and then meet with the rest of the class to share their slogans.

Making Connections Discuss the question in a group. (Answers will vary but may include ideas about how Sam might enjoy all sorts of wilderness adventures. His experience with his uncle and the bear shows he has the "wits" to survive in the wilderness.)

On Paper Have students brainstorm some answers to the prompt before they write. Have them write on their own. Students can use Practice Book p. 92 to structure their written responses, or you can send the Practice Book page home for them to complete later.

MORE PRACTICE

If you have more time, direct students to complete all the activities.

ACTIVITY 4 | Assessment Options

Passage Reading

To Do　　　**To Say**　　　　　　　　　　　　　　*10–15 minutes*

See Routine Card 6.

While some students are doing Activity 3, determine which students you want to assess this week and choose from these options.

Check fluency.

Take a two-minute timed sample of each student's oral reading.

Fluency Have a student read for two minutes from "A Lesson in Adventure." Record the number of correct words read per minute. See p. 184 for monitoring fluency. Be sure each student is assessed at least every other week.

Have students graph their progress on the Fluency Progress Chart, p. 185.

Check comprehension.

Retelling Have students reread "A Lesson in Adventure" and retell it. Prompt students if necessary. See p. 186 for monitoring retelling.

If you have time, assess every student.

Homework　　　Practice Book, p. 92, Writing

Unit 5 Week 4 *Extreme Homes*

 What do people give up to live in certain places?

Objectives *This week students will...*

Vocabulary
- build concepts and vocabulary: *adapted, architecture, burrow, extreme, homesteaders, prairie*

Phonics
- read words with vowel combinations: vowel sound in *ball* spelled *a, al, au, aw, augh, ough*
- apply knowledge of word structure to decode multisyllabic words when reading

Text Comprehension
- identify main idea to improve comprehension
- write in response to literature
- make connections across text

Fluency
- practice fluency with oral rereading

Word Work *This week's phonics focus is . . .*

Vowel Sound in *ball* Spelled *a, al, au, aw, augh, ough*

Amazing Words Concept/Amazing Words *Tested Vocabulary*

The week's vocabulary is related to the concept of extreme homes.
The first appearance of each word in the Student Reader is noted below.

adapted	changed something to fit different conditions; adjusted (p. 100)
architecture	the science and art of designing buildings (p. 95)
burrow	a hole dug in the ground by a person or an animal for shelter or protection (p. 96)
extreme	much more than usual; very great (p. 92)
homesteaders	persons who build houses on a prairie (p. 99)
prairie	a large area of level or rolling land with grass but few or no trees (p. 99)

Student Reader Unit 5 *This week students will read the following selections.*

Daily Lesson Plan

	ACTIVITIES	MATERIALS
Day 1	**Build Concepts** Weekly Concept: Extreme Homes 　Vocabulary: *adapted, architecture, burrow, extreme,* 　*homesteaders, prairie* **Read a Passage** "How We Live," pp. 86–89 　Comprehension: Use Strategies 　Reread for Fluency **Write** Response to Literature	Student Reader: Unit 5 Routine Cards 2, 4, 5 Tested Vocabulary Cards Student journals Practice Book, p. 93, Vocabulary Student Reader DVD-ROM
Day 2	**Word Work** Phonics: Vowel Sound in *ball: a, al, au, aw, augh, ough* 　Vocabulary: Deepen word meaning **Comprehension** Main Idea and Supporting Details **Read a Passage** "Living Down Under," pp. 90–93 　Reread for Fluency **Write** Response to Literature	Student Reader: Unit 5 Practice Book, p. 93, Vocabulary Graphic Organizer 1 Routine Cards 1, 2, 3, 4, 7 Practice Book, p. 94, Vowel Sound in *ball:* 　*a, al, au, aw, augh, ough* Student Reader DVD-ROM
Day 3	**Word Work** Phonics: Vowel Sound in *ball: a, al, au, aw, augh, ough* 　Vocabulary: Deepen word meaning **Comprehension** Main Idea and Supporting Details **Read a Passage** "Living Down Under," pp. 94–97 　Reread for Fluency **Write** Response to Literature	Practice Book, p. 94, Vowel Sound in *ball:* 　*a, al, au, aw, augh, ough* Tested Vocabulary Cards Student Reader: Unit 5 Graphic Organizer 1 Routine Cards 1, 2, 3, 4, 7 Practice Book, p. 95, Main Idea and Details Student Reader DVD-ROM
Day 4	**Word Work** Vocabulary: Extend word knowledge **Comprehension** Skill and Strategy Practice **Read a Passage** "A Sea of Grass," pp. 98–105 　Reread for Fluency **Write** Response to Literature	Practice Book, p. 95, Main Idea and Details Student Reader: Unit 5 Routine Cards 2, 3, 4 Student Reader DVD-ROM
Day 5	**Read a Passage** Poetry, pp. 106–107 　Comprehension: Main Idea and Supporting Details; Listening **Build Concepts** Vocabulary **Write** Response to Literature: "4 You 2 Do," p. 108 **Assessment Options** Fluency 　Comprehension	Student Reader: Unit 5 Routine Cards 3, 5, 6, 8 Fluency Progress Chart, p. 185 Practice Book, p. 96, Writing

See pp. xvi–xvii for how *My Sidewalks* integrates instructional practices for ELL.

ACTIVITY 1 Build Concepts

Amazing Words **Vocabulary**

| To Do | To Say | *10–15 minutes* |

Develop oral vocabulary.

See Routine Card 6 and p. 206.

Introduce the Concept/Amazing Words with an oral routine prior to displaying them in print. Page 206 in this Teacher's Guide provides specific guidelines for introducing each word.

Develop word meaning.

See Routine Card 5. Discuss pp. 85–89.

Have students read p. 85 and then look at the pictures on pp. 86–89. **What do you notice?** (an igloo, a palm leaf house, a house made of recycled materials, a straw bale house) **Can you use the word** *extreme* **to describe any of these pictures?** (Example: Some people might think a house built from old tires is *extreme,* but it is good for Earth.)

Scaffold instruction.

Create a concept web.

In the center of a web, write *Extreme Homes.* **This week's concept is** *extreme homes. Extreme* **means "much more than usual," or "at the farthest end of normal."** Provide an example to demonstrate meaning. **Many people ride skateboards, but** *extreme* **skateboarders take more risks and do dangerous, difficult stunts.**

Add the other vocabulary words.

Concept and Language Goals

Discuss the meaning of each word as it relates to extreme homes, using the glossary as needed. (See p. 98 of this Teacher's Guide for definitions.)

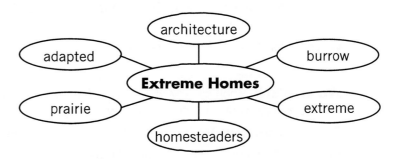

Model the multisyllabic word strategy.

Display each word. Say it as you display it.

Use the Tested Vocabulary Cards. Follow this routine for each word:

- **Look for Meaningful Parts** **Do you recognize any parts of this word? What do these parts mean? Use the parts to read the word.** As you introduce each word, be sure students notice the following: *arch-* ("chief"), *extr-* ("outside of"), *home, stead, -er* ("one who").

Point to *burrow.*

- **Chunk Words with No Recognizable Parts** Model how to chunk the word *burrow* to read it.

Think aloud.

- **Model** **I see a chunk at the beginning of the word:** *bur.* **I see a part at the end of the word:** *row.* **I say each chunk slowly:** *bur row.* **I say the chunks quickly to make a whole word:** *burrow.* **Is it a real word? Yes, I know the word** *burrow.*

- Have students practice reading each word.

Preview.

Read p. 84 with students.

Do you see any of the words we just learned on this page? Together with students, read the sentences on p. 84 describing each selection. Talk about how the concept words might be used in the selections.

MORE PRACTICE

Deepen understanding of *extreme.*

Have students demonstrate understanding by answering questions. **Which is an example of** *extreme* **weather, a day with mild temperatures, or a day with temperatures well below freezing? Why? If someone's behavior is** *extreme,* **is it ordinary behavior or unusual behavior? What makes something** *extreme?*

ACTIVITY **2** # Read a Passage

Develop Concepts "How We Live," pp. 86–89

| To Do | To Say | 10–15 minutes |

Practice strategic prereading.

See Routine Card 2.

Think aloud.

Discuss Genre Read the title on p. 86 and have students look at the photographs on pp. 86–89. Model determining genre.

The photographs are a clue that this is nonfiction. They look like photos of real houses. I think this article will tell about different kinds of houses and how they are built.

Scaffold instruction.

Review text structure.

Ask Questions What questions do you ask yourself to help you understand nonfiction? (What did I learn? What is this mainly about?) As you read this article, ask these questions and look for the answers.

Guide comprehension.

Read pp. 86–89 aloud.

Read Read the article as students follow along. Then read it a second time, having students join in. If necessary, stop at the end of each paragraph to check comprehension. Ask questions to promote discussion and develop the concept.

Develop language and concepts.

- What did people long ago rely on for house-building materials?
- Why do people on tropical islands use palm fronds to build houses?
- What are walls in recycled materials houses made from?
- What are the benefits of a straw bale house?
- What words on the concept web could help you describe extreme homes?

MORE PRACTICE

Have students reread "How We Live." As they read, tell them to list the different kinds of houses mentioned in the article to share with family members tonight.

Reread for Fluency "How We Live," p. 87

| To Do | To Say | 5 minutes |

CORRECTIVE FEEDBACK

Monitor oral reading.

Read p. 87 aloud. Reread the page three or four times so your reading gets better each time. Give feedback on students' oral reading, using the *if . . . then* statements on Routine Card 4. Model fluent reading if necessary. You may want to have students read along with the DVD-ROM.

ACTIVITY **3** # Write

Response to Literature

| To Do | To Say | 5 minutes |

Prompt journal writing.

Write on the board or a transparency: *What do people give up to live in certain places?*

Take out your journals. This week we are reading about extreme homes. Our question for this week is: *What do people give up to live in certain places?* Write an answer to this question based on what you read today. Have students write about the topic, using what they read and their own experiences.

Homework   Practice Book, p. 93, Vocabulary

Word Work

Phonics Vowel Sound in *ball*: a, al, au, aw, augh, ough

	To Do	To Say	*5–10 minutes*
Teach vowel sound in ball: a, al, au, aw, augh, ough	Write on the board or on a transparency: *It took all day to wash the laundry.*	Remember, when you read a long word, look for meaningful parts. What parts do you see in this word? *(laun dry)* The letters *au* in the first syllable of *laundry* make the sound /ò/. This is the same vowel sound that you hear in the word *ball*.	
	Write *smallest, walking, awful.*	The vowel *a*, and the letter combinations *al* and *aw* can also make the sound /ò/ that you hear in *ball*. What parts do you see in *smallest*? *(small est)* What vowel sound do you hear in the first syllable? *(/ò/)* What parts do you see in *walking*? *(walk ing)* What letters make the sound /ò/ in the first syllable? *(al)* What letters make the sound /ò/ in the first syllable of *awful*? *(aw)*	
Scaffold instruction.	Write *daughter* and *coughing.*	The letter combinations *augh* and *ough* can also make the sound /ò/ that you hear in *ball*. What parts do you see in *daughter*? *(daugh ter)* What parts do you see in *coughing*? *(cough ing)* What vowel sound do you hear in the first syllable of both words? *(/ò/)*	
CORRECTIVE FEEDBACK	Write each practice word.	Have students practice reading these words with the vowel sound in *ball*. Correct any words students miss and have them reread the list.	
		caution boardwalk fallen outlaw jawbone faulty	
MORE PRACTICE	Write more practice words.	Have students practice reading these words with the vowel sound in *ball*.	
		assault hallway install hawkish stalking pauper	

Amazing Words ## Vocabulary

	To Do	To Say	*5 minutes*
Review vocabulary.	Review the homework.	Ask students to go over answers and share their writing from Practice Book p. 93. See Routine Card 1 for Multisyllabic word routine.	
	Deepen understanding of *adapted.*	Remember, when you *adapted* to a place or situation, you changed to fit different conditions. When the weather turned cold, you wore a warmer coat. Why is this an example of *adapting*? What else is an example of *adapting*? Why?	

Comprehension

Main Idea and Supporting Details

	To Do	To Say	*5 minutes*
Scaffold instruction.	Introduce main idea and supporting details.	Today you will read about what it's like to live in an underground house. When you read, it's important to identify the main idea. The main idea is the most important idea about the topic. Supporting details can help you find the main idea.	
	Model the skill.	For example, if I know that the topic of an article is unusual homes, I need to look for details that tell what the most important idea about unusual homes is.	
	Distribute Graphic Organizer 1.	As you read "Living Down Under," look for details that help you identify the main idea. Add these details to your graphic organizers. See Routine Card 7.	

ACTIVITY 3 Read a Passage

Read for Comprehension "Living Down Under," pp. 90–93

To Do	To Say	*10–15 minutes*

Scaffold instruction.

Monitor student engagement.

See Routine Cards 2 and 3.

Read Have students read pp. 90–93. Stop at the end of each page to ask questions. Students who can read on their own can do so without stopping. After reading, ask questions to promote discussion.

Why aren't there a lot of materials to build houses around Coober Pedy? (There isn't much water, and there are few trees.)

How have people in Coober Pedy adapted to the lack of materials and the extreme heat? (Many of the buildings are underground, where it's cool.)

What originally brought people to Coober Pedy? (opals)

What do you think the rest of the article will be about? (Answers will vary. The title suggests it will tell more about underground living.)

Model summarizing.

Think aloud.

Summarize What were the first four pages mainly about? What did you learn about underground living? Think aloud to model summarizing. **I learned many details about the town of Coober Pedy, such as that temperatures there can reach 120 degrees. But the main thing I learned is that the people of the town found a good way to adapt their homes to their environment.**

Develop language and concepts.

Ask questions.

• **Why is underground living such a good idea in Coober Pedy?**

• **What kinds of buildings could you expect to find underground in Coober Pedy?**

MORE PRACTICE

Have students reread p. 92.

Reread Tell students to draw a picture that shows what an underground house or hotel might look like.

Reread for Fluency "Living Down Under," pp. 91–92

To Do	To Say	*5 minutes*

MORE PRACTICE

CORRECTIVE FEEDBACK

Pair students. Monitor paired reading.

Students read aloud pp. 91–92, switching readers at each new paragraph. Have partners reread; now the other partner begins. For optimal fluency, students should reread three or four times. Give feedback, using the *if . . . then* statements on Routine Card 4. You may want to have students read along with the DVD-ROM.

 ACTIVITY 4 Write

Response to Literature

To Do	To Say	*5 minutes*

Prompt writing.

Writing elements: support

How have the residents of Coober Pedy adapted their homes to their environment? Use details from the article to support your answer.

Homework

Practice Book, p. 94, Vowel Sound in *ball: a, al, au, aw, augh, ough*

ACTIVITY **1** Word Work

Phonics Vowel Sound in *ball*: *a, al, au, aw, augh, ough*

	To Do	**To Say**	*5 minutes*

Review vowel sound in *ball*: *a, al, au, aw, augh, ough*

Review the homework. Discuss *Australia* on p. 90 in the Student Reader.

Ask students to share answers from Practice Book p. 94.

Point out *Australia* on p. 90. **Remember, the vowel combinations *a, al, au, aw, augh,* and *ough* can stand for the vowel sound in *ball*. What parts do you see in *Australia*?** *(Au stra lia)* **What vowel sound do you hear in the first syllable?** *(/ò/)* **What letters make the vowel sound?** *(au)* Guide students in pronouncing the word correctly.

MORE PRACTICE

Model spelling words with vowel sound in *ball*.

Spell and Write Write *walls, straw,* and *Australia.* Say *walls.* **What vowel sound do you hear in this word? What letters spell that vowel sound?** Underline *al.* Continue with *straw* (*aw*) and *Australia* (*au*).

Amazing Words ### Vocabulary

	To Do	**To Say**	*5 minutes*

Build vocabulary.

Lead cumulative review.

Deepen understanding of *burrow.*

Read aloud the second paragraph on p. 96. **The author describes a *burrow* as "an underground hole." What kinds of animals live in *burrows?* Why? What are the benefits of underground living for both animals and humans?**

Use the Tested Vocabulary Cards to review words from previous weeks.

ACTIVITY **2** Comprehension

Main Idea and Supporting Details

	To Do	**To Say**	*5–10 minutes*

Scaffold instruction.

Review main idea.

Sometimes the main idea of an article is stated. Sometimes you have to identify the main idea yourself and state it in your own words. To find the main idea, ask yourself what is the most important idea discussed in the article. Look for details that support the main idea.

Guide practice.

Use Graphic Organizer 1.

Listen as I read p. 94. Notice how the author describes the opal hunters. What is the most important idea about the hunters? (They needed to find cool places to live, so they lived underground.) What is one detail that supports this idea? (Temperatures were extremely hot.) Add this detail to your graphic organizers. See Routine Card 7.

MORE PRACTICE

Have students preview pp. 94–97

Think aloud.

Read the captions and look at the photos on pp. 94–97. What do you think this section will be about? (more on the underground buildings in Coober Pedy) Why do you think so? Think aloud to model using illustrations and captions to predict.

I see pictures of underground shelters and the equipment used to build them. The captions tell about the features of the underground houses. From the pictures and captions I think the article will tell more about the underground structures in Coober Pedy.

ACTIVITY **3** # Read a Passage

Read for Comprehension "Living Down Under," pp. 94–97

To Do	To Say	

10–15 minutes

Scaffold instruction.

Monitor student engagement.

Read Have students read pp. 94–97. Stop at the end of each page to ask questions. Students who can read on their own can do so without stopping. After reading, ask questions to promote discussion.

See Routine Cards 2 and 3.

How did the opal hunters' experiences during World War I help them to find shelter in Coober Pedy? (The opal mines reminded them of the underground trenches they used to sleep in, so they used them for homes.)

What do people in Coober Pedy use to dig their underground homes? (shovels or drilling machines)

How might someone in Coober Pedy get rich while digging an underground home? (They might discover opals as they dig.)

Why is Coober Pedy often used as a movie set? (because of its extreme scenery)

Assess comprehension.

Monitor understanding.

After Reading Have students discuss the What Do You Think? question. Prompt them to identify the main idea as they tell why the people of Coober Pedy live underground. Listen as they talk to assess comprehension.

Summarize.

What is this mainly about? What did you learn? Work with students to summarize the selection.

MORE PRACTICE

Have students reread p. 96.

Reread As they read, tell students to identify the main idea of this page and note details that support it.

Reread for Fluency "Living Down Under," p. 97

To Do	To Say	

5 minutes

CORRECTIVE FEEDBACK

Monitor oral reading.

Read p. 97 aloud. Reread the page three or four times so your reading gets better each time. Give feedback on students' oral reading, using the *if . . . then* statements on Routine Card 4. Model fluent reading if necessary. You may want to have students read along with the DVD-ROM.

 ACTIVITY **4** # Write

Response to Literature

To Do	To Say	

5 minutes

MORE PRACTICE

Prompt writing.

Of all the attractions that draw visitors to Coober Pedy, which do you think is the most interesting? Why? Use details to support your opinion.

Homework

Practice Book, p. 95, Main Idea and Details

4

ACTIVITY 1   Word Work

Amazing Words   Vocabulary

	To Do	To Say
Extend word knowledge. **Teach words related to architecture.**	Write on the board or a transparency: *We admired the* <u>architecture</u> *in Italy.*	Use the word *architecture* to extend word knowledge. **Remember we read this word earlier this week.** *Architecture* means "the science and art of designing buildings." *Architecture* has its own vocabulary. **What words can you think of that have to do with buildings and** *architecture?* *(arch, attic, balcony, column, dome, pillar, spire, tower)* Write words as students name them and add some of your own. Talk about the meanings and origins of the words. Point out that the *ch* in *architecture* is pronounced /k/, while the *ch* in *arch* is pronounced /ch/. Have students practice pronouncing all of the words.
Scaffold instruction.	Develop word meaning.	**Why is** *architecture* **both a science and an art? What practical purposes must a building fulfill?**
MORE PRACTICE	Deepen understanding of *architecture* and *adapted.*	Have individual students or partners use the two words *architecture* and *adapted* in a sentence. (For example: The *architecture* of a city or town shows ways that people have *adapted* to their environment.) Share sentences. Ask: **How can** *architecture* **help people** *adapt* **to their surroundings?**

ACTIVITY 2   Comprehension

Skill and Strategy Practice

	To Do	To Say
Scaffold instruction.	Review main idea (homework).	Ask volunteers to read the passage and share answers from Practice Book p. 95. Remind students of the importance of finding the main idea. **When you read nonfiction, look for the main, or most important, idea about the topic. Sometimes the main idea is stated, and sometimes you must find it yourself. As you read, look for details that help you identify the main idea.**
Practice strategic prereading.	See Routine Card 2. Think aloud.	**Discuss Genre** Read the title and the first paragraph on p. 98 in the Student Reader. Model determining genre. **I first thought this might be nonfiction because of the pictures. They look like pictures of real people and real places. When I read the first paragraph, I knew it was nonfiction because of the information describing the United States in 1862.**
	Review text structure.	**Ask Questions** **What questions do you ask yourself to help you understand nonfiction? (What did I learn? What is this mainly about?) As you read this article, ask these questions and look for the answers.**

ACTIVITY 3 Read a Passage

Read for Comprehension "A Sea of Grass," pp. 98–105

To Do	To Say	*10–15 minutes*

Scaffold instruction.

To Do: Monitor student engagement.

See Routine Card 3.

To Say: **Read** Have students read pp. 98–105 on their own and then discuss. For students needing more help, stop after each page to discuss. After reading, ask questions.

In 1862, what did people have to do to own land in the middle of the United States? (pay a fee and live on the land for five years)

On p. 98, what was the American Dream? (owning land)

What did settlers find when they arrived on the prairie? (very few trees; a sea of grass stretching as far as they could see)

What were soddies? (prairie homes made out of sod) **What were dugouts?** (soddies built into the sides of hills)

What made life on the prairie difficult for homesteaders? (harsh weather, little medical care, lack of water, problems with pests, dirt, fire)

What were some of the challenges of living in a sod house? (Soddies were damp and dark. There were also mice, bugs, and snakes that lived in the dirt.)

Assess comprehension.

To Do: Monitor understanding.

To Say: **After Reading** Have students discuss the What Do You Think? question. Prompt them to describe what made sod houses such a good choice for homesteaders. Listen as they talk to assess comprehension.

MORE PRACTICE

Reread Have students reread pp. 100–101 and then explain how a sod house was built.

Reread for Fluency "A Sea of Grass," pp. 99–101

To Do	To Say	*5–10 minutes*

CORRECTIVE FEEDBACK

To Do: Pair students. Monitor paired reading.

To Say: Students read aloud pp. 99–101, switching readers at the end of each paragraph. Have partners reread; now the other partner begins. For optimal fluency, students should reread three or four times. Give feedback, using Routine Card 4. You may want to have students read along with the DVD-ROM.

MORE PRACTICE

To Do: **READERS' THEATER**

To Say: Work with students to adapt pp. 101–102 as an informational radio program, describing the homesteaders and the challenges they faced. Have students rehearse reading the parts of the narrator, and the husband and wife homesteaders.

ACTIVITY 4 Write

Response to Literature

To Do	To Say	*5 minutes*

Prompt expository writing.

To Do: Review p. 103.

Writing elements: support, focus, conventions

To Say: **What is the main idea of "A Sea of Grass"? Use details from the article to support your answer.** Be sure students use complete sentences, capital letters, and correct punctuation.

ACTIVITY 1 Read a Passage

Read Together Poetry, pp. 106–107

10 minutes

	To Do	**To Say**
Scaffold instruction.	Review main idea and supporting details.	Have students preview pp. 106–107. **These poems describe different houses. When you read a poem, you can try to identify the most important idea about the topic of the poem. As you read, look for details that help tell you what the most important idea is.**
	See Routine Card 3.	**Read** Read the poems as students follow along. Then read them a second time, having students join in. After reading, ask questions.
		What is the poet describing in "Old Log House"? (his great-great-grandmother's one-room log house at the edge of a wood)
		Who built the house? (pioneer men in the olden days)
		What is the main idea of "Houses"? (Houses can look like faces.)
		In "Houses," what are windows? (eyes and noses) **What are doors?** (mouths)
		What part of the house does the poet describe as "a mustache shading the chin"? (the porch)
		Which poem tells a story? ("Old Log House")
Assess comprehension.	Monitor listening comprehension.	**Summarize** Have students tell what each poem is about and what images each poet uses to create the mood of the poem.

ACTIVITY 2 Build Concepts

Amazing Words Vocabulary

5–10 minutes

	To Do	**To Say**
Review concept and vocabulary.	Display the concept web you began on Day 1.	**This week's question is *What do people give up to live in certain places?* How do this week's words relate to the question?** (Have students answer the question, using some of the vocabulary they learned this week.)
		Ask students to add more words to the concept web. Have students explain how each word relates to extreme homes. Monitor students' understanding of vocabulary as they discuss the web. See Routine Card 5.
MORE PRACTICE	Write *extreme* and *adapted* on the board.	Have students relate *extreme* and *adapted.* **Give an example of an *extreme* condition pioneers might have *adapted* to. Why is it important for people to be able to *adapt* to *extremes?* How do we learn from *adapting?***

ACTIVITY **3** Write

Response to Literature "4 You 2 Do," p. 108

To Do	To Say	*5–10 minutes*

Guide response activities.

Discuss the directions on p. 108.

Tell students to choose one activity to complete.

See Routine Card 8.

Word Play Have students complete the sentences on their own and then meet with a partner to share sentences.

Making Connections Discuss the question in a group. (Answers will vary, but some students might say that settlers in Coober Pedy and on the prairie made shelters that were adapted to the conditions in each place. Both kinds of homes were relatively easy to make with what was at hand.)

On Paper Have students brainstorm some answers to the prompt before they write on their own. Students can use Practice Book p. 96 to structure their written responses, or you can send the Practice Book page home for them to complete later.

MORE PRACTICE

If you have more time, direct students to complete all the activities.

ACTIVITY **4** Assessment Options

Passage Reading

To Do	To Say	*10–15 minutes*

See Routine Card 6.

Take a two-minute timed sample of each student's oral reading.

Check fluency.

Check comprehension.

While some students are doing Activity 3, determine which students you want to assess this week and choose from these options.

Fluency Have a student read for two minutes from "A Sea of Grass." Record the number of correct words read per minute. See p. 184 for monitoring fluency. Be sure each student is assessed at least every other week.

Have students graph their progress on the Fluency Progress Chart, p. 185.

Retelling Have students reread "A Sea of Grass" and retell it. Prompt students if necessary. See p. 186 for monitoring retelling.

If you have time, assess every student.

Homework   Practice Book, p. 96, Writing

Unit 5 Week 5 *The Moon*

 Why does the moon fascinate us?

Objectives *This week students will...*

Vocabulary
- build concepts and vocabulary: *astronaut, astronomers, craters, mission, myths, satellite*

Phonics
- read words with suffixes *-hood, -ment, -y, -en*
- apply knowledge of word structure to decode multisyllabic words when reading

Text Comprehension
- draw conclusions to improve comprehension
- write in response to literature
- make connections across text

Fluency
- practice fluency with oral rereading

Word Work *This week's phonics focus is . . .*

Suffixes *-hood, -ment, -y, -en*

Amazing Words Concept/Amazing Words *Tested Vocabulary*

The week's vocabulary is related to the concept of the moon.
The first appearance of each word in the Student Reader is noted below.

astronaut	a person who has been trained to fly in a spacecraft (p. 124)
astronomers	people who a re experts in studying the sun, moon, planets, stars, and other objects in space (p. 120)
craters	holes in the ground shaped like a bowl (p. 121)
mission	task that people are sent somewhere to do (p. 124)
myths	legends or stories, usually that attempt to explain something in nature (p. 115)
satellite	an astronomical object that revolves around a planet; a moon (p. 112)

Student Reader Unit 4 *This week students will read the following selections.*

Daily Lesson Plan

	ACTIVITIES	MATERIALS
Day 1	**Build Concepts** Weekly Concept: The Moon Vocabulary: *astronaut, astronomers, craters, mission, myths, satellite* **Read a Passage** "Phases of the Moon," pp. 112–113 Comprehension: Use Strategies Reread for Fluency **Write** Response to Literature	Student Reader: Unit 5 Routine Cards 2, 4, 5 Tested Vocabulary Cards Student journals Practice Book, p. 97, Vocabulary Student Reader DVD-ROM
Day 2	**Word Work** Phonics: Suffixes *-hood, -ment, -y, -en* Vocabulary: Deepen word meaning **Comprehension** Draw Conclusions **Read a Passage** "One Moon, Many Myths," pp. 114–117 Reread for Fluency **Write** Response to Literature	Student Reader: Unit 5 Practice Book, p. 97, Vocabulary Graphic Organizer 2 Routine Cards 1, 2, 3, 4, 7 Practice Book, p. 98, Suffixes *-hood, -ment, -y, -en* Student Reader DVD-ROM
Day 3	**Word Work** Phonics: Suffixes *-hood, -ment, -y, -en* Vocabulary: Deepen word meaning **Comprehension** Draw Conclusions **Read a Passage** "One Moon, Many Myths," pp. 118–121 Reread for Fluency **Write** Response to Literature	Practice Book, p. 98, Suffixes *-hood, -ment, -y, -en* Tested Vocabulary Cards Student Reader: Unit 5 Graphic Organizer 2 Routine Cards 1, 2, 3, 4, 7 Practice Book, p. 99, Draw Conclusions Student Reader DVD-ROM
Day 4	**Word Work** Vocabulary: Extend word knowledge **Comprehension** Skill and Strategy Practice **Read a Passage** "Saving the Moon Tree," pp. 122–129 Reread for Fluency **Write** Response to Literature	Practice Book, p. 99, Draw Conclusions Student Reader: Unit 5 Routine Cards 2, 3, 4 Student Reader DVD-ROM
Day 5	**Read a Passage** "Moon Facts," pp. 130–133 Comprehension: Draw Conclusions; Listening **Build Concepts** Vocabulary **Write** Response to Literature: "4 You 2 Do," p. 134 **Assessment Options** Fluency, Comprehension End-of-Unit Test	Student Reader: Unit 5 Routine Cards 3, 5, 8 Practice Book, p. 100, Writing Assessment Book, p. 72

See pp. xvi–xvii for how *My Sidewalks* integrates instructional practices for ELL.

Amazing Words Vocabulary

To Do	To Say		10–15 minute

Develop oral vocabulary.

See Routine Card 6 and p. 207.

Introduce the Concept/Amazing Words with an oral routine prior to displaying them in print. Page 207 in this Teacher's Guide provides specific guidelines for introducing each word.

Develop word meaning.

See Routine Card 5. Discuss pp. 111–113.

Have students read p. 111 and then look at the pictures on pp. 112–113. **What do you notice?** (different phases of the moon) **Can you use the words *moon* and *satellite* to describe any of these pictures?** (Example: The *moon* is a *satellite* of Earth.)

Scaffold instruction.

Create a concept web.

In the center of a web, write *The Moon.* **This week's concept is *the moon*. The moon is a satellite that revolves around Earth once every 29 days.** Provide an example to demonstrate meaning. ***The moon* looks bright because it reflects the light from the sun.**

Add the other vocabulary words.

Discuss the meaning of each word as it relates to the moon, using the glossary as needed. (See p. 110 in this Teacher's Guide for definitions.)

Concept and Language Goals

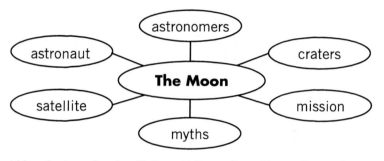

Model the multisyllabic word strategy.

Display each word. Say it as you display it.

Use the Tested Vocabulary Cards. Follow this routine for each word:

- **Look for Meaningful Parts** Remind students to look for meaningful parts. As you say each word, ask yourself: Do I see any parts I know?

- **Chunk Words with No Recognizable Parts** Model how to chunk the word *satellite* to read it.

Think aloud.

- **Model** I see a chunk at the beginning of the word: *sat.* I see a part in the middle: *el.* I see a part at the end: *lite.* I say each chunk slowly: *sat el lite.* I say the chunks fast to make a whole word: *satellite.* Is it a real word? Yes, I know the word *satellite.*

- Have students practice reading each word.

Preview.

Read p. 110 with students.

Do you see any of the words we just learned on this page? Together with students, read the sentences on p. 110 describing each selection. Talk about how the concept words might be used in the selections.

MORE PRACTICE

Deepen understanding of *satellite.*

Have students demonstrate understanding by answering questions. **Which one is a *satellite,* one of the moons of the planet Jupiter, or the space shuttle? Why? What do all *satellites* have in common?**

ACTIVITY 2 — Read a Passage

Develop Concepts "Phases of the Moon," pp. 112–113

10–15 minutes

	To Do	To Say
Practice strategic prereading.	See Routine Card 2. Think aloud.	**Discuss Genre** Read the title on p. 112 and have students look at the illustrations on pp. 112–113. Model determining genre. The photographs are a clue that this is nonfiction. They look like real photos of the moon. I think this article will describe the phases of the moon and what causes them.
Scaffold instruction.	Review text structure.	**Ask Questions** What questions do you ask yourself to help you understand nonfiction? (What did I learn? What is this mainly about?) As you read this article, ask these questions and look for the answers.
Guide comprehension. **Develop language and concepts.**	Read pp. 112–113 aloud.	**Read** Read the article as students follow along. Then read it a second time, having students join in. If necessary, stop at the end of each paragraph to check comprehension. Ask questions to promote discussion and develop the concept. • What creates the phases of the moon? • About how long does the moon take to circle the Earth? • What is a waxing moon? What is a waning moon? • What words on the concept web could help you describe the phases of the moon?

MORE PRACTICE

Have students reread "Phases of the Moon." As they read, tell them to write a description of what causes the phases of the moon to share with family members tonight.

Reread for Fluency "Phases of the Moon," p. 112

5 minutes

	To Do	To Say
CORRECTIVE FEEDBACK	Monitor oral reading.	Read p. 112 aloud. Reread the page three or four times so your reading gets better each time. Give feedback on students' oral reading, using the *if . . . then* statements on Routine Card 4. Model fluent reading if necessary. You may want to have students read along with the DVD-ROM.

ACTIVITY 3 — Write

Response to Literature

5 minutes

	To Do	To Say
Prompt journal writing.	Write on the board or a transparency: *Why does the moon fascinate us?*	Take out your journals. This week we are reading about the moon. The question for this week is: *Why does the moon fascinate us?* Write an answer to this question based on what you read today. Have students write about the topic, using what they read and their own experiences.
Homework		Practice Book, p. 97, Vocabulary

ACTIVITY 1 # Word Work

Phonics Suffixes -hood, -ment, -y, -en

	To Do	To Say	5–10 minutes

Teach suffixes -hood, -ment, -y, -en.

Write on the board or a transparency: *They visited their childhood home.*

Remember, when you read a long word, look for meaningful parts. What parts do you see in this word? Frame *child* and *hood*.

This word contains the base word, *child*, and the suffix, *-hood.* Find the base word and the suffix. Then put them together to read the word. The suffix *-hood* means "state or condition of." So *childhood* means "the condition of being a child."

Scaffold instruction.

Develop word meaning.

Have students think and converse. When does *childhood* begin and end? What comes after *childhood?*

Write *dirty, improvement,* and *wooden.*

Here are more words that contain suffixes. The suffix *-y* means "having" or "full of." The suffix *-ment* means "result, act, or condition of." The suffix *-en* means "made of."

What base word and suffix do you see in *dirty? (dirt* and *-y)* What does *dirty* mean? ("full of dirt") What base word and suffix do you see in *improvement? (improve* and *-ment)* What does *improvement* mean? ("the result of being improved") What base word and suffix do you see in *wooden? (wood* and *-en)* What does *wooden* mean? ("made of wood") Guide students in blending the word parts into the whole words.

CORRECTIVE FEEDBACK

Write each practice word.

Have students practice reading words with the suffixes *-hood, -ment, -y, -en.* Correct any words students miss and have them reread the list.

adulthood   messy   lucky   amazement   ashen   golden

MORE PRACTICE

Write more practice words.

Have students practice reading words with the suffixes *-hood, -ment, -y, -en.*

brotherhood   cloudy   salty   enjoyment   contentment   earthen

Amazing Words Vocabulary

	To Do	To Say	5 minutes

Review vocabulary.

Review the homework.

Ask students to go over answers and share their writing from Practice Book p. 97. See Routine Card 1 for multisyllabic word routine.

Deepen understanding of *myths.*

Remember, *myths* are legends or stories that attempt to explain something in nature. Some cultures believe that angry gods are responsible for bad weather. Why are these *myths?* What else is an example of a *myth?* Why?

ACTIVITY 2 # Comprehension

Draw Conclusions

	To Do	To Say	5 minutes

Scaffold instruction.

Introduce drawing conclusions.

Today you will read about different myths that relate to the moon. When you read, it's important to draw conclusions. A conclusion is a decision you make based on what you read and your own experiences.

Model the skill.

For example, if I read that people from South America believe they can see a jaguar in the moon, I can conclude that jaguars are well-known animals there.

Distribute Graphic Organizer 2.

As you read "One Moon, Many Myths," look for details that help you draw conclusions. Add these details to your graphic organizers. See Routine Card 7.

ACTIVITY **3**

Read a Passage

Read for Comprehension "One Moon, Many Myths," pp. 114–117

10–15 minutes

Scaffold instruction.	**To Do** Monitor student engagement. See Routine Cards 2 and 3.	**To Say** **Read** Have students read pp. 114–117. Stop at the end of each page to ask questions. Students who can read on their own can do so without stopping. After reading, ask questions to promote discussion. **On p. 115, what do myths about the moon explain?** (why the moon changes its shape; what people see when they look at the moon) **What do the shadowy spots on the moon look like to some people?** (faces, animals, and other things) **Why would American cowboys tell a myth about a brushfire on the moon?** (because cowboys see a lot of brushfires on the prairie) **What does Hina do with the cloth she makes from the bark of a tree?** (throws it over the Earth to make clouds) **What do you think the rest of the article will be about?** (Answers will vary. The title suggests it will tell more about different moon myths.)
Model summarizing.	Think aloud.	**Summarize** **What were the first four pages mainly about? What did you learn about moon myths?** Think aloud to model summarizing. **I learned a lot of details about moon myths, such as some people think the shadowy spots on the moon are animals. The main thing I learned is that people all over the world see the same moon, but they all see it differently and tell different stories about it.**
Develop language and concepts.	Ask questions.	• **Why do people tell stories about the moon?** • **What things affect the beliefs that different cultures have about the moon?**
MORE PRACTICE	Have students reread p. 117.	**Reread** Tell students to draw pictures that show what Hina might look like crossing the rainbow bridge to the moon or sitting on the moon making cloth.

Reread for Fluency "One Moon, Many Myths," pp. 116–117

5 minutes

MORE PRACTICE **CORRECTIVE FEEDBACK**	**To Do** Pair students. Monitor paired reading.	**To Say** Students read aloud pp. 116–117, switching readers at each new paragraph. Have partners reread; now the other partner begins. For optimal fluency, students should reread three or four times. Give feedback, using the *if . . . then* statements on Routine Card 4. You may want to have students read along with the DVD-ROM.

 ACTIVITY **4**

Write

Response to Literature

5 minutes

Prompt writing.	**To Do** Writing elements: support	**To Say** **What conclusions can you draw about Hawaiian culture based on their moon myth? Use details from the selection to support your ideas.**
Homework		Practice Book, p. 98, Suffixes *-hood, -ment, -y, -en*

ACTIVITY **1**   Word Work

Phonics Suffixes *-hood, -ment, -y, -en*

| To Do | To Say | 5 minutes |

Review suffixes -hood, -ment, -y, -en.

Review the homework. Discuss *shadowy* on p. 115 of the Student Reader.

Ask students to share answers from Practice Book p. 98.

Point out *shadowy* on p. 115, paragraph 2. **Remember, when you read a long word, look for meaningful parts. What base word and suffix do you see in this word?** (*shadow* and *-y*) Guide students in blending the word parts. **Remember, the suffix *-y* means "full of." What does *shadowy* mean?** ("full of shadows")

MORE PRACTICE

Model spelling words with suffixes.

Spell and Write Write *shadowy*. **What suffix has been added to *shadow*? Does the spelling of the base word change when the suffix is added?** Continue with *silken* and *childhood*. **Do you know other words that have a suffix?** List responses on the board.

Amazing Words ## **Vocabulary**

| To Do | To Say | 5 minutes |

Build vocabulary.

Lead cumulative review.

Deepen understanding of *astronomers* and *myths.*

Read aloud the first paragraph of p. 121. The author tells you that *astronomers* are scientists who study outer space. How might an *astronomer's* description of the moon be different from one you hear in *myths*? Why?

Use the Tested Vocabulary Cards to review words from previous weeks.

ACTIVITY **2**   Comprehension

Draw Conclusions

| To Do | To Say | 5–10 minutes |

Scaffold instruction.

Review drawing conclusions.

Remember to use details from a story or article, as well as your own experience, to draw conclusions as you read. After you draw a conclusion, ask yourself whether it makes sense and whether the evidence from the selection supports it.

Guide practice.

Use Graphic Organizer 2.

Listen as I read p. 120. Notice that the author describes what we learn about the moon from myths and from astronomers. What conclusion can you draw about information about the moon in myths, compared to information from astronomers? (Myths are entertaining, but they don't teach facts.) **How do you know?** (While myths try to explain things about the moon, we've learned facts from astronomers.) **Add these details to your graphic organizers.** See Routine Card 7.

MORE PRACTICE

Have students preview pp. 118–121.

Think aloud.

Read the captions and look at the photographs on pp. 118–121. What do you think this section will be about? (more about moon myths) **Why do you think so?** Think aloud to model using captions and illustrations to predict

The captions and photos make me think that the article will describe moon myths and characters from around the world, as well as give facts about the moon.

ACTIVITY 3 # Read a Passage

Read for Comprehension "One Moon, Many Myths," pp. 118–121

10–15 minutes

To Do	To Say

Scaffold instruction.

Monitor student engagement.

Read Have students read pp. 118–121. Stop at the end of each page to ask questions. Students who can read on their own can do so without stopping. After reading, ask questions to promote discussion.

See Routine Cards 2 and 3.

How do people in India explain moon shadows? (They say they are a mother's handprints.)

Why did the mother send her children into the sky to be the sun and moon? (She loved them so much that she wanted them to live forever.)

Why does Baloo begin to show his moon face more and more? (His courage returns, and he becomes less and less embarrassed.)

How is the moon shaped? (like an egg)

What really causes moon shadows? (craters and ancient, hardened lava flows)

Assess comprehension.

Monitor understanding.

After Reading Have students discuss the What Do You Think? question. Prompt them to draw conclusions about why people tell myths about the moon as they answer the question. Listen as they talk to assess comprehension.

Summarize.

What is this mainly about? What did you learn? Work with students to summarize the selection.

MORE PRACTICE

Have students reread p. 119.

Reread As they read, tell students to draw conclusions about what the myth tells us about Australian culture. Have them add their conclusions to their graphic organizers.

Reread for Fluency "One Moon, Many Myths," p. 120

5 minutes

To Do	To Say

CORRECTIVE FEEDBACK

Monitor oral reading.

Read p. 120 aloud. Reread the page three or four times so your reading gets better each time. Give feedback on students' oral reading, using the *if . . . then* statements on Routine Card 4. Model fluent reading if necessary. You may want to have students read along with the DVD-ROM.

 ACTIVITY 4 # Write

Response to Literature

5 minutes

To Do	To Say

MORE PRACTICE

Prompt writing.

Which do you more enjoy reading, myths about the moon, or scientific facts about the moon? Why? Support your ideas. Use complete sentences to express your thoughts.

Homework Practice Book, p. 99, Draw Conclusions

ACTIVITY 1 Word Work

Amazing Words Vocabulary

	To Do	To Say	*5–10 minutes*
Extend word knowledge.	Write on the board or a transparency: *astronaut* and *astronomers*.	Use the words *astronaut* and *astronomer* to extend word knowledge. **Remember we read these words earlier this week. We chunked the words to read them, but we might also have noticed meaningful parts.**	
Teach *astro-.* **Scaffold instruction.**		The Greek root *astro* means "star" or "space," and we can use it to read other words. *Naut* is a Greek root that means "sailor." An *astronaut* "sails," or travels, in space. A*stronomers* are scientists who study the stars and other objects in outer space. Can you think of other words that begin with *astro?* (astronomy, astrology, astronomical, astronautics, astrophysics) Write words as students name them and add some of your own. Talk about the meanings of the words and have students practice pronouncing them.	
	Develop word meaning.	**What special skills would it take to be an *astronaut* or an *astronomer?* Why?**	
MORE PRACTICE	Deepen understanding of *mission* and *astronauts.*	Have individual students or partners use the words *mission* and *astronaut* in sentences. (For example: Three *astronauts* went on *Apollo 13* in space.) Share sentences. Ask: **Why is a journey into space called a *mission?* Why are *astronauts* so important to the success of a space *mission?***	

ACTIVITY 2 Comprehension

Skill and Strategy Practice

	To Do	To Say	*5 minutes*
Scaffold instruction.	Review drawing conclusions (homework).	Ask volunteers to read the passage and share answers from Practice Book p. 99. Remind students of the importance of drawing conclusions. **When you read a story, you can draw conclusions about characters and events. As you read, ask yourself why characters behave the way they do and why events happen the way they do. Use details from the story as well as what you already know to draw conclusions. Be sure to ask yourself, "Do my conclusions make sense? Can I support them with details from the story?"**	
Practice strategic prereading.	See Routine Card 2.	**Discuss Genre** Read the title and the first paragraph on p. 122. Model determining genre.	
	Think aloud.	**I first thought this might be fiction because of the illustrations. When I read the first paragraph, I knew it was fiction because of the way the narrator speaks.**	
	Review story structure.	**Ask Questions** **What questions do you ask yourself to help you understand a fictional story?** (What is the problem or goal? How is the problem solved or the goal reached?) **As you read this story, ask these questions and look for the answers.**	

ACTIVITY 3 Read a Passage

Read for Comprehension "Saving the Moon Tree," pp. 122–129

	To Do	To Say	*10–15 minutes*

Scaffold instruction.

Monitor student engagement.

See Routine Card 3.

Read Have students read pp. 122–129 on their own and then discuss. For students who need more help, stop at the end of each page to discuss. After reading, ask questions.

Who are the main characters in this story? (Sam, Rick, Ms. Johnson, and Mr. Hardy)

Why is the sycamore tree called a moon tree? (The seed it grew from traveled to the moon on *Apollo 14*.)

How do Sam and Rick achieve their goal? (They research moon trees, get local people involved in saving the tree, and work with Mr. Hardy to save the tree.)

What happens at the end of the story? (Mr. Hardy saves the tree and dedicates it to Sam and Rick.)

Model using context for word meaning.

Read aloud the two paragraphs with *petition* on p. 126. Explain how the sentences that follow offer clues to the meaning of *petition* by describing what a petition is and how Sam and Rick use one.

Assess comprehension.

Monitor understanding.

After Reading Have students discuss the What Do You Think? question. Prompt them to draw conclusions based on details in the story. Listen as they talk to assess comprehension.

MORE PRACTICE

Reread Have students reread p. 124, tell who Stuart Roosa was, and explain how and why he becomes part of this story, set so many years later.

Reread for Fluency "Saving the Moon Tree," pp. 127–129

	To Do	To Say	*5–10 minutes*

CORRECTIVE FEEDBACK

Pair students. Monitor paired reading.

Students read aloud pp. 127–129, switching readers at the end of each paragraph. Have partners reread; now the other partner begins. For optimal fluency, students should reread three or four times. Give feedback, using Routine Card 4. You may want to have students read along with the DVD-ROM.

MORE PRACTICE

READERS' THEATER

Work with a group of students to adapt pp. 127–129 for Readers' Theater. Have students rehearse reading the parts of Sam, Mr. Hardy, Sam's mother, and a narrator. Discuss what should be cut or added to make the narration read smoothly and make sense.

ACTIVITY 4 Write

Response to Literature

	To Do	To Say	*5 minutes*

Prompt expository writing.

Writing elements: support

Why are Sam and Rick fascinated by the moon tree and its history? Use story details to support your answer.

ACTIVITY 1 — Read a Passage

Read Together "Moon Facts," pp. 130–133

10 minutes

	To Do	**To Say**
Scaffold instruction.	Review drawing conclusions.	Have students preview pp. 130–133. **This article tells why an eclipse occurs, and other interesting facts about the moon. As you read, use the information in the selection, as well as what you know, to draw conclusions about eclipses and about phases of the moon.**
	See Routine Card 3.	**Read** Read the article as students follow along. Then read it a second time, having students join in on the text. After reading, ask questions.
		What causes an eclipse of the moon? (Earth casts a shadow on the moon, which makes it seem to disappear for a time.)
		How did people long ago explain an eclipse? (They said that a dragon had eaten the moon.)
		Why do some gardeners watch the moon closely? (They believe that some crops should be planted when the moon is waxing, and others should be planted when it is waning.)
		How many people have walked on the surface of the moon? (12 people)
Assess comprehension.	Monitor listening comprehension.	**Summarize** Have one student describe what causes an eclipse while others offer additional information as needed.

ACTIVITY 2 — Build Concepts

Amazing Words Vocabulary

5–10 minutes

	To Do	**To Say**
Review concept and vocabulary.	Display the concept web you began on Day 1.	**This week's question is *Why does the moon fascinate us?* How do this week's words relate to the question?** (Have students answer the question, using some of the vocabulary they learned this week.)
		Ask students to add more words to the concept web. Have students explain how each word relates to the moon. Monitor students' understanding of vocabulary as they discuss the web. See Routine Card 5.
MORE PRACTICE	Write *crater, astronaut,* and *astronomer* on the board.	Have students relate *craters, astronaut,* and *astronomers.* **What have *astronomers* learned that explains why the moon has *craters?* In what ways have *astronauts* helped *astronomers* in their work?**

ACTIVITY **3** Write

Response to Literature "4 You 2 Do," p. 134

To Do	To Say	*5–10 minutes*

Guide response activities.

Discuss the directions on p. 134.

Tell students to choose one activity to complete.

See Routine Card 8.

Word Play Have students complete the first part on their own and then meet with partners to create space jokes using the vocabulary words.

Making Connections Discuss the question in a group. (Answers will vary, but they should show an understanding that the moon is visible to everyone and its beauty and mysteries have inspired storytellers for centuries. Scientists and astronomers want to study the moon because it is Earth's nearest neighbor in space and its only natural satellite.)

On Paper Have students brainstorm some answers to the prompt before they write. Have them write on their own. Students can use Practice Book p. 100 to structure their written responses, or you can send the Practice Book page home for them to complete later.

MORE PRACTICE

If you have more time, direct students to complete all the activities.

ACTIVITY **4** Assessment Options

End-of-Unit Test

To Do	To Say	*10–15 minutes*

Assess fluency and comprehension.

Use Assessment Book, p.72.

Options for end-of-unit assessment are available in the Assessment Book, p.72.

Homework   Practice Book, p. 100, Writing

Unit 6 Week 1 *Opportunity Knocks*

 How can we be successful?

Objectives *This week students will...*

Vocabulary
- build concepts and vocabulary: *circumstances, conviction, devised, model, procrastinates, suggested*

Phonics
- read words with syllables with vowel combinations: short *e* spelled *ea*
- apply knowledge of word structure to decode multisyllabic words when reading

Text Comprehension
- use sequence to improve comprehension
- write in response to literature
- make connections across text

Fluency
- practice fluency with oral rereading

Word Work *This week's phonics focus is . . .*

Short *e* Spelled *ea*

Amazing Words Concept/Amazing Words *Tested Vocabulary*

The week's vocabulary is related to the concept of opportunity knocks.
The first appearance of each word in the Student Reader is noted below.

circumstances	conditions that go along with some fact or event (p. 12)
conviction	a strong belief (p. 10)
devised	thought up some way of doing something; invented (p. 22)
model	a small copy of something (p. 18)
procrastinates	puts things off until later; delays (p. 18)
suggested	brought up an idea; proposed (p. 8)

Student Reader Unit 6 *This week students will read the following selections.*

Daily Lesson Plan

	ACTIVITIES	MATERIALS

Day 1	**Build Concepts** Weekly Concept: Opportunity Knocks
	   Vocabulary: *circumstances, conviction, devised, model,*
	   procrastinates, suggested
	
	Read a Passage "The Ferris Wheel," pp. 8–9
	   Comprehension: Use Strategies
	   Reread for Fluency
	
	Write Response to Literature
		Student Reader: Unit 6
		Routine Cards 2, 4, 5
		Tested Vocabulary Cards
		Student journals
		Practice Book, p. 101, Vocabulary
		Student Reader DVD-ROM

Day 2	**Word Work** Phonics: Syllables with Vowel Combinations:
	   Short *e* Spelled *ea*
	   Vocabulary: Deepen word meaning
	
	Comprehension Sequence
	
	Read a Passage "They Didn't Give Up," pp. 10–13
	   Reread for Fluency
	
	Write Response to Literature
		Student Reader: Unit 6
		Practice Book, p. 101, Vocabulary
		Graphic Organizer 5
		Routine Cards 1, 2, 3, 4, 7
		Practice Book, p. 102, Short *e* Spelled *ea*
		Student Reader DVD-ROM

Day 3	**Word Work** Phonics: Syllables with Vowel Combinations:
	   Short *e* Spelled *ea*
	   Vocabulary: Deepen word meaning
	
	Comprehension Sequence
	
	Read a Passage "They Didn't Give Up," pp. 14–17
	   Reread for Fluency
	
	Write Response to Literature
		Practice Book, p. 102, Short *e* Spelled *ea*
		Tested Vocabulary Cards
		Student Reader: Unit 6
		Graphic Organizer 5
		Routine Cards 2, 3, 4, 7
		Practice Book, p. 103, Sequence
		Student Reader DVD-ROM

Day 4	**Word Work** Vocabulary: Extend word knowledge **Comprehension** Skill and Strategy Practice **Read a Passage** "The Wright Report," pp. 18–25 Reread for Fluency **Write** Response to Literature	Practice Book, p. 103, Sequence Student Reader: Unit 6 Routine Cards 2, 3, 4 Student Reader DVD-ROM

Day 5	**Read a Passage** Poetry, pp. 26–29
	   Comprehension: Sequence; Listening
	
	Build Concepts Vocabulary
	
	Write Response to Literature: "4 You 2 Do," p. 30
	
	Assessment Options Fluency
	   Comprehension
		Student Reader: Unit 6
		Routine Cards 3, 5, 6, 8
		Fluency Progress Chart, p. 185
		Practice Book, p. 104, Writing

See pp. xvi–xvii for how *My Sidewalks* integrates instructional practices for ELL.

ACTIVITY 1 | ## Build Concepts

Amazing Words Vocabulary

| To Do | To Say | *10–15 minutes* |

Develop oral vocabulary.

See Routine Card 6 and p. 208.

Introduce the Concept/Amazing Words with an oral routine prior to displaying them in print. Page 208 in this Teacher's Guide provides specific guidelines for introducing each word.

Develop word meaning.

See Routine Card 5. Discuss pp. 7–9.

Have students read p. 7 and then look at the pictures on pp. 8–9. **What do you notice?** (Ferris wheels, the Eiffel Tower) **Can you use the word** *opportunity* **to describe any of these pictures?** (Example: I'd like to have the *opportunity* to ride the largest Ferris wheel in the world.)

Scaffold instruction.

Create a concept web.

In the center of a web, write *Opportunity Knocks.* **This week's concept is** *opportunity knocks.* **An** *opportunity* **is a good chance to do something.** Provide an example to demonstrate meaning. **We had the** *opportunity* **to hear a well-known musician perform at our school.** Discuss the metaphor: **When something knocks, where is it, usually?** (at a door) **Why do you knock on a door?** (wanting to come in) **What do you think it means when "opportunity knocks"?** (A chance to do something presents itself, wanting to come into our lives.)

Add the other vocabulary words.

Concept and Language Goals

Discuss the meaning of each word as it relates to opportunity, using the glossary as needed. (See p. 122 of this Teacher's Guide for definitions.)

Model the multisyllabic word strategy.

Display each word. Say it as you display it.

Use the Tested Vocabulary Cards. Follow this routine for each word:

- **Look for Meaningful Parts** **Do you recognize any parts of this word? What do these parts mean? Use the parts to read the word.** As you introduce the words, be sure students notice the following: *convict, suggest, -tion, -ed.*

- **Chunk Words with No Recognizable Parts** Model how to chunk the word *procrastinates* to read it.

Think aloud.

- **Model** **I see a chunk at the beginning of the word:** *pro.* **I see a part in the middle:** *cras.* **I see another part:** *ti.* **I see a part at the end:** *nates.* **I say the chunks slowly:** *pro cras ti nates.* **I say the chunks fast to make a whole word:** *procrastinates.* **Is it a real word? Yes, I know the word** *procrastinates.*

- Have students practice reading each word.

Read p. 6 with students.

Do any of the words we just learned seem to fit on this page? Together with students, read the sentences on p. 6 describing each selection. Talk about how the concept words might be used in the selections.

MORE PRACTICE

Deepen understanding of *opportunity.*

Have students demonstrate understanding by answering questions. **If you have an** *opportunity* **to try something new, should you take it? Why or why not? Do** *opportunities* **come along every day, or are they rare? Explain.**

ACTIVITY 2 Read a Passage

Develop Concepts "The Ferris Wheel," pp. 8–9

| To Do | To Say | *10–15 minutes* |

Practice strategic prereading.

See Routine Card 2.

Think aloud.

Discuss Genre Read the title on p. 8 and have students look at the illustrations on pp. 8–9. Model determining genre.

The photographs are a clue that this is nonfiction. They look like photos of real Ferris wheels and a real place, the Eiffel Tower. I think this article will tell me about the Ferris wheel and how it was invented.

Scaffold instruction.

Review text structure.

Ask Questions What questions do you ask yourself to help you understand nonfiction? (What did I learn? What is this mainly about?) As you read this article, ask these questions and look for the answers.

Guide comprehension.

Read pp. 8–9 aloud.

Read Read the article as students follow along. Then read it a second time, having students join in. If necessary, stop at the end of each paragraph to check comprehension. Ask questions to promote discussion and develop the concept.

Develop language and concepts.

- Who was George Ferris?
- Why did the people of Chicago want to build something as wonderful as the Eiffel Tower?
- What was the Ferris wheel designed to do?
- What words on the concept web could help you describe the invention of the Ferris wheel?

MORE PRACTICE

Have students reread "The Ferris Wheel." As they read, tell them to write a brief explanation of why George Ferris invented the Ferris wheel to share with family members tonight.

Reread for Fluency "The Ferris Wheel," p. 9

| To Do | To Say | *5 minutes* |

CORRECTIVE FEEDBACK

Monitor oral reading.

Read p. 9 aloud. Reread the page three or four times so your reading gets better each time. Give feedback on students' oral reading, using the *if . . . then* statements on Routine Card 4. Model fluent reading if necessary. You may want to have students read along with the DVD-ROM.

ACTIVITY 3 Write

Response to Literature

| To Do | To Say | *5 minutes* |

Prompt journal writing.

Write on the board or a transparency: *How can we be successful?*

Take out your journals. This week we are reading about ways that opportunity knocks. Our question for this week is: *How can we be successful?* Write an answer to this question based on what you read today. Have students write about the topic, using what they read and their own experiences.

Homework

Practice Book, p. 101, Vocabulary

ACTIVITY 1 Word Work

Phonics Short e Spelled ea

To Do	To Say	5–10 minutes

Teach syllables with vowel combinations: short e spelled ea.

Teach syllables with vowel combinations: short e spelled ea.	Write on the board or a transparency: *The weather looked threatening.*	Remember, when you read a long word, look for meaningful parts. What parts do you see in *weather?* Frame *weath* and *er.* Listen to the vowel sound in the first syllable of *weather.* The vowel combination *ea* stands for the sound short *e.* Now look at *threatening.* What vowel sound do you hear in the first syllable? (short *e*) What vowel combination makes the sound short *e? (ea)*
Scaffold instruction.	Develop word meaning.	Have students think and converse. If the *weather* looks *threatening,* should you be outside? Why?
	Write *instead.*	Here is another word with the vowel combination *ea.* What vowel sound do you hear in the second syllable of *instead?* (short *e*)
CORRECTIVE FEEDBACK	Write each practice word.	Have students practice reading these words with short *e* spelled *ea.* Correct any words students miss and have them reread the list.

head	gingerbread	unhealthy	sweating	heavier	spread

MORE PRACTICE	Write more practice words.	Have students practice reading these words with short *e* spelled *ea.*

ready	headline	wealth	feather	heaven	breath

Amazing Words Vocabulary

To Do	To Say	5 minutes

Review vocabulary.	Review the homework.	Ask students to go over answers and share their writing from Practice Book p. 101. See Routine Card 1 for the multisyllabic word routine.
	Deepen understanding of *suggested.*	Remember, to *suggest* something means to bring up an idea. If someone *suggested* a change to you, would you be more likely to accept that suggestion if things were going fine, or if they weren't? Why? Is a *suggestion* always helpful? Explain.

ACTIVITY 2 Comprehension

Sequence

To Do	To Say	5 minutes

Scaffold instruction.	Introduce sequence.	Today you will read about real people who became successes because they refused to give up on their dreams. As you read about how they achieved success, keep track of the sequence, or order of events. Keeping track of the sequence can help you better understand what you read. Words such as *first, next,* and *finally,* as well as dates and times, can give you clues to the sequence.
	Model the skill.	For example, if I read that an author *finally* had her book published, I need to pay attention to the sequence to help me understand what events happened to her before that.
	Distribute Graphic Organizer 5.	As you read "They Didn't Give Up," look for details to help you track the sequence of events in these people's lives. Add these details to your graphic organizers. See Routine Card 7.

ACTIVITY 3 Read a Passage

Read for Comprehension "They Didn't Give Up," pp. 10–13

10–15 minutes

	To Do	To Say
Scaffold instruction.	Monitor student engagement. See Routine Cards 2 and 3.	**Read** Have students read pp. 10–13. Stop at the end of each page to ask questions. Students who can read on their own can do so without stopping. After reading, ask questions to promote discussion. **How did Ted Geisel finally get his story published?** (by sending it to more than forty different publishers until one said "yes") **What was Ted Geisel convinced of that made him keep trying?** (He was sure that kids would love his story.) **What made Joanne Rowling continue writing?** (She was convinced that success would mean a better life for her and her daughter.) **What do you think the rest of the article will be about?** (Answers will vary. The title suggests that it will tell about others who found success after refusing to give up on their dreams.)
Model summarizing.	Think aloud.	**Summarize** What were the first four pages mainly about? What did you learn about people who refused to give up? Think aloud to model summarizing. I learned a lot of details about Ted Geisel and J.K. Rowling, such as that they both had difficulty getting their first books published. But the main thing I learned is that sometimes success comes only after a long time of trying.
Develop language and concepts.	Ask questions.	• **How can a strong belief in yourself lead to success?** • **How were Ted Geisel and J.K. Rowling similar?**
MORE PRACTICE	Have students reread p. 10.	**Reread** Have students draw a picture that shows what Ted Geisel might have looked like as he listened to the rhythm of the ship and wrote his story.

Reread for Fluency "They Didn't Give Up," pp. 12–13

5 minutes

	To Do	To Say
MORE PRACTICE **CORRECTIVE FEEDBACK**	Pair students. Monitor paired reading.	Students read aloud pp. 12–13, switching readers at each new page. Have partners reread; now the other partner begins. For optimal fluency, students should reread three or four times. Give feedback, using the *if . . . then* statements on Routine Card 4. You may want to have students read along with the DVD-ROM.

ACTIVITY 4 Write

Response to Literature

5 minutes

	To Do	To Say
Prompt writing.	Writing elements: support	**How did Ted Geisel and J.K. Rowling achieve success? Include details from the article to support your ideas.**
Homework		Practice Book, p. 102, Short *e* Spelled *ea*

ACTIVITY 1 Word Work

Phonics Short e Spelled *ea*

	To Do	**To Say**	5 minutes

Review syllables with vowel combinations: short e spelled *ea*.

Scaffold instruction.

Review the homework. Discuss *steady* on p. 10 in the Student Reader.

Ask students to share answers from Practice Book p. 102.

Point out *steady* on p. 10, paragraph 1. **Remember, the vowel combination *ea* sometimes stands for the sound short *e*. What parts do you see in *steady*? (stead y) What vowel sound do you hear in the first syllable? (short *e*)** Guide students in blending the word parts and pronouncing the word.

Then point to *read* on p. 11, paragraph 2. **What vowel sound do you hear in *read*? (short *e*) What vowel combination makes the sound short *e*? (ea)** Point out that *read* is pronounced /red/ only when the past tense of the verb is used.

MORE PRACTICE

Model spelling words with the short *e* sound spelled *ea*.

Spell and Write Write *head*. Say *head*. **What vowel sound do you hear in this word? What letters spell the vowel sound? Underline *ea*. What other words do you know where *ea* spells the short *e* sound?** List responses on the board.

Amazing Words Vocabulary

	To Do	**To Say**	5 minutes

Build vocabulary.

Deepen understanding of *circumstances*.

Read aloud the first paragraph on p. 12. **Remember that *circumstances* are the "conditions that go along with some fact or event." Write *circumstances*. Why were the *circumstances* of the young mother and her daughter not very good? (They were living in a cold apartment in Scotland.) Say a sentence using *circumstances*. How might bad *circumstances* help people succeed?**

Lead cumulative review.

Use the Tested Vocabulary Cards to review words from previous weeks.

ACTIVITY 2 Comprehension

Sequence

	To Do	**To Say**	5–10 minutes

Scaffold instruction.

Review sequence.

An author may give clues to the sequence. Look for dates, phrases, and words such as *first, then, next,* or *at last*. As you read, look for sequence.

Guide practice.

Use Graphic Organizer 5.

Listen as I read the second paragraph on p. 14. Notice that the author is describing events in the life of a young man. Read the paragraph aloud. Then ask: **What did the Johnson family do in the 1930s? (They moved from Arkansas to Chicago.) What did John do next? (He became an excellent student at two of Chicago's best universities.) What did he do after that? (He wanted to start a magazine for African Americans.) Add these details to your graphic organizers.** See Routine Card 7.

MORE PRACTICE

Have students preview pp. 14–17.

Read the captions and look at the photos on pp. 14–17. What do you think this section will be about? (more about people who worked hard and refused to give up their dreams for success) Why do you think so? Think aloud to model using captions and illustrations to predict.

Think aloud.

The pictures and captions make me think that the article will tell about two more successful men and how they overcame challenges in order to succeed.

ACTIVITY 3 Read a Passage

Read for Comprehension "They Didn't Give Up," pp. 14–17

10–15 minutes

	To Do	To Say
Scaffold instruction.	Monitor student engagement. See Routine Cards 2 and 3.	**Read** Have students read pp. 14–17. Stop at the end of each page to ask questions. Students who can read on their own can do so without stopping. After reading, ask questions to promote discussion. **Why did John Johnson's family move north?** (They believed their circumstances would improve, and there would be more opportunities for them.) **Why didn't banks want to lend money to John Johnson?** (They didn't think his idea would be successful.) **How did hearing the word *no* help John Johnson succeed?** (It made him work even harder.) **What did Walt Disney do after World War I?** (He worked as an artist at his own company.) **What happened in 1928 that changed Walt's life?** (Walt made a cartoon movie starring Mickey Mouse.)
Assess comprehension.	Monitor understanding. Summarize.	**After Reading** Have students discuss the What Do You Think? question. Prompt them to use sequence words in telling how a person achieved success. Listen as they talk to assess comprehension. **What is this mainly about? What did you learn?** Work with students to summarize the selection.
MORE PRACTICE	Have students reread p. 17.	**Reread** As they read, tell students to note sequence words. *(finally, today)* Have students add these words to their graphic organizers. After they read, have them retell how Walt Disney achieved success.

Reread for Fluency "They Didn't Give Up," p. 15

5 minutes

	To Do	To Say
CORRECTIVE FEEDBACK	Monitor oral reading.	Read p. 15 aloud. Reread the page three or four times so your reading gets better each time. Give feedback on students' oral reading, using the *if . . . then* statements on Routine Card 4. Model fluent reading if necessary. You may want to have students read along with the DVD-ROM.

ACTIVITY 4 Write

Response to Literature

5 minutes

	To Do	To Say
MORE PRACTICE	Prompt writing.	**What do all the people described in "They Didn't Give Up" have in common?** (Students should focus their ideas on the topic.)
Homework		Practice Book, p. 103, Sequence

Word Work

Amazing Words Vocabulary

	To Do	To Say
Extend word knowledge.	Write on the board or a transparency: *His <u>conviction</u> was that children would love the story.*	Use the word *conviction* to extend word knowledge. **Remember we read this word earlier this week. We looked for meaningful parts and we noticed the word *convict*. That is a related word because they both share the Latin root *vict*. We can use this root and another form of it, *vinc,* to read other words.**
Teach Latin root *vict*.		**The root words *vict* and *vinc* mean "to conquer or overcome." A *conviction* is a strong belief. Can you think of other words with the root *vict* or *vinc*?** *(victor, victory, victorious, evict, eviction, convince, invincible)* **Write words as students name them and add some of your own. Talk about the meanings of the words and practice pronouncing them.**
Scaffold instruction.	Develop word meaning.	**How can a *conviction* or strong belief help you conquer or overcome something?**
MORE PRACTICE	Deepen understanding of *conviction*.	Have students use the word *conviction* in sentences. (For example: It was my father's *conviction* that the traffic would be bad, so we left earlier.) Share sentences. Ask: **What *conviction* do you have if you carry an umbrella even though the sun is out? What kind of *conviction* does an inventor need to have in order to be successful? Why?**

Comprehension

Skill and Strategy Practice

	To Do	To Say
Scaffold instruction.	Review sequence (homework).	Ask volunteers to read the passage and share answers from Practice Book p. 103. Remind students of the importance of following the sequence. **When you read a biography or a story, the sequence of events is often important. Look for clue words to the order in which things happen. It may also help you to picture in your mind the events as they happen.**
Practice strategic prereading.	See Routine Card 2.	**Discuss Genre** Read the title and the first paragraph on p. 18 in the Student Reader. Model determining genre.
	Think aloud.	**I first thought this might be fiction because of the illustrations. When I read the first paragraph, I knew it was fiction because the narrator mentions David's dream.**
	Review story structure.	**Ask Questions** What questions do you ask yourself to help you understand a fictional story? (What is the problem or goal? How is the problem solved or the goal reached?) **As you read this story, ask these questions and look for the answers.**

ACTIVITY 3 Read a Passage

Read for Comprehension "The Wright Report," pp. 18–25

	To Do	To Say	*10–15 minutes*

Scaffold instruction.

To Do: Monitor student engagement.

See Routine Card 3.

To Say: **Read** Have students read pp. 18–25 on their own and then discuss. For students who need more help, stop at the end of each page to discuss. After reading, ask questions.

What problem does David have? (He procrastinates when it comes to doing his schoolwork.)

How do David's parents know he can do good work? (He builds model planes.)

What assignment does Mrs. Sanger give David's class? (They must select a book on a famous person and write a report on it.)

Review the phonics skill.

To Do: Point out *breakfast* on p. 18, paragraph 2.

To Say: Remind students that the vowel combination *ea* can stand for the sound short *e*. Frame the word parts *break* and *fast* and have students blend the parts to read the word. Explain: **This really is the word *break* (/brāk/), but when it's combined with *fast* to make the word *breakfast*, it's pronounced /brek/.**

Why does David choose a book about Orville and Wilbur Wright? (They were pioneers in airplane flight, and David loves airplanes.)

Assess comprehension.

To Do: Monitor understanding.

To Say: **After Reading** Have students discuss the What Do You Think? question. Prompt them to use sequence words to respond. Listen as they talk to assess comprehension.

MORE PRACTICE

Reread Have students reread p. 20 and explain why David is procrastinating about choosing a topic.

Reread for Fluency "The Wright Report," pp. 23–24

	To Do	To Say	*5–10 minutes*

CORRECTIVE FEEDBACK

To Do: Pair students. Monitor paired reading.

To Say: Students read aloud pp. 23–24, switching readers at the end of each page. Have partners reread; now the other partner begins. For optimal fluency, students should reread three or four times. Give feedback, using Routine Card 4. You may want to have students read along with the DVD-ROM.

ACTIVITY 4 Write

Response to Literature

	To Do	To Say	*5 minutes*

Prompt expository writing.

To Do: Review pp. 18–25.

Writing elements: organization, conventions

To Say: **What is the sequence of events in the story that makes David become an eager student? Include sequence words such as *first, then,* and *finally* to show the order of events. Use complete sentences to express your ideas.**

ACTIVITY 1 Read a Passage

Read Together Poetry, pp. 26–29

	To Do	To Say	*10 minutes*
Scaffold instruction.	Review sequence.	Have students preview pp. 26–29. **These poems are about trying hard to get what you want and following your dreams. As you read, pay attention to the order of the steps the girl takes to learn something new and the way that a person climbs a ladder to the sky.**	
	See Routine Card 3.	**Read** Read the poems as students follow along. Then read them a second time, having students join in. After reading, ask questions.	
		What happens after the little girl puts the roller skates on? (She stands up and almost flops over backwards.)	
		What does she do after she falls? (She gets up and keeps trying.)	
		In "Ladder to the Sky," what should you do after you lean a ladder against the moon? (climb high)	
		What do you do after climbing a rainbow? (ride the rainbow slide back home)	
		What do both of these poems have in common? (They both describe taking opportunities to try to excel at something.)	
Assess comprehension.	Monitor listening comprehension.	**Summarize** Have one student describe the images the poet uses to create or reinforce the mood and message in each poem.	

ACTIVITY 2 Build Concepts

Amazing Words Vocabulary

	To Do	To Say	*5–10 minutes*
Review concept and vocabulary.	Display the concept web you began on Day 1.	**This week's question is *How can we be successful?* How do this week's words relate to the question?** (Have students answer the question, using some of the vocabulary they learned this week.)	
		Ask students to add more words to the concept web. Have students explain how each word relates to opportunity knocks. Monitor students' understanding of vocabulary as they discuss the web. See Routine Card 5.	
MORE PRACTICE	Write *opportunity* and *devise* on the board.	Have students relate *opportunity* and *devise*. **Give me an example of a plan you might *devise* in order to succeed at something. If an *opportunity* doesn't present itself to you, can you *devise* your own plan for making something happen? How?**	

ACTIVITY **3** Write

Response to Literature "4 You 2 Do," p. 30

To Do	To Say	*5–10 minutes*

Guide response activities.

Discuss the directions on p. 30.

Tell students to choose one activity to complete. See Routine Card 8.

Word Play Have students work individually to unscramble the words and use them in the sentences.

Making Connections Discuss the question in a group. (Answers will vary, but students should include details that led to success for the people they choose.)

On Paper Have students brainstorm some answers to the prompt before they write. Have them write on their own. Students can use Practice Book p. 104 to structure their written responses, or you can send the Practice Book page home for them to complete later.

MORE PRACTICE

If you have more time, direct students to complete all the activities.

ACTIVITY **4** Assessment Options

Passage Reading

To Do	To Say	*10–15 minutes*

See Routine Card 6.

While some students are doing Activity 3, determine which students you want to assess this week and choose from these options.

Check fluency.

Take a two-minute timed sample of each student's oral reading.

Fluency Have a student read for two minutes from "The Wright Report." Record the number of correct words read per minute. See p. 184 for monitoring fluency. Be sure each student is assessed at least every other week.

Have students graph their progress on the Fluency Progress Chart, p. 185.

Check comprehension.

Retelling Have students reread "The Wright Report" and retell it. Prompt students if necessary. See p. 186 for monitoring retelling.

If you have time, assess every student.

Homework

Practice Book, p. 104, Writing

Unit 6 Week 2 *Challenges*

 How can we overcome obstacles to reach our goals?

Objectives *This week students will...*

Vocabulary
- build concepts and vocabulary: *achieved, furious, hurdles, perseverance, personality, timid*

Phonics
- read words with vowels *oo* in *foot, u* in *put*
- apply knowledge of word structure to decode multisyllabic words when reading

Text Comprehension
- draw conclusions to improve comprehension
- write in response to literature
- make connections across text

Fluency
- practice fluency with oral rereading

Word Work *This week's phonics focus is . . .*

Vowels *oo* in *foot, u* in *put*

Amazing Words Concept/Amazing Words *Tested Vocabulary*

The week's vocabulary is related to the concept of challenges.
The first appearance of each word in the Student Reader is noted below.

achieved	carried out to a successful end; accomplished; did (p. 37)
furious	very angry (p. 48)
hurdles	things that stand in the way; difficulties (p. 37)
perseverance	an aim; never giving up what you have set out to do (p. 34)
personality	an individual quality that makes someone different from another person (p. 48)
timid	easily frightened; shy (p. 46)

Student Reader Unit 6 *This week students will read the following selections.*

34	**The Secret of Success**	Biography
38	**Hurdles to Success**	Biography
46	**Sammy the Sofa**	Humorous Fiction
54	**Climbing to the Top of the World**	Expository Nonfiction
56	**4 You 2 Do**	Activity Page

Daily Lesson Plan

	ACTIVITIES	MATERIALS
Day 1	**Build Concepts** Weekly Concept: Challenges Vocabulary: *achieved, furious, hurdles, perseverance, personality, timid* **Read a Passage** "The Secret of Success," pp. 34–37 Comprehension: Use Strategies Reread for Fluency **Write** Response to Literature	Student Reader: Unit 6 Routine Cards 2, 4, 5 Tested Vocabulary Cards Student journals Practice Book, p. 105, Vocabulary Student Reader DVD-ROM
Day 2	**Word Work** Phonics: Vowels *oo* in *foot, u* in *put* Vocabulary: Deepen word meaning **Comprehension** Draw Conclusions **Read a Passage** "Hurdles to Success," pp. 38–41 Reread for Fluency **Write** Response to Literature	Student Reader: Unit 6 Practice Book, p. 105, Vocabulary Graphic Organizer 2 Routine Cards 1, 2, 3, 4, 7 Practice Book, p. 106, Vowels *oo* as in *foot, u* as in *put* Student Reader DVD-ROM
Day 3	**Word Work** Phonics: Vowels *oo* in *foot, u* in *put* Vocabulary: Deepen word meaning **Comprehension** Draw Conclusions **Read a Passage** "Hurdles to Success," pp. 42–45 Reread for Fluency **Write** Response to Literature	Practice Book, p. 106, Vowels *oo* as in *foot, u* as in *put* Tested Vocabulary Cards Student Reader: Unit 6 Graphic Organizer 2 Routine Cards 2, 3, 4, 7 Practice Book, p. 107, Draw Conclusions Student Reader DVD-ROM
Day 4	**Word Work** Vocabulary: Extend word knowledge **Comprehension** Skill and Strategy Practice **Read a Passage** "Sammy the Sofa," pp. 46–53 Reread for Fluency **Write** Response to Literature	Practice Book, p. 107, Draw Conclusions Student Reader: Unit 6 Routine Cards 2, 3, 4 Student Reader DVD-ROM
Day 5	**Read a Passage** "Climbing to the Top of the World," pp. 54–55 Comprehension: Draw Conclusions; Listening **Build Concepts** Vocabulary **Write** Response to Literature: "4 You 2 Do," p. 56 **Assessment Options** Fluency Comprehension	Student Reader: Unit 6 Routine Cards 3, 5, 6, 8 Fluency Progress Chart, p. 185 Practice Book, p. 108, Writing

See pp. xvi–xvii for how *My Sidewalks* integrates instructional practices for ELL.

Build Concepts

Amazing Words Vocabulary

	To Do	To Say	*10–15 minutes*

Develop oral vocabulary.

See Routine Card 6 and p. 209.

Introduce the Concept/Amazing Words with an oral routine prior to displaying them in print. Page 209 in this Teacher's Guide provides specific guidelines for introducing each word.

Develop word meaning.

See Routine Card 5.

Discuss pp. 33–37.

Have students read p. 33 and then look at the pictures on pp. 34–37. **What do you notice?** (Thomas Edison and some of his inventions) **Can you use the word** *challenge* **to describe any of these pictures?** (Example: Thomas Edison had to overcome *challenges* in order to invent new things.)

Scaffold instruction.

Create a concept web.

In the center of a web, write *Challenges*. **This week's concept is** *challenges*. *Challenges* **are things that test your skill.** Provide an example to demonstrate meaning. **It was a** *challenge* **to ski down the mountain, but we went slowly and made it without falling down.**

Add the other vocabulary words.

Concept and Language Goals

Discuss the meaning of each word as it relates to challenges, using the glossary as needed. (See p. 134 in this Teacher's Guide for definitions.)

Model the multisyllabic word strategy.

Display each word. Say it as you display it.

Use the Tested Vocabulary Cards. Follow this routine for each word:

- **Look for Meaningful Parts** **Do you recognize any parts of this word? What do these parts mean? Use the parts to read the word.** As you introduce each word, be sure students notice the following: *fur(y), -ous* ("full of"), *persever(e), -ance, person, -ality.*

Point to *hurdles.*

- **Chunk Words with No Recognizable Parts** Model how to chunk the word *hurdles* to read it.

Think aloud.

- **Model** **I see a chunk at the beginning of the word:** *hur.* **I see a part at the end of the word:** *dles.* **I say each chunk slowly:** *hur dles.* **I say the chunks quickly to make a whole word:** *hurdles.* **Is it a real word? Yes, I know the word** *hurdles.*

- Have students practice reading each word.

Preview.

Read p. 32 with students.

Do any of the words we just learned seem to fit on this page? Together with students, read the sentences on p. 32 describing each selection. Talk about how the vocabulary words might be used in the selections.

MORE PRACTICE

Deepen understanding of *challenges.*

Have students demonstrate understanding by answering questions. **Which one is a** *challenge,* **learning your lines for a school play, or talking to your friends? Why? If something is a** *challenge,* **is it easy to do, or difficult? What makes something** *challenging?*

ACTIVITY 2 Read a Passage

Develop Concepts "The Secret of Success," pp. 34–37

To Do	To Say	10–15 minutes

Practice strategic prereading.

See Routine Card 2.

Discuss Genre Read the title on p. 34 and have students look at the illustrations on pp. 34–37. Model determining genre.

Think aloud.

The photographs are a clue that this is nonfiction. They look like real pictures of Thomas Edison and his inventions. I think this article will tell about how Edison achieved success as an inventor.

Scaffold instruction.

Review text structure.

Ask Questions What questions do you ask yourself to help you understand nonfiction? (What did I learn? What is this mainly about?) As you read this article, ask these questions and look for the answers.

Guide comprehension.

Read pp. 34–37 aloud.

Read Read the article as students follow along. Then read it a second time, having students join in. If necessary, stop at the end of each paragraph to check comprehension. Ask questions to promote discussion and develop the concept.

Develop language and concepts.

- What was Edison's secret to success?

- What led Edison to become an inventor?

- In what ways is Edison a good example of what hard work can accomplish?

- What words on the concept web could help you describe challenges?

MORE PRACTICE

Have students reread "The Secret of Success." As they read, tell them to make lists of the qualities that helped Thomas Edison to succeed as an inventor to share with family members tonight.

Reread for Fluency "The Secret of Success," p. 36

To Do	To Say	5 minutes

CORRECTIVE FEEDBACK

Monitor oral reading.

Read p. 36 aloud. Reread the page three or four times so your reading gets better each time. Give feedback on students' oral reading, using the *if . . . then* statements on Routine Card 4. Model fluent reading if necessary. You may want to have students read along with the DVD-ROM.

ACTIVITY 3 Write

Response to Literature

To Do	To Say	5 minutes

Prompt journal writing.

Write on the board or a transparency: *How can we overcome obstacles to reach our goals?*

Take out your journals. This week we are reading about challenges. Our question for this week is: *How can we overcome obstacles to reach our goals?* Write an answer to this question based on what you read today. Have students write about the topic, using what they read and their own experiences.

Homework

Practice Book, p. 105, Vocabulary

ACTIVITY 1 Word Work

Phonics Vowels *oo* in *foot*, *u* in *put*

	To Do	**To Say**	*5–10 minutes*

Teach vowels *oo* in *foot* and *u* in *put*.

Write on the board or a transparency: *It was warm enough to walk <u>barefoot</u> on the beach.*

Remember, when you read a long word, look for meaningful parts. What parts do you see in this word? Frame *bare* and *foot*. What vowel sound do you hear in the second syllable of *barefoot*? (/u̇/) What letters make the vowel sound? (*oo*)

When the vowels *oo* appear together in a word or syllable, they can make the sound /u̇/ that you hear in the word *foot*. The vowel *u* alone can also make the sound /u̇/ that you hear in the word *foot* and in the word *put*.

Scaffold instruction.

Write *input*.

What parts do you see in *input*? *(in put)* What vowel sound do you hear in the second syllable? (/u̇/) Guide students in blending word parts into the whole word.

Develop word meaning.

Have students think and converse. If someone asks for your *input*, they want your comments or opinion. In what type of situations might your *input* be valued? Why?

CORRECTIVE FEEDBACK

Write each practice word.

Have students practice reading words with vowels *oo* and *u*. Correct any words students miss and have them reread the list.

unhook	goodness	cookie	underfoot	output	pushed

MORE PRACTICE

Write more practice words.

Have students practice reading words with vowels *oo* and *u*.

driftwood	outlook	boyhood	putting	cookbook	crooked

Vocabulary

	To Do	**To Say**	*5 minutes*

Review vocabulary.

Review the homework.

Ask students to go over answers and share their writing from Practice Book p. 105. See Routine Card 1 for the multisyllabic word routine.

Deepen understanding of *perseverance*.

Remember, *perseverance* is "never giving up what you have set out to do." Although the runner grew tired in the middle of the race, she kept going all the way to the finish line. Why is this *perseverance*? What else is an example of *perseverance*? Why?

ACTIVITY 2 Comprehension

Draw Conclusions

	To Do	**To Say**	*5 minutes*

Scaffold instruction.

Introduce drawing conclusions.

Today you will read about three real people who overcame obstacles to achieve success. Drawing conclusions about the information in an article can help you better understand what you read. A conclusion is a decision you make based on what you read and your own experiences.

Model the skill.

For example, if I read that a person who had a difficult childhood grew up to be a doctor, I can draw the conclusion that this person had the perseverance to overcome obstacles.

Distribute Graphic Organizer 2.

As you read "Hurdles to Success," look for details that help you draw conclusions about the lives of the three people the author describes. Add these details to your graphic organizers. See Routine Card 7.

ACTIVITY 3

Read a Passage

Read for Comprehension "Hurdles to Success," pp. 38–41

	To Do	To Say	*10–15 minutes*

Scaffold instruction.

Monitor student engagement.

See Routine Cards 2 and 3.

Read Have students read pp. 38–41. Stop at the end of each page to ask questions. Students who can read on their own can do so without stopping. After reading, ask questions to promote discussion.

What challenges did Ben Carson face as a boy? (He didn't feel smart, he got in trouble at school, and his mother had to work several jobs at once.)

What did Ben's mother do to change Ben's situation? (She didn't let him watch much TV and she made him do his homework, read more, and write two book reports each week.)

How did Ben achieve success? (through hard work, knowledge, and perseverance)

What hurdles did Ann Carl have to get over as a child? (She was shy and not very confident.)

What do you think the rest of the article will be about? (Answers will vary. The title suggests that it will tell about how others overcame problems to find success.)

Model summarizing.

Think aloud.

Summarize What were the first four pages mainly about? What did you learn about hurdles to success? Think aloud to model summarizing. I learned many details about Ben Carson and Ann Carl, such as that they both lacked confidence in childhood. But the main thing I learned is that you have to work hard and persevere if you want to have success.

Develop language and concepts.

Ask questions.

- **How did Ben Carson's mother help contribute to his success?**
- **How did Ann Carl's experience at her uncle's ranch help her to gain confidence?**

MORE PRACTICE

Have students reread p. 41.

Reread Tell students to draw a picture that shows what Ann might have looked like as she went to the pasture to get the cows in.

Reread for Fluency "Hurdles to Success," pp. 39–40

	To Do	To Say	*5 minutes*

MORE PRACTICE

CORRECTIVE FEEDBACK

Pair students. Monitor paired reading.

Students read aloud pp. 39–40, switching readers at each new paragraph. Have partners reread; now the other partner begins. For optimal fluency, students should reread three or four times. Give feedback, using the *if . . . then* statements on Routine Card 4. You may want to have students read along with the DVD-ROM.

 ACTIVITY 4

Write

Response to Literature

	To Do	To Say	*5 minutes*

Prompt writing.

Writing elements: organization

How were Ann Carl and Ben Carson similar? How were they different? Use words that compare and contrast, such as *both* and *unlike*, to show similarities and differences.

Homework

Practice Book, p. 106, Vowels *oo* as in *foot, u* as in *put*

ACTIVITY 1   Word Work

Phonics Vowels *oo* in *foot*, *u* in *put*

	To Do	To Say	5 minutes
Review vowels *oo* in *foot* and *u* in *put*. **Scaffold instruction.**	Review the homework. Discuss *book* on p. 39 in the Student Reader.	Ask students to share answers from Practice Book p. 106. Point out *book* on p. 39, paragraph 2. **Remember, the vowel combination *oo* and the vowel *u* can both can make the sound /u̇/ that you hear in the word *foot*. What vowel sound do you hear in *book*?** (/u̇/) **What vowel combination makes the sound /u̇/?** *(oo)* Guide students in pronouncing the word. Then point to *put* on p. 44, paragraph 1. **What vowel sound do you hear in *put*?** (/u̇/) **What vowel makes the sound /u̇/?** *(u)*	
MORE PRACTICE	Model spelling words with vowel sound *oo* in *foot*.	**Spell and Write** Write *foot*. Say *foot*. **What vowel sound do you hear in this word? What letters spell that vowel sound? Underline *oo*. What other words do you know that have the same vowel sound as *foot*?** List responses on the board.	

★ Amazing Words ★   Vocabulary

	To Do	To Say	5 minutes
Build vocabulary. **Lead cumulative review.**	Deepen understanding of *hurdles*.	Read aloud the first paragraph on p. 41. **The author gives a clue to the meaning of *hurdles* when she says that "Ann Baumgartner Carl had her own hurdles to get over." Give an example of a physical *hurdle*. How do you get over a physical *hurdle*? Give an example of a mental *hurdle*. How do you get over a mental *hurdle*? How are they similar?** Use the Tested Vocabulary Cards to review words from previous weeks.	

ACTIVITY 2   Comprehension

Draw Conclusions

	To Do	To Say	5–10 minutes
Scaffold instruction.	Review drawing conclusions.	**Remember to use details from the article, as well as your own experiences, to draw conclusions. After you draw conclusions, ask yourself whether your conclusions make sense, and whether they can be supported with details from the selection.**	
Guide practice.	Use Graphic Organizer 2.	**Listen as I read p. 42, paragraph 1. Notice that the author is describing Ann Carl's life. Was Ann Carl confident as an adult?** (yes) **How do you know?** (She joined the Air Force so she could fly planes when people thought only men should fly.) **Add these details to your graphic organizers.** See Routine Card 7.	
MORE PRACTICE	Have students preview pp. 42–45. Think aloud.	**Read the captions and look at the photos on pp. 42–45. What do you think this section will be about?** (more on overcoming obstacles to achieve success) **Why do you think so?** Think aloud to model using captions and illustrations to predict. **The captions make me think the article will tell more about people achieving their goals despite difficult challenges. From the pictures I think this section will tell about two women who overcame hurdles to become successful.**	

ACTIVITY 3   Read a Passage

Read for Comprehension "Hurdles to Success," pp. 42–45

10–15 minutes

To Do	To Say
Scaffold instruction. Monitor student engagement.	**Read** Have students read pp. 42–45. Stop at the end of each page to ask questions. Students who can read on their own can do so without stopping. After reading, ask questions to promote discussion.
See Routine Cards 2 and 3.	**What was Ann chosen to be?** (the first woman test pilot)
	As a girl, how did Dolores Huerta learn about the lives of migrant workers? (She grew up around migrant workers and later became a teacher of the children of many migrant workers.)
	What did Dolores Huerta hope to achieve? (She wanted migrant workers to get better pay, better places to live, and better health care.)
Model using context for word meaning.	Read aloud the paragraph with *migrants* on p. 43. Explain how the sentences "They came for the harvest. Then they traveled on to other farms or returned home" provide clues to the meaning of *migrants* by explaining how migrant workers live and work.
Assess comprehension. Monitor understanding.	**After Reading** Have students discuss the What Do You Think? question. Prompt them to find similarities in how all three people persevered. Listen as they talk to assess comprehension.
Summarize.	**What is this mainly about? What did you learn?** Work with students to summarize the selection.
MORE PRACTICE Have students reread pp. 44–45.	**Reread** As they read, tell students to note the hurdles that Dolores, as well as Ann and Ben, had to overcome. Have them draw conclusions about what motivated each to persevere. Have them add these details to their graphic organizers.

Reread for Fluency "Hurdles to Success," p. 43

5 minutes

To Do	To Say
CORRECTIVE FEEDBACK Monitor oral reading.	**Read p. 43 aloud. Reread the page three or four times so your reading gets better each time.** Give feedback on students' oral reading, using the *if . . . then* statements on Routine Card 4. Model fluent reading if necessary. You may want to have students read along with the DVD-ROM.

ACTIVITY 4   Write

Response to Literature

5 minutes

To Do	To Say
MORE PRACTICE Prompt writing.	**Think about what you have learned about challenges and success. What does it take to overcome hurdles and achieve success?** (Students should include information that supports their ideas.)
Homework	Practice Book, p. 107, Draw Conclusions

Word Work

Amazing Words Vocabulary

	To Do	To Say	5–10 minutes
Extend word knowledge.	Write: *She had the right <u>personality</u> to work in the medical field.*	Use the word *personality* to extend word knowledge. **Remember we read this word earlier this week. We looked for meaningful parts, and we noticed the base word** *person.* **We can use the word** *person* **to read other words.**	
Teach words related to *person.*		A *person* **is any human being: man, woman, or child. Can you think of other words related to** *person? (personable, personal, personally, personify, personnel)* **Write words as students name them and add some of your own. Have students talk about the meanings of the words and practice pronouncing them.**	
Scaffold instruction.	Develop word meaning.	**Can people share** *personality* **traits? Can they have the same** *personality?* **Why?**	
MORE PRACTICE	Deepen understanding of *timid* and *personality.*	Have students use the two words *timid* and *personality* together in sentences. (For example: *He had a timid personality, but when he spoke in public he was very confident.*) Share sentences. Ask: **What challenges might someone with a** *timid personality* **face in trying to overcome obstacles? Why?**	

Comprehension

Skill and Strategy Practice

	To Do	To Say	5 minutes
Scaffold instruction.	Review drawing conclusions (homework).	Ask volunteers to read the passage and share answers from Practice Book p. 107. Remind students of the importance of drawing conclusions. **When you read a story, you can draw conclusions about characters and events. As you read, ask yourself why certain events take place and why characters behave as they do. Use the details in the story and what you already know to draw conclusions.**	
Practice strategic prereading.	See Routine Card 2.	**Discuss Genre** Read the title and the first paragraph on p. 46 in the Student Reader. Model determining genre.	
	Think aloud.	**I first thought this might be fiction because of the illustrations. When I read the first paragraphs, I knew it was fiction because of the casual tone of the narrator.**	
	Review story structure.	**Ask Questions** **What questions do you ask yourself to help you understand a fictional story? (What is the problem or goal? How is the problem solved or the goal reached?) As you read this story, ask these questions and look for the answers.**	

ACTIVITY 3 | Read a Passage

Read for Comprehension "Sammy the Sofa," pp. 46–53

10–15 minutes

	To Do	**To Say**
Scaffold instruction.	Monitor student engagement.	**Read** Have students read pp. 46–53 on their own and then discuss. For students who need more help, stop at the end of each page to discuss. After reading, ask questions.
Guide reading.	See Routine Card 3.	**Who is telling this story?** (Ronnie, Sammy's older sister)
		What is the setting? (Ronnie and Sammy's house)
		What problem does Sammy have? (He is very shy and hides behind the sofa all the time.)
		What does Monica want Sammy to do? (try out for the school play) **Why?** (He has a great singing voice.)
		How has Sammy changed by the end of the story? (He is very timid at the beginning, but by the end he finds the courage to try out for the play and gets a role as a singing sofa.)
Assess comprehension.	Monitor understanding.	**After Reading** Have students discuss the What Do You Think? question. Prompt them to think about why Sammy tried out for the play. Listen as they talk to assess comprehension.
MORE PRACTICE		**Reread** Have students reread pp. 47–48 and describe how Sammy behaves differently with his loyal friends than he does with other people.

Reread for Fluency "Sammy the Sofa," pp. 49–51

5–10 minutes

	To Do	**To Say**
CORRECTIVE FEEDBACK	Pair students. Monitor paired reading.	Students read aloud pp. 49–51, switching readers after each paragraph. Have partners reread; now the other partner begins. For optimal fluency, students should reread three or four times. Give feedback, using Routine Card 4. You may want to have students read along with the DVD-ROM.
MORE PRACTICE	**READERS' THEATER**	Work with a group of three students to adapt pp. 49–52 as a Readers' Theater scene. Have students rehearse reading the parts, with one student as Ronnie (narrator), one as Sammy, and one as Monica. Students should decide in advance which narrative lines each should read.

ACTIVITY 4 | Write

Response to Literature

5 minutes

	To Do	**To Say**
Prompt expository writing.	Review pp. 46–53. Writing elements: focus, organization	**How does Sammy overcome obstacles to win a part in the school play?** Use details that support your main ideas. Include transitional words that connect your ideas.

ACTIVITY 1 | Read a Passage

Read Together "Climbing to the Top of the World," pp. 54–55

	To Do	To Say
Scaffold instruction.	Review draw conclusions.	Have students preview pp. 54–55. **This article tells about people who have climbed the tallest mountain in the world, Mount Everest. Drawing conclusions about people can help you better understand how they overcame obstacles to achieve success. As you read the article, look for details about the people who have climbed Mount Everest so that you can draw conclusions about them.**
	Read pp. 54–55 aloud.	**Read** Read the article as students follow along. Then read it a second time, having students join in on the text. After reading, ask questions.
	See Routine Card 3.	**What did Radhanath Sickdhar set out to do in 1852?** (measure the height of Mount Everest)
		Why is it such a challenge to climb Mount Everest? (It's the tallest mountain in the world, and the conditions on the mountain are very dangerous.)
		What abilities do climbers need to climb Mount Everest successfully? (perseverance, physical fitness, common sense)
		Why will people continue to try to climb Mount Everest? (Its height is a challenge to climbers.)
Assess comprehension.	Monitor listening comprehension.	**Summarize** Have one student explain what makes Mount Everest such a challenge to climb and what abilities are necessary to climb it safely.

ACTIVITY 2 | Build Concepts

Amazing Words Vocabulary

	To Do	To Say
Review concept and vocabulary.	Display the concept web you began on Day 1.	**This week's question is *How can we overcome obstacles to reach our goals?* How do this week's words relate to the question?** (Have students answer the question, using some of the vocabulary they learned this week.)
		Ask students to add more words to the concept web. Have students explain how each word relates to challenges. Monitor students' understanding of vocabulary as they discuss the web. See Routine Card 5.
MORE PRACTICE	Write *achieved, challenges,* and *perseverance* on the board.	Have students relate *achieved, challenges* and *perseverance*. **Give an example of a goal you can *achieve* through *perseverance*. Why is *perseverance* so important when you are faced with *challenges*? Which is more important in *achieving* success, talent or *perseverance*? Why?**

ACTIVITY 3 | Write

Response to Literature "4 You 2 Do," p. 56

To Do	To Say	5–10 minutes

Guide response activities.

Discuss the directions on p. 56. Tell students to choose one activity to complete. See Routine Card 8.

Word Play Have students find the synonym matches on their own and then meet with a partner to share their answers.

Making Connections Discuss the question in a group. (Answers may vary but should mention people doing what they are interested in or are good at, believing in themselves, wanting to help others, or making dreams come true.)

On Paper Have students brainstorm some answers to the prompt before they write. Have them write on their own. Students can use Practice Book p. 108 to structure their written responses, or you can send the Practice Book page home for them to complete later.

MORE PRACTICE

If you have more time, direct students to complete all the activities.

ACTIVITY 4 | Assessment Options

Passage Reading

To Do	To Say	10–15 minutes

See Routine Card 6.

While some students are doing Activity 3, determine which students you want to assess this week and choose from these options.

Check fluency.

Take a two-minute timed sample of each student's oral reading.

Fluency Have a student read for two minutes from "Hurdles to Success." Record the number of correct words read per minute. See p. 184 for monitoring fluency. Be sure each student is assessed at least every other week.

Have students graph their progress on the Fluency Progress Chart, p. 185.

Check comprehension.

Retelling Have students reread "Hurdles to Success" and retell it. Prompt students if necessary. See p. 186 for monitoring retelling.

If you have time, assess every student.

Homework   Practice Book, p. 108, Writing

Unit 6 Week 3 *American Journeys*

 How can moving change our view of the world?

Objectives *This week students will...*

Vocabulary
- build concepts and vocabulary: *appreciate, awkward, barrier, immigration, international, occupations*

Phonics
- read words with syllables with vowel combinations: long *i: ind, ild*; long *o: ost, old*
- apply knowledge of word structure to decode multisyllabic words when reading

Text Comprehension
- draw conclusions to improve comprehension
- write in response to literature
- make connections across text

Fluency
- practice fluency with oral rereading

Word Work *This week's phonics focus is . . .*

Long *i: -ind, -ild*   Long *o: -ost, -old*

Amazing Words Concept/Amazing Words *Tested Vocabulary*

The week's vocabulary is related to the concept of American journeys.
The first appearance of each word in the Student Reader is noted below.

appreciate	to think highly of; recognize the worth of (p. 73)
awkward	embarrassing (p. 72)
barrier	something that stands in the way (p. 66)
immigration	coming into a foreign country to live there (p. 65)
international	between or among two or more countries (p. 62)
occupations	the work people do regularly or to earn a living (p. 73)

Student Reader Unit 6 *This week students will read the following selections.*

Daily Lesson Plan

	ACTIVITIES	MATERIALS
Day 1	**Build Concepts** Weekly Concept: American Journeys Vocabulary: *appreciate, awkward, barrier, immigration, international, occupations* **Read a Passage** "Immigration," pp. 60–61 Comprehension: Use Strategies Reread for Fluency **Write** Response to Literature	Student Reader: Unit 6 Routine Cards 2, 4, 5 Tested Vocabulary Cards Student journals Practice Book, p. 109, Vocabulary Student Reader DVD-ROM
Day 2	**Word Work** Phonics: Vowel Combinations: Long *i: -ind, -ild;* Long *o: -ost, -old* Vocabulary: Deepen word meaning **Comprehension** Draw Conclusions **Read a Passage** "A Shooting Star from China," pp. 62–65 Reread for Fluency **Write** Response to Literature	Student Reader: Unit 6 Practice Book, p. 109, Vocabulary Graphic Organizer 2 Routine Cards 1, 2, 3, 4, 7 Practice Book, p. 110, Long *i: -ind, -ild;* Long *o: -ost, -old* Student Reader DVD-ROM
Day 3	**Word Work** Phonics: Vowel Combinations: Long *i: -ind, -ild;* Long *o: -ost, -old* Vocabulary: Deepen word meaning **Comprehension** Draw Conclusions **Read a Passage** "A Shooting Star from China," pp. 66–69 Reread for Fluency **Write** Response to Literature	Practice Book, p. 110, Long *i: -ind, -ild;* Long *o: -ost, -old* Tested Vocabulary Cards Student Reader: Unit 6 Graphic Organizer 2 Routine Cards 1, 2, 3, 4, 7 Practice Book, p. 111, Draw Conclusions Student Reader DVD-ROM
Day 4	**Word Work** Vocabulary: Extend word knowledge **Comprehension** Skill and Strategy Practice **Read a Passage** "Becoming an American," pp. 70–77 Reread for Fluency **Write** Response to Literature	Practice Book, p. 111, Draw Conclusions Student Reader: Unit 6 Routine Cards 2, 3, 4 Student Reader DVD-ROM
Day 5	**Read a Passage** "Traditional Clothing," pp. 78–81 Comprehension: Draw Conclusions; Listening **Build Concepts** Vocabulary **Write** Response to Literature: "4 You 2 Do," p. 82 **Assessment Options** Fluency Comprehension	Student Reader: Unit 6 Routine Cards 3, 5, 6, 8 Fluency Progress Chart, p. 185 Practice Book, p. 112, Writing

See pp. xvi–xvii for how *My Sidewalks* integrates instructional practices for ELL.

Build Concepts

Amazing Words **Vocabulary**

| To Do | To Say | *10–15 minutes* |

Develop oral vocabulary.

See Routine Card 6 and p. 210.

Introduce the Concept/Amazing Words with an oral routine prior to displaying them in print. Page 210 in this Teacher's Guide provides specific guidelines for introducing each word.

Develop word meaning.

See Routine Card Discuss pp. 59–61.

Have students read p. 59 and then look at the pictures on pp. 60–61. **What do you notice?** (luggage, and immigrants arriving in the United States) **Can you use the words *immigration* and *journeys* to describe any of these pictures?** (Example: *Immigration* requires people to make long *journeys* from their homes to the United States.)

Scaffold instruction.

Create a concept web.

In the center of a web, write *American Journeys*. **This week's concept is *American journeys*. A *journey* is a long trip from one place to another.** Provide an example to demonstrate meaning. **Many immigrants took a *journey* by ship from Europe to the United States.**

Add the other vocabulary words.

Concept and Language Goals

Discuss the meaning of each word as it relates to American journeys, using the glossary as needed. (See p. 146 in this Teacher's Guide for definitions.)

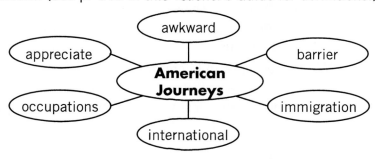

Model the multisyllabic word strategy.

Display each word. Say it as you display it.

Use the Tested Vocabulary Cards. Follow this routine for each word:

- **Look for Meaningful Parts** Do you recognize any parts of this word? What do these parts mean? Use the parts to read the word. As you introduce each word, be sure students notice the following: *migrat(e)*, *-ion*, *inter-* ("among" or "between"), *national*.

Point to *barrier*.

- **Chunk Words with No Recognizable Parts** Model how to chunk the word *barrier* to read it.

Think aloud.

- **Model** I see a chunk at the beginning of the word: *bar.* I see a part in the middle: *ri.* I see a part at the end of the word: *er.* I say each chunk slowly: *bar ri er.* I say the chunks quickly to make a whole word: *barrier.* Is it a real word? Yes, I know the word *barrier.*

- Have students practice reading each word.

Read p. 58 with students.

Do you see any of the words we just learned on this page? Together with students, read the sentences on p. 58 describing each selection. Talk about how the vocabulary words might be used in the selections.

MORE PRACTICE

Deepen understanding of *immigration.*

Have students demonstrate understanding by answering questions. **Which one is an example of *immigration,* moving to a new house in your town or moving to a new country? Why? What benefits can *immigration* bring to people who come to live in America?**

ACTIVITY 2 — Read a Passage

Develop Concepts "Immigration," pp. 60–61

10–15 minutes

	To Do	**To Say**
Practice strategic prereading.	See Routine Card 2. Think aloud.	**Discuss Genre** Read the title on p. 60 and have students look at the pictures on pp. 60–61. Model determining genre. The photographs are a clue that this is nonfiction. They look like photos of real people. I think this article will tell me about immigration to the United States.
Scaffold instruction.	Review text structure.	**Ask Questions** What questions do you ask yourself to help you understand nonfiction? (What did I learn? What is this mainly about?) As you read this article, ask these questions and look for the answers.
Guide comprehension.	Read pp. 60–61 aloud.	**Read** Read the article as students follow along. Then read it a second time, having students join in. If necessary, stop at the end of each paragraph to check comprehension. Ask questions to promote discussion and develop the concept.
Develop language and concepts.		• Up until 1930, where did most immigrants to America come from? How did they travel? • Why did immigrants leave the countries where they were born? • Where do most of today's immigrants come from? • What words on the concept web could help you describe immigration?

MORE PRACTICE

Have students reread "Immigration." As they read, tell them to make lists of the reasons why people immigrate to share with family members tonight.

Reread for Fluency "Immigration," p. 61

5 minutes

	To Do	**To Say**
CORRECTIVE FEEDBACK	Monitor oral reading.	Read p. 61 aloud. Reread the page three or four times so your reading gets better each time. Give feedback on students' oral reading, using the *if . . . then* statements on Routine Card 4. Model fluent reading if necessary. You may want to have students read along with the DVD-ROM.

ACTIVITY 3 — Write

Response to Literature

5 minutes

	To Do	**To Say**
Prompt journal writing.	Write on the board or a transparency: *How can moving change our view of the world?*	Take out your journals. This week we are reading about American journeys. Our question for this week is: *How can moving change our view of the world?* Write an answer to this question based on what you read today. Have students write about the topic, using what they read and their own experiences.
Homework		Practice Book, p. 109, Vocabulary

ACTIVITY 1 Word Work

Phonics Long *i*: -ind, -ild; Long *o*: -ost, -old

| | **To Do** | **To Say** | *5–10 minutes* |

Teach vowel combinations: long i: -ind, -ild; long o: -ost, -old.

Write on the board or a transparency: *The photos <u>remind</u> her of her <u>childhood</u> home.*

Remember, when you read a long word, look for meaningful parts. What parts do you see in *remind?* Frame *re* and *mind.*

The *i* in the second syllable of *remind* makes the sound long *i*. When *i* is followed by *nd* or *ld*, or when *o* is followed by *st* or *ld*, the vowel is usually long. What parts do you see in *childhood?* (child hood) What vowel sound do you hear in the first syllable? (long *i*)

Scaffold instruction.

Develop word meaning.

Have students think and converse. What objects do people keep to *remind* them of past times? Why?

Write *household* and *almost.*

Here are two more words. What parts do you see in *household?* (house hold) What vowel sound do you hear in the second syllable? (long *o*) What parts do you see in *almost?* (al most) What vowel sound do you hear in the second syllable? (long *o*) Guide students in blending the word parts into the whole word.

CORRECTIVE FEEDBACK

Write each practice word.

Have students practice reading these words with long *i* and long *o*. Correct any words students miss and have them reread the list.

grinder   rewind   wildlife   ghostly   hostess   resold

MORE PRACTICE

Write more practice words.

Have students practice reading these words with long *i* and long *o*.

kindness   findings   mildly   outpost   utmost   behold

Amazing Words Vocabulary

| | **To Do** | **To Say** | *5 minutes* |

Review vocabulary.

Review the homework.

Ask students to go over answers and share their writing from Practice Book p. 109. See Routine Card 1 for the multisyllabic word routine.

Deepen understanding of *international.*

Remember, *international* means "between two or more nations." An airline flight between the United States and another country is called an *international* flight. Why? Give an example of an *international* sport. What makes it *international?*

ACTIVITY 2 Comprehension

Draw Conclusions

| | **To Do** | **To Say** | *5 minutes* |

Scaffold instruction.

Introduce drawing conclusions.

Today you will read about an international sports star. Drawing conclusions about the information in the article can help you better understand what you read. A conclusion is a decision you make based upon what you read and on your own experience.

Model the skill.

For example, if I read that people immigrated to the United States in search of education, I can draw the conclusion that there were not as many educational opportunities in their old countries.

Distribute Graphic Organizer 2.

As you read "A Shooting Star from China," look for details that can help you draw conclusions. Add these details to your graphic organizers. See Routine Card 7.

ACTIVITY 3 · Read a Passage

Read for Comprehension "A Shooting Star from China," pp. 62–65

10–15 minutes

	To Do	To Say
Scaffold instruction.	Monitor student engagement. See Routine Cards 2 and 3.	**Read** Have students read pp. 62–65. Stop at the end of each page to ask questions. Students who can read on their own may do so without stopping. After reading, ask questions to promote discussion. **Who is Yao Ming?** (a basketball star from China who plays for the Houston Rockets) **What was unusual about the school that Yao Ming attended?** (He was allowed to practice basketball there for many hours a day.) **Why do you think Yao Ming's parents left China with him?** (They wanted to stay together as a family.) **What do you think the rest of the article will be about?** (Answers will vary. The title suggests it will tell more about Yao Ming and his American journey.)
Model summarizing.	Think aloud.	**Summarize** What were the first four pages mainly about? What did you learn about Yao Ming? Think aloud to model summarizing. I learned many details about Yao Ming's life, such as that his parents were both basketball players. But the main thing I learned is that even though he is a basketball star, he still has challenges to overcome as an immigrant.
Develop language and concepts.	Ask questions.	• **Why did Yao Ming want to come to the United States?** • **What would Yao Ming's life probably be like if he had stayed in China?**
MORE PRACTICE	Have students reread p. 63.	**Reread** Tell students to draw a picture showing what the young Yao Ming might have looked like riding the bus.

Reread for Fluency "A Shooting Star from China," pp. 64–65

5 minutes

	To Do	To Say
MORE PRACTICE **CORRECTIVE FEEDBACK**	Pair students. Monitor paired reading.	Students read aloud pp. 64–65, switching readers at each new paragraph. Have partners reread; now the other partner begins. For optimal fluency, students should reread three or four times. Give feedback, using the *if . . . then* statements on Routine Card 4. You may want to have students read along with the DVD-ROM.

ACTIVITY 4 · Write

Response to Literature

5 minutes

	To Do	To Say
Prompt writing.	Writing elements: conventions	Yao's arrival in the United States was different from that of many immigrants. What conclusions can you draw about how many immigrants may feel when they arrive in the United States? Use information from your reading to support your ideas. Express your ideas clearly with correct spelling and punctuation.
Homework		Practice Book, p. 110, Long *i: -ind, -ild*; Long *o: -ost, -old*

ACTIVITY **1** # Word Work

Phonics Long *i: -ind, -ild;* Long *o: -ost, -old*

	To Do	To Say
Review vowel combinations: long i: -ind, -ild; long o: -ost, -old. **Scaffold instruction.**	Review the homework. Discuss *most* on p. 69.	Ask students to share answers from Practice Book p. 110. Point out *most* on p. 69, paragraph 1. **Remember, when *i* is followed by *nd* or *ld*, or when *o* is followed by *st* or *ld*, the vowel is usually long. What vowel sound do you hear in *most*?** (long *o*) Ask students to think of other words that have syllables with long *i* spelled *ind, ild* or long *o* spelled *ost, old.*
MORE PRACTICE	Model spelling words with long *i* and long *o*.	**Spell and Write** Write *find* and *wild.* Say the words. **What vowel sound do you hear in these words? What letters stand for that vowel sound?** Underline *ind* and *ild.* Continue with *most (ost)* and *gold (old).* **What are some rhyming words that have the same vowel sound and pattern?** List responses on the board.

Amazing Words ## Vocabulary

	To Do	To Say
Build vocabulary. **Lead cumulative review.**	Deepen understanding of *barrier.*	Read aloud the first sentence on p. 66. **What language *barrier* did Yao face?** (He spoke only a little English.) **Say a sentence using *barrier.* Can you think of a synonym for *barrier*? (obstacle). What other *barriers* might immigrants face?** Use the Tested Vocabulary Cards to review words from previous weeks.

ACTIVITY **2** # Comprehension

Draw Conclusions

	To Do	To Say
Scaffold instruction.	Review drawing conclusions.	**Remember to use details from a story or article, as well as your own experience, to draw conclusions as you read. After you draw a conclusion, ask yourself whether your conclusion makes sense, and whether it can be supported with details from the selection.**
Guide practice.	Use Graphic Organizer 2.	**Listen as I read the following paragraphs on pp. 66–67. Notice that the author is describing one of the challenges Yao Ming faced when he moved to the United States. Read p. 66, paragraph 2, and p. 67, paragraph 1. Why do you think Yao felt nervous about his driving test?** (He was worried that he wouldn't do well.) **How do you know?** (The article says that Yao had to learn to drive and that his family had never owned a car before.) **Add these details to your graphic organizers.** See Routine Card 7.
MORE PRACTICE	Have students preview pp. 66–69.	**Read the captions and look at the photos on pp. 66–69. What do you think this section will be about?** (more about the challenges Yao Ming faced) **Why do you think so?** Think aloud to model using illustrations and captions to predict.
	Think aloud.	**The pictures and captions make me think the article is about how life in China was different for Yao Ming and how he has learned to adapt to America.**

Read a Passage

Read for Comprehension "A Shooting Star from China," pp. 66–69

| **To Do** | **To Say** | *10–15 minutes* |

Scaffold instruction.

Monitor student engagement.

Read Have students read pp. 66–69. Stop at the end of each page to ask questions. Students who can read on their own can do so without stopping. After reading, ask questions to promote discussion.

See Routine Cards 2 and 3.

Why did Yao need a translator at the games? (to help him communicate with players, coaches, and reporters)

What do basketball players communicate with besides words? (with moves and gestures)

Why was living in the spotlight a challenge for Yao? (He is a shy person.)

Why did Yao play for China in the 2004 Olympics? (He feels he owes much to China because that is where he grew up and learned to play basketball.)

Point out *impossible* on p. 69, paragraph 2.

Demonstrate with your finger how to circle the base word *possible* and then the prefix *im-*. Blend the word parts to read the whole word. Discuss with students the meaning of *impossible*. See Routine Card 1.

Assess comprehension.

Monitor understanding.

After Reading Have students discuss the What Do You Think? question. Prompt them to draw conclusions about why Yao worked so hard to improve his English. Listen as they talk to assess comprehension.

Summarize.

What is this mainly about? What did you learn? Work with students to summarize the selection.

MORE PRACTICE

Have students reread p. 69.

Reread As they read, tell students to note the ways that Yao maintained his ties to China. After they read, have them draw conclusions about his feelings for China, and list the details that support their conclusions.

Reread for Fluency "A Shooting Star from China," p. 69

| **To Do** | **To Say** | *5 minutes* |

CORRECTIVE FEEDBACK

Monitor oral reading.

Read p. 68 aloud. Reread the page three or four times so your reading gets better each time. Give feedback on students' oral reading, using the *if . . . then* statements on Routine Card 4. Model fluent reading if necessary. You may want to have students read along with the DVD-ROM.

 Write

Response to Literature

| **To Do** | **To Say** | *5 minutes* |

MORE PRACTICE

Prompt writing.

How did Yao Ming prove that "with time, anything is possible"? Provide specific examples from the selection that show Yao Ming's obstacles and how he overcame them.

Homework

Practice Book, p. 111, Draw Conclusions

ACTIVITY **1** Word Work

Amazing Words **Vocabulary**

	To Do	To Say	5–10 minutes

Extend word knowledge. — Write on the board or a transparency: *The Olympics is an* <u>international</u> *athletic event.* — Use the word *international* to extend word knowledge. **Remember we read this word earlier this week. We looked for meaningful parts, and we noticed the word** *national.* **Today I want you to notice the prefix** *inter-.* **We can use this prefix to read other words.**

Teach the prefix *inter-*. — **The prefix** *inter-* **means "among" or "between." Can you think of other words that begin with** *inter-?* (*interact, interchange, intercultural, interstate*) **Write words as students name them and add some of your own. Talk about the meanings of the words and practice pronouncing them.**

Scaffold instruction. — Develop word meaning. — **What can you learn from** *international* **travel?**

MORE PRACTICE — Deepen understanding of *occupations.* — Have individual students or partners use the word *occupation* in sentences. (For example: His *occupation* as a marine biologist allowed him to spend many hours in the ocean.) Ask: **How do you choose an** *occupation?* **Do the citizens of all countries have similar** *occupations* **to choose from? Why or why not?**

ACTIVITY **2** Comprehension

Skill and Strategy Practice

	To Do	To Say	5 minutes

Scaffold instruction. — Review drawing conclusions (homework). — Ask volunteers to read the passage and share answers from Practice Book p. 111. Remind students of the importance of drawing conclusions. **When you read a story, you can draw conclusions about characters and events. As you read, ask yourself why certain events take place and why characters behave as they do. Use the details in the story and what you already know to draw conclusions.**

Practice strategic prereading. — See Routine Card 2. — **Discuss Genre** Read the title and the first two journal entries on pp. 70–71. Model determining genre.

— Think aloud. — **I first thought this might be nonfiction because the illustrations are all photographs and the writing sounds like diary or journal entries by real people. But when I read both entries I realized the selection is comparing a boy in 1907 with a girl in 2007, and I changed my mind. Now I think this is fiction written to sound like real diaries or journals.**

— Review story structure. — **Ask Questions** What questions do you ask yourself to help you understand a fictional story? (What is the problem or goal? How is the problem solved or the goal reached?) **As you read this story, ask these questions and look for the answers.**

ACTIVITY 3 Read a Passage

Read for Comprehension "Becoming an American," pp. 70–77

To Do	To Say	

10–15 minutes

Scaffold instruction.

Monitor student engagement.

See Routine Card 3.

Read Have students read pp. 70–77 on their own and then discuss. For students who need more help, stop at the end of each page to discuss. After reading, ask questions.

How is the story told? (through journal entries)

Who are the authors of the journal entries? (Albert and Elena)

During what year is Albert's journal written? (1907) **During what year is Elena's journal written?** (2007)

What similar problems do Albert and Elena face? (Both are new to America; they have language barriers to overcome; they have to get used to American ways.)

What conclusions can you draw about the kind of people Albert and Elena are? (Both like being in America; both are curious and enthusiastic, but a bit nervous; both try to adapt to their new homes.)

Assess comprehension.

Monitor understanding.

After Reading Have students discuss the What Do You Think? question. Prompt them to draw conclusions about what Albert and Elena like best about living in the United States. Listen as they talk to assess comprehension.

MORE PRACTICE

Reread Have students reread p. 72 and list reasons why Albert might feel awkward trying to speak with the American kids in his class.

Reread for Fluency "Becoming an American," pp. 74–75

To Do	To Say	

5–10 minutes

CORRECTIVE FEEDBACK

Pair students. Monitor paired reading.

Students read aloud pp. 74–75, switching readers at the end of each paragraph. Have partners reread; now the other partner begins. For optimal fluency, students should reread three or four times. Give feedback, using Routine Card 4. You may want to have students read along with the DVD-ROM.

MORE PRACTICE

READERS' THEATER

Work with a group of students to adapt pp. 70–77 as a radio play. Have students rehearse reading the parts, with two girls alternating as Elena and two boys alternating as Albert. (They can switch after each sentence or after each entry.) Then have them perform for the class.

ACTIVITY 4 Write

Response to Literature

To Do	To Say	

5 minutes

Prompt personal narrative.

Review pp. 70–77.

Writing elements: support

Albert and Elena's feelings about moving to a new place change over time. How would you feel if you moved to a new place? Include details that support your thoughts and describe your experiences.

ACTIVITY 1 Read a Passage

Read Together "Traditional Clothing," pp. 78–81

10 minutes

	To Do	**To Say**
Scaffold instruction.	Review drawing conclusions.	Have students preview pp. 78–81. **This article tells about traditional outfits from four different cultures. As you read, use details from the article as well as what you know to draw conclusions about traditional clothing and what it reveals about different cultures.**
	See Routine Card 3.	**Read** Read the article as students follow along. Then read it a second time, having students join in on the text. After reading, ask questions.
		What is a Japanese kimono made of? (silk)
		Why does it take so long to get dressed in a kimono? (because it has several different pieces that need to be worn correctly)
		Why are dashikis good clothing to wear in hot weather? (They are loose fitting and comfortable.)
		What is the oldest traditional dress in the world? (the Indian sari)
		What items of clothing are worn with the Greek *foustanela?* (a white shirt, woolen vest, sash, and shoes with large pompoms)
Assess comprehension.	Monitor listening comprehension.	**Summarize** Have one student describe each of the traditional outfits from the selection and why it is significant.

ACTIVITY 2 Build Concepts

Amazing Words Vocabulary

5–10 minutes

	To Do	**To Say**
Review concept and vocabulary.	Display the concept web you began on Day 1.	**This week's question is *How can moving change our view of the world?* How do this week's words relate to the question?** (Have students answer the question, using some of the vocabulary they learned this week.)
		Ask students to add more words to the concept web. Have students explain how each word relates to American journeys. Monitor students' understanding of vocabulary as they discuss the web. See Routine Card 5.
MORE PRACTICE	Write *awkward* and *barrier* on the board.	Have students relate *awkward* and *barrier.* **Give an example of a *barrier* that can make someone from another country feel *awkward.* How can *barriers* be overcome?**

ACTIVITY 3 Write

Response to Literature "4 You 2 Do," p. 82

| To Do | To Say | 5–10 minutes |

Guide response activities.

Discuss the directions on p. 82. Tell students to choose one activity to complete.

See Routine Card 8.

Word Play Have students unscramble the words on their own and then meet with partners to share their answers.

Making Connections Discuss the question in a group. (Possible answers: Yao Ming came to the United States as a celebrity. Everyone knew who he was. Elena and Albert didn't know anyone and didn't have a lot of money. They all had to learn a new language.)

On Paper Have students brainstorm some answers to the prompt before they write. Have them write on their own. Students can use Practice Book p. 112 to structure their written responses, or you can send the Practice Book page home for them to complete later.

MORE PRACTICE

If you have more time, direct students to complete all the activities.

 ACTIVITY 4 Assessment Options

Passage Reading

| To Do | To Say | 10–15 minutes |

Check fluency.

See Routine Card 6.

Take a two-minute timed sample of each student's oral reading.

While some students are doing Activity 3, determine which students you want to assess this week and choose from these options.

Fluency Have a student read for two minutes from "A Shooting Star from China." Record the number of correct words read per minute. See p. 184 for monitoring fluency. Be sure each student is assessed at least every other week.

Have students graph their progress on the Fluency Progress Chart, p. 185.

Check comprehension.

Retelling Have students reread "A Shooting Star from China" and retell it. Prompt students if necessary. See p. 186 for monitoring retelling.

If you have time, assess every student.

Homework

Practice Book, p. 112, Writing

Unit 6 Week 4 *Grand Gestures*

 When do people choose to make sacrifices?

Objectives *This week students will...*

Vocabulary
- build concepts and vocabulary: *apply, determined, distinguishes, efficient, headway, progress*

Phonics
- read words with syllables V/V
- apply knowledge of word structure to decode multisyllabic words when reading

Text Comprehension
- identify main idea to improve comprehension
- write in response to literature
- make connections across text

Fluency
- practice fluency with oral rereading

Word Work *This week's phonics focus is . . .*

V/V Syllables

Amazing Words Concept/Amazing Words *Tested Vocabulary*

The week's vocabulary is related to the concept of grand gestures.
The first appearance of each word in the Student Reader is noted below.

apply	to set to work and stick to it (p. 90)
determined	with your mind made up (p. 87)
distinguishes	makes something clearly different from other similar things (p. 86)
efficient	able to do something without waste of time, energy, or materials (p. 91)
headway	progress (p. 87)
progress	to move forward; to go ahead (p. 87)

Student Reader Unit 6 *This week students will read the following selections.*

86	**Grand Gestures**	Expository Nonfiction
88	**Library Hero**	Narrative Nonfiction
96	**A Simple Gift**	Expository Nonfiction
104	**A Birthday Give-Away**	Expository Nonfiction
108	**4 You 2 Do**	Activity Page

Daily Lesson Plan

	ACTIVITIES	MATERIALS
Day 1	**Build Concepts** Weekly Concept: Grand Gestures Vocabulary: *apply, determined, distinguishes, efficient, headway, progress* **Read a Passage** "Grand Gestures," pp. 86–87 Comprehension: Use Strategies Reread for Fluency **Write** Response to Literature	Student Reader: Unit 6 Routine Cards 2, 4, 5 Tested Vocabulary Cards Student journals Practice Book, p. 113, Vocabulary Student Reader DVD-ROM
Day 2	**Word Work** Phonics: Syllables V/V Vocabulary: Deepen word meaning **Comprehension** Main Idea **Read a Passage** "Library Hero," pp. 88–91 Reread for Fluency **Write** Response to Literature	Student Reader: Unit 6 Practice Book, p. 113, Vocabulary Graphic Organizer 1 Routine Cards 1, 2, 3, 4, 7 Practice Book, p. 114, Syllables V/V Student Reader DVD-ROM
Day 3	**Word Work** Phonics: Syllables V/V Vocabulary: Deepen word meaning **Comprehension** Main Idea **Read a Passage** "Library Hero," pp. 92–95 Reread for Fluency **Write** Response to Literature	Practice Book, p. 114, Syllables V/V Tested Vocabulary Cards Student Reader: Unit 6 Graphic Organizer 1 Routine Cards 1, 2, 3, 4, 7 Practice Book, p. 115, Main Idea and Supporting Details Student Reader DVD-ROM
Day 4	**Word Work** Vocabulary: Extend word knowledge **Comprehension** Skill and Strategy Practice **Read a Passage** "A Simple Gift," pp. 96–103 Reread for Fluency **Write** Response to Literature	Practice Book, p. 115, Main Idea and Supporting Details Student Reader: Unit 6 Routine Cards 2, 3, 4 Student Reader DVD-ROM
Day 5	**Read a Passage** "A Birthday Give-Away," pp. 104–107 Comprehension: Main Idea; Listening **Build Concepts** Vocabulary **Write** Response to Literature: "4 You 2 Do," p. 108 **Assessment Options** Fluency Comprehension	Student Reader: Unit 6 Routine Cards 3, 5, 6, 8 Fluency Progress Chart, p. 185 Practice Book, p. 116, Writing

See pp. xvi–xvii for how *My Sidewalks* integrates instructional practices for ELL.

Amazing Words** Vocabulary

| To Do | To Say | *10–15 minutes* |

Develop oral vocabulary.

See Routine Card 6 and p. 211.

Introduce the Concept/Amazing Words with an oral routine prior to displaying them in print. Page 211 in this Teacher's Guide provides specific guidelines for introducing each word.

Develop word meaning.

See Routine Card 5. Discuss pp. 85–87.

Have students read p. 85 and then look at the pictures on pp. 86–87. **What do you notice?** (kids at a museum, girl holding a jar of money) **Can you use the word** *gesture* **or the phrase** *grand gesture* **to describe what you see?** (Examples: Giving a gift is a nice *gesture.* This girl might be making a *grand gesture* by giving her savings to a group that helps others or to another worthwhile cause.)

Scaffold instruction.

Create a concept web.

In the center of a web, write *Grand Gestures.* **This week's concept is** *Grand Gestures.* **Grand means "great."** *Gestures* **are actions to express feelings. People make** *grand gestures* **when they give up something to help others.** Provide an example to demonstrate meaning. **Volunteering to help at the nursing home is a** *grand gesture.*

Add the other vocabulary words.

Concept and Language Goals

Discuss the meaning of each word as it relates to *grand gestures,* using the glossary as needed. (See p. 158 in this Teacher's Guide for definitions.)

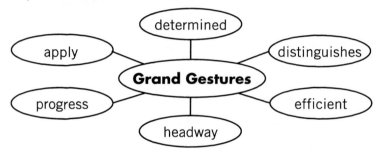

Model the multisyllabic word strategy.

Display each word. Say it as you display it.

Think aloud.

Use the Tested Vocabulary Cards. Follow this routine for each word:

- **Look for Meaningful Parts** Do you recognize any parts of this word? What do the parts mean? Be sure students notice the following: *head, way.*

- **Model** I recognize the word *head* at the beginning of *headway.* I know that if you're at the *head* of the line, you're at the front or beginning. I also see the word *way* in *headway.* I know that if I am making my *way* across the park, it means that I am making progress. So I think *headway* must have something to do with getting ahead or making progress. Discuss other words that contain *head: heading, headlight, headline, headfirst, head-on,* and so on.

Point to *efficient.*

- **Chunk Words with No Recognizable Parts** Model how to chunk the word *efficient* to read it. I see a chunk at the beginning of the word: *ef.* I see a part in the middle: *fi.* I see a chunk at the end: *cient.* I say each chunk slowly: *ef fi cient.* I say the chunks fast to make a whole word: *efficient.* Is it a real word? Yes, I know the word *efficient.*

- Have students practice reading each word.

Preview.

Read p. 84 with students.

Do any of the words we just learned seem to fit on this page? Together with students, read the sentences on p. 84 describing each selection. Talk about how the vocabulary words might be used in the selections.

MORE PRACTICE

Deepen understanding of *grand gestures.*

Have students demonstrate understanding by answering questions. **Which of the following two** *gestures* **is an example of a** *grand gesture:* **taking out the trash after dinner, or spending part of a Saturday picking up trash in the park? Why?**

ACTIVITY 2 # Read a Passage

Develop Concepts "Grand Gestures," pp. 86–87

	To Do	**To Say**	*10–15 minutes*
Practice strategic prereading.	See Routine Card 2. Think aloud.	**Discuss Genre** Read the title and look at the pictures on pp. 86–87. Model determining genre. The photographs are a clue that this is nonfiction. They seem to show real kids and a real museum. I think this article will tell why the girl has a jar of money and how it relates to the kids at the museum.	
Scaffold instruction.	Review text structure.	**Ask Questions** What questions do you ask yourself to help you understand nonfiction? (What did I learn? What is this mainly about?) As you read this article, ask these questions and look for the answers.	
Guide comprehension. **Develop language and concepts.**	Read pp. 86–87 aloud.	**Read** Read the article as students follow along. Then read it a second time, having students join in. If necessary, stop at the end of each paragraph to check comprehension. Ask questions to promote discussion and develop the concept. • What is a grand gesture? • What distinguishes a grand gesture from a nice gesture? • How might giving up some of your savings be a grand gesture? • What words on the concept web could help you describe grand gestures?	

MORE PRACTICE Have students reread "Grand Gestures." As they read, tell them to think about the difference between a nice gesture and a grand gesture. They can share their ideas with family members tonight.

Reread for Fluency "Grand Gestures," p. 87

	To Do	**To Say**	*5 minutes*
CORRECTIVE FEEDBACK	Monitor oral reading.	Read p. 87 aloud. Reread the page three or four times so your reading gets better each time. Give feedback on students' oral reading, using the *if . . . then* statements on Routine Card 4. Model fluent reading if necessary. You may want to have students read along with the DVD-ROM.	

ACTIVITY 3 # Write

Response to Literature

	To Do	**To Say**	*5 minutes*
Prompt journal writing.	Write on the board or a transparency: *When do people choose to make sacrifices?*	Take out your journals. This week we are reading about grand gestures. Our question for the week is: *When do people choose to make sacrifices?* Write an answer to this question based on what you read today. Also write about sacrifices you've made. Have students write about the topic, using what they read and their own experiences.	
Homework		Practice Book, p. 113, Vocabulary	

ACTIVITY **1** Word Work

Phonics Syllables V/V

	To Do	**To Say**	*5–10 minutes*

Teach syllables V/V.

Write on the board or a transparency: *We watched the* <u>meteor</u> *shower.*

Read the sentence aloud. The word *meteor* **has two vowels in the middle. If a word has two vowels together that stand for two different sounds, divide between the two vowels. Draw a line between** *e* **and** *o.* **Read the syllables one at a time:** *me te or.* **Blend them to make a word:** *meteor.*

Write *fuel.*

Here is another word with two vowels in the middle. How would you divide the word *fuel*? (between *u* and *e*)

Scaffold instruction.

CORRECTIVE FEEDBACK

Develop word meaning.

Have students think and converse. Is *fuel* **necessary for all types of flight? What do birds use as** *fuel*?

Write each practice word.

Have students practice reading these words with syllables V/V. Correct any words students miss and have them reread the list.

   radio   piano   realize   ruined   poetry   react

MORE PRACTICE

Write more practice words.

Have students practice reading these words with syllables V/V.

   sundial   rodeo   diary   violets   triumph   iodine

Vocabulary

	To Do	**To Say**	*5 minutes*

Review vocabulary.

Review the homework.

Ask students to go over answers and share their writing from Practice Book p. 113. See Routine Card 1 for the multisyllabic word routine.

Deepen understanding of *determined.*

Remember, *determined* **means "with your mind made up." If you are** *determined* **to raise money by selling candy, does it mean that you will most likely succeed or fail? Why? How can being** *determined* **to succeed actually help you succeed?**

ACTIVITY **2** Comprehension

Main Idea

	To Do	**To Say**	*5 minutes*

Scaffold instruction.

Introduce main idea.

Today you will read about a real boy named Jonathan. When you read nonfiction, identifying the main idea can help you better understand what you read. To find the main idea, ask yourself: Who or what is this article about? What is the most important idea about the topic? What are some details that support the main idea?

Model the skill.

For example, if I know that the topic of an article is a boy named Jonathan Marrero, in order to find the main idea, I need to identify the most important idea about Jonathan.

Distribute Graphic Organizer 1.

As you read "Library Hero," look for the most important ideas about the topic, as well as details that support it. Add these details to your graphic organizers. See Routine Card 7.

ACTIVITY **3** # Read a Passage

Read for Comprehension "Library Hero," pp. 88–91

To Do	To Say	*10–15 minutes*

Scaffold instruction.

Monitor student engagement.

Read Have students read pp. 88–91. Stop at the end of each page to ask questions. Students who can read on their own can do so without stopping. After reading, ask questions to promote discussion.

See Routine Cards 2 and 3.

What problem did the Salem, Massachusetts, school system face? (It was running out of money.)

What was the first thing Jonathan did after learning about the school system's problems? (He wrote a note and took it, along with his money, to his school's librarian.)

What were some ways Jonathan earned money for the schools in Salem? (He had other kids help him ask for donations; he sold hot chocolate and lollipops; he shoveled driveways and sidewalks.)

What do you think the rest of the article will be about? (Answers will vary. The title suggests that it will tell how Jonathan became a "hero" to the library.)

Model summarizing.

Think aloud.

Summarize **What were the first four pages mainly about? What did you learn about Jonathan?** Think aloud to model summarizing. **I learned a lot of details about Jonathan and the ways he helped his school system when he learned it was running out of money. But the main thing I learned about Jonathan is that he was very determined to make a difference.**

Develop language and concepts.

Ask questions.

- **What three words would you use to describe Jonathan?** (Example: generous, caring, determined)
- **What are some grand gestures Jonathan made?** (Example: He tried to give away his own money to the library; he worked with other kids and by himself to raise money for the school system.)

MORE PRACTICE

Have students reread p. 88.

Reread Tell students to draw a picture showing how Jonathan felt when he learned that his school system was running out of money.

Reread for Fluency "Library Hero," pp. 88–89

To Do	To Say	*5 minutes*

MORE PRACTICE

CORRECTIVE FEEDBACK

Pair students. Monitor paired reading.

Students read aloud pp. 88–89, switching readers at each new paragraph. Have partners reread; now the other partner begins. For optimal fluency, students should reread three or four times. Give feedback, using the *if . . . then* statements on Routine Card 4. You may want to have students read along with the DVD-ROM.

ACTIVITY **4** # Write

Response to Literature

To Do	To Say	*5 minutes*

Prompt writing.

Writing elements: support

What is the main idea of the first four pages of "Library Hero"? Use details from the article to support your answer.

Homework   Practice Book, p. 114, Syllables V/V   **DAY 2** Grand Gestures   163

ACTIVITY **1** Word Work

Phonics Syllables V/V

To Do	To Say	*5 minutes*

Review syllables V/V.

Scaffold instruction.

Review the homework. Discuss *librarian* on p. 93 in the Student Reader.

Ask students to share answers from Practice Book p. 114.

Point out *librarian* on p. 93, paragraph 2. **Remember, if a word has two vowels together that make two different sounds, divide between the two vowels. How would you divide *librarian*?** *(li brar i an)* Guide students in blending the word parts into the word.

Then point to *radio* on p. 88, paragraph 1. **Where would you divide *radio*?** *(ra di o)*

MORE PRACTICE

Model spelling words with syllables V/V

Spell and Write Write *real* and *quiet.* Underline *ea* in *real* and say the word. **What vowel sounds do you hear in this word?** Point out that the word is divided into syllables between the vowels, so each vowel letter stands for a vowel sound. Continue with *quiet* and *ie.*

Amazing Words Vocabulary

To Do	To Say	*5 minutes*

Build vocabulary.

Deepen understanding of *apply.*

Read aloud the last paragraph on p. 90. **When the author says Jonathan Marrero needed to *apply* himself even harder, what does he mean?** (to make himself work harder to achieve his goal) **What does Jonathan do to *apply* himself?** (He sells hot chocolate and lollipops; he shovels snow after a snowstorm.)

Lead cumulative review.

Use the Tested Vocabulary Cards to review words from previous weeks.

ACTIVITY **2** Comprehension

Main Idea

To Do	To Say	*5–10 minutes*

Scaffold instruction.

Review main idea.

To identify the main idea, ask yourself what the most important idea about the topic is. Sometimes the author states the main idea. Sometimes you have to figure out the main idea and state it in your own words.

Guide practice.

Use Graphic Organizer 1.

Listen as I read p. 92, paragraph 2. I want you to think about the main idea of this paragraph. Read the paragraph. **What is the most important idea in this paragraph?** (By giving up his time and savings, Jonathan made a big difference.) **What is one detail that supports this idea?** (He saved 47 of the 80 jobs that were due to be cut.) See Routine Card 7.

MORE PRACTICE

Have students preview pp. 92–95.

Look at the illustrations on pp. 92–95. What do you think this section will be about? (more about Jonathan and how he helped the school system) **Why do you think so?** Think aloud to model using illustrations to predict.

Think aloud.

The pictures make me think that the article will tell more about Jonathan and the different things he did to help his school system.

ACTIVITY 3 · Read a Passage

Read for Comprehension "Library Hero," pp. 92–95

10–15 minutes

	To Do	To Say
Scaffold instruction.	Monitor student engagement. See Routine Cards 2 and 3.	**Read** Have students read pp. 92–95 on their own. Stop at the end of each page to ask questions. Students who can read on their own can do so without stopping. After reading, ask questions to promote discussion. **How did Jonathan inspire other people?** (Other people saw what he was doing and decided to help too.) **What did the governor of Massachusetts do when he heard about Jonathan?** (He praised him for "stepping up" and helping the schools; he gave him a pin.) **How did Jonathan help students in his class take a trip to Boston?** (He held a yard sale to raise money. He gave the money to the class to help the kids who weren't able to raise enough money for the trip.)
Assess comprehension.	Monitor understanding. Summarize.	**After Reading** Have students discuss the What Do You Think? question. Prompt them to find details in the article to support their responses. Listen as they talk to assess comprehension. **What is this mainly about? What did you learn?** Work with students to summarize the selection.
MORE PRACTICE	Have students reread p. 95.	**Reread** As students read, ask them to explain why Jonathan gave up his time and savings to help others.

Reread for Fluency "Library Hero," p. 94

5 minutes

	To Do	To Say
CORRECTIVE FEEDBACK	Monitor oral reading.	Read p. 94 aloud. Reread the page three or four times so your reading gets better each time. Give feedback on students' oral reading, using the *if . . . then* statements on Routine Card 4. Model fluent reading if necessary. You may want to have students read along with the DVD-ROM.

ACTIVITY 4 · Write

Response to Literature

5 minutes

	To Do	To Say
MORE PRACTICE	Prompt writing.	After he helped save the library, a national group chose Jonathan as its "Amazing Kid" of the month. What makes Jonathan an "amazing kid"? Include specific details and vivid language that support your ideas.
Homework		Practice Book, p. 115, Main Idea and Supporting Details

ACTIVITY 1 | Word Work

 **Vocabulary**

	To Do	**To Say**	5–10 minutes
Extend word knowledge.	Write on the board or a transparency: *We made quick progress on our journey.*	Use the word *progress* to extend word knowledge. **Remember, we read this word earlier this week. We also talked about finding meaningful parts in a word. Today I want you to notice the Latin word part *pro-*. We can use this word part to read other words.**	
Teach Latin word part *pro-*.		**The Latin word part *pro-* means "forward." So *progress* means "to move forward." Can you think of other words with the word part *pro-*?** (Possible answers: *proceed, procession, promote, propel*) **Write words as students name them and add some of your own. Talk about the meanings of the words.**	
Scaffold instruction.	Develop word meaning.	**Imagine taking a trip to Antarctica. What kinds of things could stop you from making *progress* on your journey? What might you do to improve your *progress*?**	
MORE PRACTICE	Deepen understanding of *progress* and *headway*.	**Have individual students or partners use the words *progress* and *headway* in sentences. (For example: All *progress* halted when the dogs found it impossible to make *headway* against the strong winds.) Share sentences. *Progress* and *headway* are synonyms. They mean almost the same thing. What is another synonym of *progress* and *headway*?** (Possible answers: *improvement, growth*)	

ACTIVITY 2 | Comprehension

Skill and Strategy Practice

	To Do	**To Say**	5 minutes
Scaffold instruction.	Review main idea (homework).	Ask volunteers to read the passage and share answers from Practice Book p. 115. **Remind students of the importance of finding the main idea. Sometimes an author will state the main idea directly. Other times, the author will leave it up to the reader to find the main idea. When you look for the main idea, ask yourself "What is the most important idea about the topic?" After you identify the main idea, look for details that support it.**	
Practice strategic prereading.	See Routine Card 2.	**Discuss Genre** Read the title and paragraph on p. 96 in the Student Book. Look at the pictures on pp. 96–103. Model determining genre.	
	Think aloud.	**The photographs are a clue that this is nonfiction. They look like photos of real people and places. The paragraph makes me think this article will tell about a grand gesture having to do with cows and children.**	
	Review text structure.	**Ask Questions** What questions do you ask yourself to help you understand nonfiction? (What did I learn? What is this mainly about?) As you read this article, ask these questions and look for answers.	

ACTIVITY 3   Read a Passage

Read for Comprehension "A Simple Gift," pp. 96–103

10–15 minutes

	To Do	To Say
Scaffold instruction.	Monitor student engagement. See Routine Card 3.	**Read** Have students read pp. 96–103 on their own and then discuss. For students who need more help, stop at the end of each page to discuss. After reading, ask questions. **Why did Dan West want to send cows across the ocean?** (He knew the cows could provide hungry families with milk.) **What does the group Heifer International do?** (They provide cows, goats, chickens, sheep, and other animals to people around the world.) **How did a cow change an entire village?** (A Ugandan woman received a cow from Heifer. The cow helped feed people in her village. She hired a teacher with the money she made selling milk. As a result, the children of the village could go to school.)
Review the phonics skill.	Point out *nutrient* on p. 101.	Remind students that if a word has two vowels together that make two different sounds, divide between the two vowels. Demonstrate framing the word parts *nu tri ent.* Have students blend the parts to read the word.
Assess comprehension.	Monitor understanding.	**After Reading** Have students discuss the What Do You Think? question. Prompt them to explain how Heifer International helps people make grand gestures. Listen as they talk to assess comprehension.
MORE PRACTICE		**Reread** Have students reread pp. 100–101 and then explain to partners how the gift of different kinds of animals can help in different ways.

Reread for Fluency "A Simple Gift," pp. 100–102

5–10 minutes

	To Do	To Say
CORRECTIVE FEEDBACK	Pair students. Monitor paired reading.	Students read aloud pp. 100–102, switching readers at the end of each paragraph. Have partners reread; now the other partner begins. For optimal fluency, students should reread three or four times. Give feedback, using Routine Card 4. Model fluent reading if necessary. You may want to have students read along with the DVD-ROM.
MORE PRACTICE	**READERS' THEATER**	Work with a group of students to adapt pp. 100–103 as an international radio program. Will they switch announcers after each sentence or each paragraph? Do they need to add anything at the beginning to let their radio audience know what this program is about?

ACTIVITY 4   Write

Response to Literature

5 minutes

	To Do	To Say
Prompt expository writing.	Writing elements: support, conventions	**The group Heifers for Relief changed over the years. In what ways did it change? Support your ideas with information from the text. Use complete sentences to express your ideas.**

ACTIVITY 1 · Read a Passage

Read Together "A Birthday Give-Away," pp. 104–107

	To Do	**To Say**	*10 minutes*
Scaffold instruction.	Review main idea.	Have students preview pp. 104–107. **This article tells about a kind of birthday party that is called a "give-away party." As you read, ask yourself what the most important idea about give-away parties is, and look for details that support this idea.**	
	See Routine Card 3.	**Read** Read the article as students follow along. Then read it a second time, having students join in on the script. After reading, ask questions.	
		What is a give-away party? (a party in which guests bring gifts they want to donate to a group that helps others)	
		What kinds of gifts do people bring to a give-away party? (money or items for a group that helps others, such as pet supplies for an animal shelter)	
		Why do people have give-away parties? (They want to help people or animals in need.)	
		How is hosting a give-away party an example of making a grand gesture? (At a give-away party, the host gives something up—birthday presents, for example—to help others.)	
Assess comprehension.	Monitor listening comprehension.	**Summarize** Have students describe the purpose of a give-away party and explain how this type of party helps others.	

ACTIVITY 2 · Build Concepts

Amazing Words Vocabulary

	To Do	**To Say**	*5–10 minutes*
Review concept and vocabulary.	**Concept and Language Goals**	**This week's question is *When do people choose to make sacrifices?* How do this week's words relate to the question?** (Have students answer the question using some of the vocabulary they learned this week.)	
	Display the concept web you began on Day 1.	Ask students to add more words to the concept web. Have students explain how each word relates to the concept of grand gestures. Monitor students' understanding of vocabulary as they discuss the web. See Routine Card 5.	
MORE PRACTICE	Write *efficient* and *apply* on the board.	Have students relate *efficient* and *apply*. **How is hosting your own give-away party an *efficient* way to *apply* what you've learned about making grand gestures? What makes hosting a give-away party an *efficient* way to help others?**	

ACTIVITY 3 | Write

Response to Literature "4 You 2 Do," p. 108

		10–15 minutes
	To Do	**To Say**

Guide response activities.

To Do: Discuss the directions on p. 108. Tell students to choose one activity to complete. See Routine Card 8.

To Say:

Word Play Have students make a word chain on their own and then meet with partners to share their work.

Making Connections Discuss the question in a group. (Answers will vary, but suggestions should reflect an understanding of Jonathan's work and the work of Heifer International.)

On Paper Have students brainstorm answers to the prompt before they write. Then have them write on their own. Students can use Practice Book p. 116 to structure their written responses, or you can send the Practice Book page home for them to complete later.

MORE PRACTICE

If you have more time, direct students to complete all the activities.

ACTIVITY 4 | Assessment Options

Passage Reading

10–15 minutes

To Do | **To Say**

Check fluency.

To Do: See Routine Card 6.

Take a two-minute timed sample of each student's oral reading.

To Say:

While some students are doing Activity 3, determine which students you want to assess this week and choose from these options.

Fluency Have a student read for two minutes from "Library Hero." Record the number of correct words read per minute. See p. 184 for monitoring fluency. Be sure each student is assessed at least every other week.

Have students graph their progress on the Fluency Progress Chart, p. 185.

Check comprehension.

Retelling Have students reread "Library Hero" and retell it. Prompt students if necessary. See p. 186 for monitoring retelling.

If you have time, assess every student.

Homework   Practice Book, p. 116, Writing

Unit 6 Week 5 *Space*

 How do we reach for the stars?

Objectives *This week students will...*

Vocabulary
- build concepts and vocabulary: *complex, futuristic, galaxy, scientific, telescope, universe*

Phonics
- read related words
- apply knowledge of word structure to decode multisyllabic words when reading

Text Comprehension
- compare and contrast to improve comprehension
- write in response to literature
- make connections across text

Fluency
- practice fluency with oral rereading

Word Work *This week's phonics focus is . . .*

Related Words

Amazing Words Concept/Amazing Words *Tested Vocabulary*

The week's vocabulary is related to the concept of space.
The first appearance of each word in the Student Reader is noted below.

complex	hard to understand; made up of a number of parts that work together (p. 119)
futuristic	of or like something in the future (p. 119)
galaxy	a group of billions of stars forming one system (p. 124)
scientific	using the facts and laws of science (p. 125)
telescope	a device you look through that makes things far away seem nearer and larger (p. 112)
universe	everything there is, including all space and matter (p. 115)

Student Reader Unit 6 *This week students will read the following selections.*

Daily Lesson Plan

	ACTIVITIES	MATERIALS
Day 1	**Build Concepts** Weekly Concept: Space Vocabulary: *complex, futuristic, galaxy, scientific, telescope, universe* **Read a Passage** "What's Out There?" pp. 112–115 Comprehension: Use Strategies Reread for Fluency **Write** Response to Literature	Student Reader: Unit 6 Routine Cards 2, 4, 5 Tested Vocabulary Cards Student journals Practice Book, p. 117, Vocabulary Student Reader DVD-ROM
Day 2	**Word Work** Phonics: Related Words Vocabulary: Deepen word meaning **Comprehension** Compare and Contrast **Read a Passage** "Spaceships from Hollywood," pp. 116–119 Reread for Fluency **Write** Response to Literature	Student Reader: Unit 6 Practice Book, p. 117, Vocabulary Graphic Organizer 3 Routine Cards 1, 2, 3, 4, 7 Practice Book, p. 118, Related Words Student Reader DVD-ROM
Day 3	**Word Work** Phonics: Related Words Vocabulary: Deepen word meaning **Comprehension** Compare and Contrast **Read a Passage** "Spaceships from Hollywood," pp. 120–123 Reread for Fluency **Write** Response to Literature	Practice Book, p. 118, Related Words Tested Vocabulary Cards Student Reader: Unit 6 Graphic Organizer 3 Routine Cards 2, 3, 4, 7 Practice Book, p. 119, Compare and Contrast Student Reader DVD-ROM
Day 4	**Word Work** Vocabulary: Extend word knowledge **Comprehension** Skill and Strategy Practice **Read a Passage** "Searching the Universe," pp. 124–131 Reread for Fluency **Write** Response to Literature	Practice Book, p. 119, Compare and Contrast Student Reader: Unit 6 Routine Cards 2, 3, 4 Student Reader DVD-ROM
Day 5	**Read a Passage** "The Sounds of Space," pp. 132–133 Comprehension: Compare and Contrast; Listening **Build Concepts** Vocabulary **Write** Response to Literature: "4 You 2 Do," p. 134 **Assessment Options** Fluency, Comprehension End-of-Unit Test	Student Reader: Unit 6 Routine Cards 3, 5, 8 Practice Book, p. 120, Writing Assessment Book, p. 84

See pp. xvi–xvii for how *My Sidewalks* integrates instructional practices for ELL.

Build Concepts

Amazing Words Vocabulary

	To Do	**To Say**
Develop oral vocabulary.	See Routine Card 6 and p. 212.	Introduce the Concept/Amazing Words with an oral routine prior to displaying them in print. Page 212 in this Teacher's Guide provides specific guidelines for introducing each word.
Develop word meaning.	See Routine Card 5. Discuss pp. 111–115.	Have students read p. 111 and then look at the pictures on pp. 112–115. **What do you notice?** (galaxies, stars, moons, telescopes, the planet Jupiter, astronauts repairing a telescope in space) **Can you use the words** *space* **and** *telescope* **to describe any of these pictures?** (Example: Powerful *telescopes* allow us to see and learn a great deal about outer *space*.)
Scaffold instruction.	Create a concept web. Add the other vocabulary words. **Concept and Language Goals**	In the center of a web, write *Space*. **This week's concept is** *space*. *Space* **is the unlimited room or emptiness that exists in all directions.** Provide an example to demonstrate meaning. **The rocket traveled through** *space* **and landed on the moon.** Discuss the meaning of each word as it relates to space, using the glossary as needed. (See p. 170 in this Teacher's Guide for definitions.)

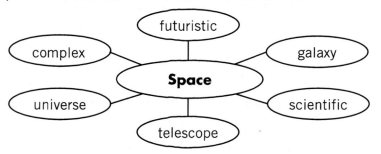

Model the multisyllabic word strategy.	Display each word. Say it as you display it.	Use the Tested Vocabulary Cards. Follow this routine for each word: • **Look for Meaningful Parts** **Do you recognize any parts of this word? What do these parts mean? Use the parts to read the word.** As you introduce each word, be sure students notice the following: *futur(e)*, *scien(ce)*, *tele-* ("over a long distance"), *scope*.
	Point to *galaxy*.	• **Chunk Words with No Recognizable Parts** Model how to chunk the word *galaxy* to read it.
	Think aloud.	• **Model** I see a chunk at the beginning of the word: *gal*. I see a part in the middle: *ax*. I see a part at the end of the word: *y*. I say each chunk slowly: *gal ax y*. I say the chunks quickly to make a whole word: *galaxy*. Is it a real word? Yes, I know the word *galaxy*. • Have students practice reading each word.
Preview.	Read p. 110 with students.	**Do you see any of the words we just learned on this page?** Together with students, read the sentences on p. 110 describing each selection. Talk about how the vocabulary words might be used in the selections.
MORE PRACTICE	Deepen understanding of *space* and *telescope*.	Have students demonstrate understanding by answering questions. **Give an example of something you might see in** *space* **using a** *telescope*. **What have we been able to learn about** *space* **by using** *telescopes*? **What can** *space* **exploration teach us about Earth?**

ACTIVITY **2** # Read a Passage

Develop Concepts "What's Out There?" pp. 112–115

10–15 minutes

	To Do	To Say

Practice strategic prereading.

See Routine Card 2.

Think aloud.

Discuss Genre Read the title on p. 112 and have students look at the illustrations on pp. 112–115. Model determining genre.

The photographs are a clue that this is nonfiction. They look like real pictures of things in outer space. I think this article will tell how telescopes work and what we have learned about the universe by using them.

Scaffold instruction.

Review text structure.

Ask Questions **What questions do you ask yourself to help you understand nonfiction? (What did I learn? What is this mainly about?) As you read this article, ask these questions and look for the answers.**

Guide comprehension.

Read pp. 112–115 aloud.

Read Read the article as students follow along. Then read it a second time, having students join in. If necessary, stop at the end of each paragraph to check comprehension. Ask questions to promote discussion and develop the concept.

Develop language and concepts.

- When was the first telescope invented?
- How did Galileo improve the telescope?
- How did Bernhard Schmidt's invention change how scientists get information about space?
- What words on the concept web could help you describe telescopes?

MORE PRACTICE

Have students reread "What's Out There?" As they read, tell them to make a list of developments in telescope capability over time to share with family members tonight.

Reread for Fluency "What's Out There?" p. 113

5 minutes

	To Do	To Say

CORRECTIVE FEEDBACK

Monitor oral reading.

Read p. 113 aloud. Reread the page three or four times so your reading gets better each time. Give feedback on students' oral reading, using the *if . . . then* statements on Routine Card 4. Model fluent reading if necessary. You may want to have students read along with the DVD-ROM.

ACTIVITY **3** # Write

Response to Literature

5 minutes

	To Do	To Say

Prompt journal writing.

Write on the board or a transparency: *How do we reach for the stars?*

Take out your journals. This week we are reading about space. The question for this week is: *How do we reach for the stars?* Would you like to explore space? Why or why not? Write an answer to these questions based on what you read today, as well as on your own knowledge. Have students write about the topic, using what they read and their own experiences.

Homework   Practice Book, p. 117, Vocabulary

ACTIVITY 1 Word Work

Phonics Related Words

	To Do	**To Say**	*5–10 minutes*

Teach related words.

Write on the board or a transparency: *Telescopes allow us to explore the universe.*

Write *relative*.

One way to understand a long word is to look for meaningful parts. Another way is to look for related words. Related words are words that belong to the same family. A related word can help you understand the meaning of the original word. What words can you think of that are related to *universe*? (*universal, university*)

Some related words have parts that are spelled the same but are pronounced differently. What words can you think of that are related to *relative*? (*relate, relationship*) Have students practice pronouncing the words.

Scaffold instruction.

CORRECTIVE FEEDBACK

Develop word meaning.

Write each practice word.

Have students think and converse. How does the way that you *relate* to other people affect your *relationship* with them? Why?

Have students practice finding related words. They may need to use dictionaries for help. Correct any words students miss and have them reread the list.

conclusion   imagination   variety   production   scientist   family

MORE PRACTICE

Write more practice words.

Have students practice finding related words.

donation   healthy   realistic   future   discover   astronomy

Vocabulary

	To Do	**To Say**	*5 minutes*

Review vocabulary.

Review the homework.

Deepen understanding of *complex*.

Ask students to go over answers and share their writing from Practice Book p. 117. See Routine Card 1 for the multisyllabic word routine.

Remember, *complex* means "hard to understand" or "made up of a number of parts that work together." In that sense, it's the opposite of *simple*. When you read a book with many different characters and plots, you might describe it as a *complex* book. Why? What else is an example of something that is *complex*? Why?

ACTIVITY 2 Comprehension

Compare and Contrast

	To Do	**To Say**	*5 minutes*

Scaffold instruction.

Introduce compare and contrast.

Model the skill.

Distribute Graphic Organizer 3.

Today you will read about how television and movies influence our ideas about outer space. When you read about two or more things, you can compare and contrast them to understand better what you are reading. As you read, look for similarities and differences between two or more things.

For example, if I read that both a robot and a computer can be programmed to do something, I've identified one way that they are alike. But if a robot is designed to move and a computer isn't, that's one way that they are different.

As you read "Spaceships from Hollywood," look for similarities and differences between the TV shows and movies. Add these details to your graphic organizers. See Routine Card 7.

ACTIVITY **3** Read a Passage

Read for Comprehension "Spaceships from Hollywood," pp. 116–119

	To Do	To Say	

10–15 minutes

Scaffold instruction.

Monitor student engagement.

See Routine Cards 2 and 3.

Read Have students read pp. 116–119. Stop at the end of each page to ask questions. Students who can read on their own can do so without stopping. After reading, ask questions to promote discussion.

How did the Robinson family become lost in space? (A spy tried to stop them from completing their mission; their ship went off course.)

What time period was the *Star Trek* TV series set in? (the 23rd century)

How did the *Star Trek* stories make the show seem believable? (They dealt with real problems, such as crime, love, and power.)

What do you think the rest of the article will be about? (Answers will vary. The title suggests it will tell more about how outer space is depicted in Hollywood TV shows and movies.)

Model summarizing.

Think aloud.

Summarize What were the first four pages mainly about? What did you learn about Hollywood and space? Think aloud to model summarizing. **I learned many details about some of the more popular TV shows and movies that deal with outer space, such as *Star Trek*. But the main thing I learned is that they can influence the ideas people have about outer space.**

Develop language and concepts.

Ask questions.

• **What sorts of details can make science fiction seem believable?**

• **In what ways is science fiction similar to other kinds of fiction? In what ways is it different?**

MORE PRACTICE

Have students reread p. 119.

Reread Tell students to draw a picture of one of their favorite characters from a science-fiction TV show or movie or invent one of their own.

Reread for Fluency "Spaceships from Hollywood," pp. 116–117

	To Do	To Say	

5 minutes

MORE PRACTICE

CORRECTIVE FEEDBACK

Pair students. Monitor paired reading.

Students read aloud pp. 116–117, switching readers at each new paragraph. Have partners reread; now the other partner begins. For optimal fluency, students should reread three or four times. Give feedback, using the *if . . . then* statements on Routine Card 4. You may want to have students read along with the DVD-ROM.

ACTIVITY **4** Write

Response to Literature

	To Do	To Say	

5 minutes

Prompt writing.

Writing elements: organization

Compare and contrast the movies and TV shows described in this part of "Spaceships from Hollywood" Use words such as *both* and *different* to show similarities and differences.

Homework

Practice Book, p. 118, Related Words

3

Word Work

Phonics Related Words

	To Do	To Say	*5 minutes*
Review related words. **Scaffold instruction.**	Review the homework. Discuss *scenes* on p. 121 in the Student Reader.	Ask students to share answers from Practice Book p. 118. Point out *scenes* on p. 121. **Remember, related words are words that belong to the same family. What words can you think of that are related to *scenes*?** *(scenic, scenery, scenario)* Guide students in pronouncing the words. Explain that the letter combination *sc* in these words is pronounced /s/. Then point to *images* on p. 123, paragraph 2. **What words can you think of that are related to *images*?** *(imagine, imagination, imagery, imaginary)*.	
MORE PRACTICE	Model spelling related words.	**Spell and Write** Write *invent*. **What words do you know that are related to *invent*?** (invention, inventor, inventive) Continue with *science* (scientific, scientists).	

Amazing Words Vocabulary

	To Do	To Say	*5 minutes*
Build vocabulary. **Lead cumulative review.**	Deepen understanding of *futuristic*.	Read aloud p. 118 and the first paragraph on p. 119. **The author gives a clue to the meaning of *futuristic*. What clue tells you that the show takes place in the future?** (The author says that the show is set in the 23rd century.) Write *futuristic*. **Say a sentence using *futuristic*. Would you want to live in a *futuristic* world? Why or why not?** Use the Tested Vocabulary Cards to review words from previous weeks.	

Comprehension

Compare and Contrast

	To Do	To Say	*5–10 minutes*
Scaffold instruction. **Guide practice.**	Review compare and contrast. Use Graphic Organizer 3.	**Remember, comparing and contrasting two or more things can help you better understand what you're reading. Look for clue words such as *like*, *also*, *unlike*, and *however* that may signal a similarity or difference. Remember that not all comparisons are signaled by clue words.** **Listen as I read p. 121. Notice that the author is describing the movie *Star Wars*. What does the author compare *Star Wars* with?** (movies made before *Star Wars*) **How is *Star Wars* different from movies that were made before it?** (The scenes are very realistic; the movie used new computer technology to create special effects.) **Add these details to your graphic organizers.** See Routine Card 7.	
MORE PRACTICE	Have students preview pp. 120–123. Think aloud.	**Read the captions and look at the photos on pp. 120–123. What do you think this section will be about?** (more TV shows and movies that are about outer space) **Why do you think so?** Think aloud to model using headings, captions, and illustrations to predict. **The captions and photos make me think that the article will tell more about TV shows and movies that take place in outer space, such as *Star Wars* and *E.T.*, and how these shows and movies affect how we think about outer space.**	

Read a Passage

Read for Comprehension "Spaceships from Hollywood," pp. 120–123

10–15 minutes

	To Do	To Say
Scaffold instruction.	Monitor student engagement.	**Read** Have students read pp. 120–123. Stop at the end of each page to ask questions. Students who can read on their own can do so without stopping. After reading, ask questions to promote discussion.
	See Routine Cards 2 and 3.	**What was the role of the Jedi Knights?** (to protect weaker star systems from the giant evil Empire)
		Why was *Star Wars* so popular? (It was like no movie anyone had ever seen before.)
		Why does E.T. travel to Earth? (to study plants) **Why does he need Elliot's help?** (His spaceship leaves him and he has to find a way home.)
	Model using context for word meaning.	Read aloud the paragraph with *humorous* on p. 123. Explain how the antonym *serious* in the sentence that follows provides clues to the meaning of *humorous*.
Assess comprehension.	Monitor understanding.	**After Reading** Have students discuss the What Do You Think? question. Prompt them to compare and contrast details from the article to answer the question. Listen as they talk to assess comprehension.
	Summarize.	**What is this mainly about? What did you learn?** Work with students to summarize the selection.
MORE PRACTICE	Have students reread p. 120.	**Reread** As they read, tell students to note how Luke Skywalker was similar to and different from earlier heroes. (Similarities: He battled evil, and he was a knight. Differences: He was a Jedi and protected star systems in space.) Have students add these details to their graphic organizers.

Reread for Fluency "Spaceships from Hollywood," p. 122

5 minutes

	To Do	To Say
CORRECTIVE FEEDBACK	Monitor oral reading.	Read p. 122 aloud. Reread the page three or four times so your reading gets better each time. Give feedback on students' oral reading, using the *if . . . then* statements on Routine Card 4. Model fluent reading if necessary. You may want to have students read along with the DVD-ROM.

Write

Response to Literature

5 minutes

	To Do	To Say
MORE PRACTICE	Prompt writing.	**How have TV and movie images of space changed through the years? How have they stayed the same? Include details that support your ideas.**
	Homework	Practice Book, p. 119, Compare and Contrast

ACTIVITY **1** Word Work

Amazing Words Vocabulary

	To Do	**To Say**	*5–10 minutes*

Extend word knowledge.

Write on the board or a transparency: *The scientists used the telescope to view the stars.*

Use the word *telescope* to extend word knowledge. **Remember we read this word earlier this week. We looked for meaningful parts, and we noticed the word *scope*. The word *scope* comes from a Greek word that means "to see." Today I want you to notice the prefix *tele-*. We can use this prefix to read other words.**

Teach the prefix *tele-*.

The prefix *tele-* means "over a long distance." So a *telescope* is an instrument used to see things that are a long distance away. Can you think of other words that begin with *tele-*? (*telecommute, telephone, telegraph, telegram, telepathy*) Write words as students name them and add some of your own. Talk about the meanings of the words, and then practice pronouncing them.

Scaffold instruction.

Develop word meaning.

A *microscope* is an instrument that makes small objects look larger. How is a *microscope* similar to a *telescope*? How is it different?

MORE PRACTICE

Deepen understanding of *telescope* and *galaxy*.

Have individual students or partners use the words *telescope* and *galaxy* together in sentences. (For example: A modern *telescope* can allow a scientist to study a *galaxy* in great detail.) Share sentences. Ask: What does a *galaxy* look like when viewed through a *telescope*? Do all *galaxies* look the same?

ACTIVITY **2** Comprehension

Skill and Strategy Practice

	To Do	**To Say**	*5 minutes*

Scaffold instruction.

Review compare and contrast (homework).

Ask volunteers to read the passage and share answers from Practice Book p. 119. Remind students of the importance of comparing and contrasting. **When you read a story, you can compare and contrast characters, events, problems, and settings to help you better understand what you read. You can also compare and contrast what happens in a story to something that happens in another story or in real life.**

Practice strategic prereading.

See Routine Card 2.

Discuss Genre Read the title and the first paragraph on p. 124 in the Student Reader. Model determining genre.

Think aloud.

I first thought this might be fiction because of the illustrations. When I read the first paragraph, I knew it was fiction because of the way the narrator speaks about Brian.

Review story structure.

Ask Questions What questions do you ask yourself to help you understand a fictional story? (What is the problem or goal? How is the problem solved or the goal reached?) **As you read this story, ask these questions and look for the answers.**

ACTIVITY 3 Read a Passage

Read for Comprehension "Searching the Universe," pp. 124–131

10–15 minutes

	To Do	**To Say**
Scaffold instruction.	Monitor student engagement. See Routine Card 3.	**Read** Have students read pp. 124–131 on their own and then discuss. For students who need more help, stop at the end of each page to discuss. After reading, ask questions. **What is Brian's dream?** (to discover a new planet) **Why does Brian sketch what he sees through his telescope?** (to capture the image so he could compare it to images in books) **What does Grandpa think Brian saw?** (a lunar eclipse) **Why does Brian disagree with that idea?** (Brian knows enough about astronomy to know that it wasn't possible that a lunar eclipse happened that night.) **What new information solves the mystery?** (Grandpa reads in the paper that scientists discovered a new planet similar to what Brian saw.) **What puzzle remains in Brian's mind?** (Is his telescope more powerful than he thought it was? Did he really see the image or did he imagine it?)
Assess comprehension.	Monitor understanding.	**After Reading** Have students discuss the What Do You Think? question. Prompt them to respond by comparing and contrasting details in the story. Listen as they talk to assess comprehension.
MORE PRACTICE		**Reread** Have students reread p. 129 and explain what prevents Brian from sleeping.

Reread for Fluency "Searching the Universe," pp. 126–128

5–10 minutes

	To Do	**To Say**
CORRECTIVE FEEDBACK	Pair students. Monitor paired reading.	Students read aloud pp. 126–128, switching readers at the end of each page. Have partners reread; now the other partner begins. For optimal fluency, students should reread three or four times. Give feedback, using Routine Card 4. You may want to have students read along with the DVD-ROM.
MORE PRACTICE	**READERS' THEATER**	Work with a group of students to adapt pp. 126–128 as a radio play. Have students rehearse reading the parts: narrator, Brian, Grandpa, and Mom. Then have them perform for the class.

ACTIVITY 4 Write

Response to Literature

5 minutes

	To Do	**To Say**
Prompt narrative writing.	Review pp. 126–131. Writing elements: focus, support	**How does Brian explore space? Provide specific examples from the selection that support your main ideas.**

ACTIVITY 1 — Read a Passage

Read Together "The Sounds of Space," pp. 132–133

10 minutes

	To Do	**To Say**
Scaffold instruction.	Review compare and contrast.	Have students preview pp. 132–133. **This article tells about how sound travels in space. Comparing and contrasting information in an article can help you better understand what you read. As you read, use the information in the article to compare and contrast the way sound travels through space with the way it travels on Earth.**
	See Routine Card 3.	**Read** Read the article as students follow along. Then read it a second time, having students join in on the text. After reading, ask questions.
		What do a phone call to Japan, a soccer game in Germany, and music from Brazil have in common? (They have all traveled into outer space.)
		How do we see and hear things from thousands of miles away? (Satellites that circle Earth send and receive signals from telephones, televisions, and radios.)
		Can we hear sounds in space? (No, but there are radio waves.)
		What do converted radio waves sound like? (whistling or hissing)
Assess comprehension.	Monitor listening comprehension.	**Summarize** Have one student explain how we can hear things from far away on Earth; have another explain how NASA can hear things in space.

ACTIVITY 2 — Build Concepts

Amazing Words ★ Vocabulary

5–10 minutes

	To Do	**To Say**
Review concept and vocabulary.	Display the concept web you began on Day 1.	**This week's question is *How do we reach for the stars?* How do this week's words relate to the question?** (Have students answer the question, using some of the vocabulary they learned this week.)
		Ask students to add more words to the concept web. Have students explain how each word relates to space. Monitor students' understanding of vocabulary as they discuss the web. See Routine Card 5.
MORE PRACTICE	Write *scientific* and *futuristic* on the board.	Have students relate *scientific* and *futuristic*. **How do *scientific* advances encourage people to have *futuristic* ideas and goals? In what ways might *futuristic* ideas inspire *scientific* investigation? Explain.**

ACTIVITY 3 Write

Response to Literature "4 You 2 Do," p. 134

| To Do | To Say | 5–10 minutes |

Guide response activities.

Discuss the directions on p. 134. Tell students to choose one activity to complete. See Routine Card 8.

Word Play Have students work in pairs or small groups to create movie titles using the vocabulary words.

Making Connections Discuss the question in a group. (Possible response: Because of his interest in astronomy, Brian might like a documentary that shows scientists making discoveries, or a science fiction movie about a boy who discovers a new planet by experimenting with radio telescopes and sound waves.)

On Paper Have students brainstorm some answers to the prompt before they write. Have them write on their own. Students can use Practice Book p. 120 to structure their written responses, or you can send the Practice Book page home for them to complete later.

MORE PRACTICE

If you have more time, direct students to complete all the activities.

ACTIVITY 4 Assessment Options

End-of-Unit Test

| To Do | To Say | 10–15 minutes |

Assess fluency and comprehension.

Use Assessment Book, p. 84.

Options for end-of-unit assessment are available in the Assessment Book, p. 84.

Homework Practice Book, p. 120, Writing

Resources

Contents

Monitoring Fluency

Ongoing assessment of student reading fluency is one of the most valuable measures we have of students' reading skills. One of the most effective ways to assess fluency is taking timed samples of students' oral reading and measuring the number of words correct per minute (WCPM).

Fluency Goals

Level D End-of-Year Goal =
110–130 WCPM

Target Goals by Unit:

Unit 1 60 to 80 WCPM

Unit 2 70 to 90 WCPM

Unit 3 80 to 100 WCPM

Unit 4 90 to 110 WCPM

Unit 5 100 to 120 WCPM

Unit 6 110 to 130 WCPM

How to Measure Words Correct Per Minute—WCPM

Timed Reading of the Text

Make a copy of the text for yourself and have one for the student. Tell the student: **As you read this aloud, I want you to do your best reading. Read as quickly as you can without making mistakes. That doesn't mean it's a race. Just do your best reading. When I say** *begin,* **start reading.**

As the student reads, follow along in your copy. Mark words that are read incorrectly. Definitions and examples of these reading errors are given on p. 192.

Incorrect	Correct
• omissions	• self-corrections within 3 seconds
• substitutions	• repeated words
• mispronunciations	
• insertions	

After One Minute

At the end of one minute, draw a line after the last word that was read. Have the student finish reading but don't count any words beyond one minute. Arrive at the words correct per minute—WCPM—by counting the total number of words that the student read correctly in one minute.

Fluency Progress Chart

Copy the chart on the next page. Use it to record each student's progress across the year. Assist students in recording their scores on the chart and setting goals for the future.

Interpreting Results

Fluency goals are estimates, and students will vary considerably in their progress based on many factors. Also, student progress will depend greatly on where they start with respect to WCPM. Level D End-of-Year goals are the same as for students without reading difficulties at the end of Grade 4.

Fluency Progress Chart, Level D

Student's Name _____

140																				
135																				
130																				
125																				
120																				
115																				
110																				
105																				
100																				
95																				
90																				
85																				
80																				
75																				
70																				
65																				
60																				
55																				
50																				
45																				
	1	2	3*	4	5*	1	2	3*	4	5*	1	2	3*	4	5*	1	2	3*	4	5*
	Unit 1					**Unit 2**					**Unit 3**					**Unit 4**				

1	2	3*	4	5*	1	2	3*	4	5*
Unit 5					**Unit 6**				

* = Fluency Assessment Using Unfamiliar Text

Monitoring Retelling

Retelling is a way to monitor and assess comprehension. Through retelling, students show whether they understand story grammar and can follow sequence, grasp main ideas, and draw conclusions about what they read. Help students learn how to retell by giving them many opportunities to retell stories and nonfiction selections. Scaffold their retellings by prompting them to tell more.

How to Do a Retelling

Have the student read quietly. If the student has difficulty with the passage, you may read it aloud.

Tell the student: **Read the story quietly to yourself. When you finish reading, I will ask you to tell me about what you read.**

When the student has finished, or when you have finished reading aloud, ask:

- (For fiction) **What happened in the story?**
- (For nonfiction) **What was the selection mostly about?**

Prompts for Retelling

If a retelling is incomplete, use prompts to encourage the student to tell more.

Narrative Prompts

- **Who is in the story?**
- **Where and when does the story take place?**
- **What is the problem or goal?**
- **How is the problem solved or the goal reached?**

Expository Prompts

- **What did you learn about _____?**
- **What are the most important ideas?**

Looking Back

Encourage students to look back in the text to find answers or to confirm their answers.

- **Let's check the book to make sure.**
- **Show me where the book tells you that.**
- **Where can we look in the book to find the answer?**

See Assessment Book, pp. 12–13, for scoring rubrics for retelling. Use the rubrics to help students move toward a fluent retelling.

Using End-of-Unit Assessment Results

To make instructional decisions at the end of each unit, consider scores for

- Unit Test
- Benchmark Reader reading

Record Scores

Several forms are provided for recording students' progress across the year.

- Record Sheet for Unit Tests: Record scores for each Unit Test. See the Assessment Book, p. 16.
- Fluency Progress Chart: Record each student's WCPM across the year. See p. 185.
- Retelling Charts: Record the student's retelling scores for each unit. See the Assessment Book, pp. 12–14.

Questions to Consider

- Has the student's performance met expectations for daily lessons?
- What can the student read alone? What can the student read with supervision?
- Is the student progressing toward grade-level goals?

Evaluate Student Progress

To move into the next unit of _My Sidewalks_, the student should

- score 80% or better on the Unit Test
- be able to read and retell the end-of-unit Benchmark Reader accurately
- be capable of working in the Level D group based on teacher judgment

---

If . . . the student's scores indicate a specific weakness in one area of literacy, such as fluency or comprehension,

then . . . focus the student's instruction and practice on that area.

If . . . the student has not met the fluency benchmarks for the unit,

then . . . consider that the benchmark WCPM at the high end of the range are more typical of on-level students, and students in intensive intervention may be progressing well even if they are not meeting fluency benchmarks.

The student may be more appropriately placed in _My Sidewalks_, Level C if the student

- scores 60% or lower on Unit Tests
- is struggling to keep up with the Level D group
- is unable to decode the simplest word types

Exiting MY SiDEWALKS

In Level D of *My Sidewalks,* there are two opportunities for students to exit the program—at midyear and at the end of the year. Many factors govern decisions concerning instruction for individual students. Understandably, guidelines in your school or district regarding adequate yearly progress, in addition to processes such as Individualized Education Plans, will influence each student's placement in or exit from any intervention program.

Midyear Exit Criteria

Has the student scored 80% or above on Unit Tests?

YES   NO continue in *My Sidewalks*

Is the student able to profit from instruction in the regular classroom?

YES   NO continue in *My Sidewalks*

Is the student performing successfully in a classroom reading program with or without extra support?

YES   NO continue in *My Sidewalks*

Check Reading of On-Level Material

- Select the next unread fictional passage from the classroom reading text.
- Briefly discuss the passage and preteach words identified in the program teacher's guide.
- Read aloud the title and the first paragraph.
- Ask the student to reread the first paragraph and to continue reading for three minutes.
- As the student reads, record errors.
- After reading, ask the student to retell what was read.

Determine Accuracy At the end of the reading, count the number of words read and the number of errors. Did the student read with 85% accuracy?

YES   NO continue in *My Sidewalks*

Determine Comprehension Was the student able to retell effectively?

YES   NO continue in *My Sidewalks*

Students who can read the classroom text accurately and with comprehension may exit *My Sidewalks*. If you are hesitant to exit the student, follow the Check Reading procedure on more than one occasion. If all data confirm that the student is ready to exit *My Sidewalks,* then exit the student with confidence. If results are mixed, then continue the student in the program.

End-of-Year Exit Criteria

Has the student scored 80% or above on Unit Tests?

YES   NO continue in *My Sidewalks*

Is the student able to profit from instruction in the regular classroom?

YES   NO continue in *My Sidewalks*

Is the student performing successfully in a classroom reading program with or without extra support?

YES   NO continue in *My Sidewalks*

Based on your school or district end-of-year assessment, is the student making adequate yearly progress?

YES   NO continue in *My Sidewalks*

Students who are making adequate yearly progress on school or district end-of-year assessments may be prepared to exit *My Sidewalks*.

Matching Students to Text

Providing students with reading materials they can and want to read is an important step toward developing fluent readers. A fluency test allows you to determine each student's instructional and independent reading level. Information on how to take a fluency test is provided on pp. 191–192.

Instructional Reading Level

Only approximately 1 in 10 words will be difficult when reading a selection from the Student Reader for students in the *My Sidewalks* intervention program. Students reading at their instructional level need teacher support and benefit from guided instruction.

Independent Reading Level

Students should read regularly in independent-level texts in which no more than approximately 1 in 20 words is difficult for the reader. Other factors that make a book easy to read include the student's interest in the topic, the amount of text on a page, how well illustrations support meaning, and the complexity and familiarity of the concepts.

Guide students in learning how to self-select books at their independent reading level. As you talk about a book with students, discuss the challenging concepts in it, list new words students find in sampling the book, and ask students about their familiarity with the topic. A blackline master to help students evaluate books for independent reading is provided on p. 190.

Self-Selected/Independent Reading

While oral reading allows you to assess students' reading level and fluency, independent reading is of crucial importance to students' futures as readers and learners. Students need to develop their ability to read independently for increasing amounts of time.

- Specify the amount of time you wish students to read independently each week. During the year, gradually increase the amount of time devoted to independent reading.

- Encourage students to read to a partner or a family member.

- Help students track the amount of time they read independently and the number of pages they read in a given amount of time. Tracking will help motivate them to gradually increase their duration and speed. A blackline master for tracking independent reading is provided on p. 190. Check it on a regular basis to monitor progress.

Choosing a Book for Independent Reading

When choosing a book, story, or article for independent reading, consider these questions:

_____ 1.   Do I know something about this topic?

_____ 2.   Am I interested in this topic?

_____ 3.   Do I like reading this kind of book (fiction, fantasy, biography, or whatever)?

_____ 4.   Have I read other things by this author? Do I like this author?

If you say "yes" to at least one of the questions above, continue:

_____ 5.   In reading the first page, was only about 1 of every 20 words hard?

If you say "yes," continue:

_____ 6.   Does the number of words on a page look about right to me?

If you say "yes," the book or article is probably at the right level for you.

Silent Reading

Record the date, the title of the book or article you read, the amount of time you spent reading, and the number of pages you read during that time.

Date	Title	Minutes	Pages

Matching Students to Text

Taking a Fluency Test

A fluency test is an assessment of a student's oral reading accuracy and oral reading fluency. Reading accuracy is based on the number of words read correctly. Reading fluency is based on the reading rate (the number of words correct per minute) and the degree to which a student reads with a "natural flow."

How to Measure Reading Accuracy

1. Choose a text of about 100 to 140 words that is unfamiliar to the student.

2. Make a copy of the text for yourself. Make a copy for the student or have the student read aloud from a book.

3. Give the student the text and have the student read aloud. (You may wish to record the student's reading for later evaluation.)

4. On your copy of the text, mark any miscues or errors the student makes while reading. See the fluency test sample on p. 192, which shows how to identify and mark miscues.

5. Count the total number of words in the text and the total number of errors made by the student. Note: If a student makes the same error more than once, such as mispronouncing the same word multiple times, count it as one error. Self-corrections do not count as actual errors. Use the following formula to calculate the percentage score, or accuracy rate:

$$\frac{\text{Total Number of Words} - \text{Total Number of Errors}}{\text{Total Number of Words}} \times 100 = \text{percentage score}$$

Interpreting the Results

- A student who reads 95–100% of the words correctly is reading at an independent level and may need more challenging text.

- A student who reads 90–94% of the words correctly is reading at an instructional level and will likely benefit from guided instruction.

- A student who reads 89% or fewer of the words correctly is reading at a frustrational level and may benefit most from targeted instruction with lower-level texts and further intervention.

How to Measure Reading Rate (WCPM)

1. Follow Steps 1–3 above.

2. Note the exact times when the student begins and finishes reading.

3. Use the following formula to calculate the number of words correct per minute (WCPM):

$$\frac{\text{Total Number of Words Read Correctly}}{\text{Total Number of Seconds}} \times 60 = \text{words correct per minute}$$

Interpreting the Results

An appropriate reading rate for an on-level fourth-grader is 120–130 WCPM.

Matching Students to Text

Fluency Test Sample

Fluency Test Sample

Ms. Abbot read the list of student pairs.
She said, "The last student pair is Miguel
and Emi." Miguel groaned aloud.

"What is she going to teach me?" he
asked loudly. "She doesn't even speak
English!"

Ms. Abbot stared hard at Miguel.

"Miguel, I think this project has a lot to
teach you," she said.

My family just moved here from
Japan three weeks ago. I am shy about
talking to the other students. I have not
made any friends.

At this school, students come from all
different backgrounds. I wanted to meet
them. But I didn't feel comfortable speaking
English. I learned some English in Japan.
But, there are still so many words I don't
know. My mother says I am just homesick.

—from *Paper Birds and Plantains*
My Sidewalks Student Reader, Level D

Miscues

Hesitation
The student hesitates over a word, and the teacher provides the word. Wait several seconds before telling the student what the word is.

Insertion
The student inserts words or parts of words that are not in the text.

Self-Correction
The student reads a word incorrectly but then corrects the error. Do not count self-corrections as actual errors. However, noting self-corrections will help you identify words the student finds difficult.

Mispronunciation/Misreading
The student pronounces or reads a word incorrectly.

Omission
The student omits words or word parts.

Substitution
The student substitutes words or parts of words for the words in the text.

Fluency Test Results ▶	**Reading Accuracy** ▶	**Reading Rate—WCPM**
Total Number of Words: **124**	$\dfrac{124-5}{124} = \dfrac{119}{124} = .959 = 96\%$	$\dfrac{119}{61} \times 60 = 117.04 = 117$ words correct per minute
Number of Errors: **5**		
Reading Time: **61 seconds**	Accuracy Percentage Score: **96%**	Reading Rate: **117 WCPM**

Scope and Sequence

Concepts of Print and Print Awareness	Level A	Level B	Level C	Level D	Level E
Develop awareness that print represents spoken language and conveys and preserves meaning	•				
Identify parts of a book and their functions (front cover, title, page numbers)	•				
Understand the concept of letter and word (including constancy of words and word boundaries)	•				
Track print (front to back of book, top to bottom of page, left to right on line, sweep back left for next line)	•				
Match spoken to printed words	•				
Know capital and lowercase letter names and match them	•				
Write capital and lowercase letters	•				

Phonemic Awareness	Level A	Level B	Level C	Level D	Level E
Identify sounds that are the same or different	•				
Identify and isolate initial, final, and medial sounds	•				
Blend sounds orally	•	•			
Segment a word into sounds	•	•			
Add or delete phonemes	•	•			

Phonics	Level A	Level B	Level C	Level D	Level E
Understand and apply the *alphabetic principle* that spoken words are composed of sounds that are represented by letters	•				
Know letter-sound relationships	•	•	•		
Blend sounds of letters to decode					
Consonants	•	•			
Consonant blends	•	•	•		

Consonant digraphs	●	●	●		
Vowels					
Short	●	●	●	●	●
Long	●	●	●	●	●
r-Controlled	●	●	●	●	●
Digraphs	●	●	●	●	●
Diphthongs		●	●	●	●
Other vowel patterns	●	●	●	●	●
Phonograms/word families	●	●	●		
Decode words with common word parts					
Base words and inflected endings	●	●	●	●	●
Contractions	●	●	●	●	●
Possessives	●	●			
Compounds	●	●	●	●	●
Suffixes and prefixes		●	●	●	●
Blend syllables to decode words					
VC/CV	●	●	●	●	●
Consonant + *le*	●	●	●	●	●
VC/V and V/CV	●	●	●	●	●
VCCCV			●	●	●
V/V			●	●	●

Spelling	Level A	Level B	Level C	Level D	Level E
Use sound-letter knowledge to spell	●	●	●	●	●
Use knowledge of word structure to spell	●	●	●	●	●
Blend multisyllabic words	●	●	●	●	●
Reading Fluency	**Level A**	**Level B**	**Level C**	**Level D**	**Level E**
Read aloud fluently with accuracy, comprehension, and appropriate pace/rate	●	●	●	●	●
Practice fluency in a variety of ways, including choral reading, partner/paired reading, repeated oral reading, tape-assisted reading, and Readers' Theater	●	●	●	●	●
Work toward appropriate fluency goals	40–60 WCPM	70–90 WCPM	100–120 WCPM	110–130 WCPM	120–140 WCPM
Vocabulary (Oral and Written)	**Level A**	**Level B**	**Level C**	**Level D**	**Level E**
Recognize regular and irregular high-frequency words automatically	●	●			
Recognize and understand lesson vocabulary	●	●	●	●	●
Develop vocabulary through direct instruction, concrete experiences, reading, and listening to text read aloud	●	●	●	●	●
Use concept vocabulary	●	●	●	●	●
Use speaking vocabulary	●	●			
Use knowledge of word structure to figure out word meaning		●	●	●	●
Use context clues					
to confirm word identification	●	●	●		
to determine word meaning of multiple-meaning words, homonyms, homographs			●	●	●
to determine word meaning of unfamiliar words			●	●	●
Understand synonyms and antonyms			●	●	●

Text Comprehension	Level A	Level B	Level C	Level D	Level E
Comprehension Strategies					
Preview the text	●	●	●	●	●
Set and monitor purpose for reading	●	●	●	●	●
Activate and use prior knowledge	●	●	●	●	●
Make predictions	●	●	●	●	●
Ask and answer questions	●	●	●	●	●
Look back in text for answers			●	●	●
Recognize story structure: characters, plot, setting	●	●	●	●	●
Summarize text by retelling stories or identifying main ideas	●	●	●	●	●
Use graphic and semantic organizers			●	●	●
Comprehension Skills					
Compare and contrast	●	●	●	●	●
Draw conclusions		●	●	●	●
Main idea and supporting details	●	●	●	●	●
Sequence of events	●	●	●	●	●
Write in response to text	●	●	●	●	●

Oral Vocabulary Routine

Let's Learn Amazing Words

Use this Oral Vocabulary Routine along with the definitions, examples, letter-sounds, and word parts provided on the following pages to introduce each Amazing Word.

ABOUT ORAL VOCABULARY A student's oral vocabulary development is a predictor of future reading success. Oral vocabulary development boosts students' comprehension as they become fluent readers. Oral vocabulary is informally assessed.

Routine

Introduce the Word Relate the word to the selection in which it appears. Supply a student-friendly definition. Have students say the word. Example:
- In the story, the puzzle is a *challenge*. A *challenge* is a hard task or a test of someone's abilities. You can also *challenge* someone by inviting or daring him or her to do something, such as take part in a competition. Say the word *challenge* with me, *challenge*.

Demonstrate Provide familiar examples to demonstrate meaning. When possible, use gestures to help convey meaning. Examples:
- Running in the 5K race was a *challenge*. It was a *challenge* to write a two-page report. Our school will *challenge* another school to a basketball game.

Apply Have students demonstrate understanding with a simple activity. Example:
- Tell me something that is a *challenge* for you. How else might one school *challenge* another?

Display the Word/Letter-Sounds Write the word on a card and display it on a classroom Amazing Words board. Have students identify some familiar letter-sounds or word parts. Example:
- This word is *challenge*. Run your hand under the two word parts *chal-lenge* as you read the word.

Use the Word Ask students to use the word in a sentence. Model a sentence if students need help. Example:
- Eating with chopsticks is a *challenge* for me.

Oral Vocabulary Unit 4 Week 1

Let's Learn Amazing Words

Routine *Oral Vocabulary*

illusion

1 An *illusion* is something that appears to be different from what it really is.

2 **EXAMPLES** The rabbit didn't really disappear; it was an *illusion*. The glass floor created the *illusion* that we were walking on air

3 **APPLY TO THE INSTRUCTION** Point out that most magic tricks rely on *illusions*. Have students give examples.

4 **WORD PARTS** Run your hand under the three word parts *il-lu-sion* as students read each part and then read the whole word.

invisible

1 If something is *invisible*, you can't see it with your eyes.

2 **EXAMPLE** The lion was *invisible* to the hunters because it was hidden behind the trees.

3 **APPLY TO THE INSTRUCTION** Have students name something that is *invisible*.

4 **WORD PARTS** Run your hand under the four word parts *in-vis-i-ble* as students read each part and then read the whole word.

magician

1 A *magician* is someone who performs tricks.

2 **EXAMPLES** The *magician* entertained us with tricks at the party. The *magician* showed us an amazing card trick.

3 **APPLY TO THE INSTRUCTION** Have students describe a *magician's* trick they have seen or read about.

4 **SOUND-SPELLINGS** Run your hand under the three word parts *ma-gi-cian* as students read each part and then read the whole word.

mysterious

1 Something that is *mysterious* is hard to explain or understand.

2 **EXAMPLE** The *mysterious* sounds frightened us; we didn't know what made them.

3 **APPLY TO THE INSTRUCTION** Have students tell about something *mysterious* they have thought or heard about.

4 **SOUND-SPELLINGS** Run your hand under the four word parts *mys-ter-i-ous* as students read each part and then read the whole word.

perception

1 *Perception* is understanding. *Perception* can also be the act of being aware of something.

2 **EXAMPLES** She had a clear *perception* of the problem and knew how to solve it. His *perception* of time became confused when he traveled from New York to London.

3 **APPLY TO THE INSTRUCTION** Show students several optical illusions and ask volunteers to describe their *perception* of them.

4 **WORD PARTS** Run your hand under the three word parts *per-cep-tion* as students read each part and then read the whole word.

vanish

1 To *vanish* means to disappear suddenly.

2 **EXAMPLE** The mouse *vanished* when it saw the cat.

3 **APPLY TO THE INSTRUCTION** Have students write a word in pencil on a piece of paper. Then tell them to find a way to make it *vanish*.

4 **SOUND-SPELLINGS** Identify the sound-spellings /van/*van* and /ish/*ish*. Students can decode *vanish*.

Oral Vocabulary Unit 4 Week 2

Let's Learn Amazing Words

Routine *Oral Vocabulary*

communication

1. *Communication* is the way people and animals exchange information.

2. **EXAMPLES** The telephone is used for *communication*. Text messaging is a new form of *communication*.

3. **APPLY TO THE INSTRUCTION** Have students identify which of these relate to *communication*: babies crying, birds singing, cats running, newspapers, spiders crawling, dogs barking, people waving, trains, walkie-talkies.

4. **WORD PARTS** Run your hand under the five word parts *com-mu-ni-ca-tion* as students read each part and then read the whole word.

instinct

1. *Instinct* is a way of acting that an animal is born with, not learned.

2. **EXAMPLE** Spiders have an *instinct* for spinning webs.

3. **APPLY TO THE INSTRUCTION** Ask: Which of these is an *instinct*: a dog doing a trick or a dog barking at a noise.

4. **WORD PARTS** Run your hand under the two word parts *in-stinct* as students read each part and then read the whole word.

protect

1. If you *protect* something, you keep it safe.

2. **EXAMPLE** Wearing a helmet and knee pads can *protect* you if you fall while skate boarding.

3. **APPLY TO THE INSTRUCTION** Have students use *protect* to describe things that *protect* them.

4. **WORD PARTS** Students can identify the syllable *pro-*. Students can decode *protect*.

relationships

1. *Relationships* are connections between people, groups and other things.

2. **EXAMPLE** She has good *relationships* with all her friends.

3. **APPLY TO THE INSTRUCTION** Have students tell about *relationships* between different groups, such as coaches and players, dogs and cats, people and animals.

4. **WORD PARTS** Run your hand under the four word parts *re-la-tion-ships* as students read each part and then read the whole word.

response

1. A *response* is an answer by saying, writing, or doing something.

2. **EXAMPLE** Her *response* to bumping her foot was to say, "Ouch!"

3. **APPLY TO THE INSTRUCTION** Ask students what their *response* is to a question, such as "How are you?" and "How's the weather?"

4. **WORD PARTS** Run your hand under the word parts *re-sponse* as students read each part and then read the whole word.

sense

1. If you *sense* something, you feel it or are aware of it.

2. **EXAMPLES** The rabbit *sensed* danger, so it ran away. I could *sense* that you were nervous.

3. **APPLY TO THE INSTRUCTION** Have students list things an animal might *sense*.

4. **SOUND-SPELLINGS** Identify the sound-spelling /s/*s*. Students can decode *sense*.

young

1. The children of people and animals are their *young*. *Young* can also mean not old.

2. **EXAMPLE** One way animals protect their *young* is by warning them of danger. A kitten is a *young* cat.

3. **APPLY TO THE INSTRUCTION** Have students list names of different animal *young*, such as cubs, chicks, and kittens.

4. **SOUND-SPELLINGS** Identify the sound-spelling /y/*y*.

Let's Learn Amazing Words

Routine *Oral Vocabulary*

conceals

1 *Conceals* means hides.

2 **EXAMPLES** The leafy tree *conceals* a family of squirrels. The box *conceals* the gift inside.

3 **APPLY TO THE INSTRUCTION** Have students name one word that means the opposite of *conceals*, and another word that means about the same as *conceals*.

4 **WORD PARTS** Run your hand under the two word parts *con-ceals* as students read each part and then read the whole word.

creative

1 If you are *creative*, you are able to think of new things or ideas.

2 **EXAMPLE** The author was very *creative* and wrote many books.

3 **APPLY TO THE INSTRUCTION** Have students give examples of *creative* things they or others have done.

4 **WORD PARTS** Run your hand under the three word parts *cre-a-tive* as students read each part and then read the whole word.

exchange

1 To *exchange* means to give and take things of the same kind.

2 **EXAMPLES** She had to *exchange* the small shoes for a larger pair. We agreed to *exchange* books after we read them.

3 **APPLY TO THE INSTRUCTION** Have students write a scrambled word on a piece of paper. Then say: *Exchange* papers and unscramble the words.

4 **SOUND-SPELLINGS** Identify the sound-spelling /ex/ex. Students can decode *exchange*.

interprets

1 When you *interpret* something, you explain the meaning of it.

2 **EXAMPLE** The guide at the museum *interprets* all of the signs for the visitors.

3 **APPLY TO THE INSTRUCTION** Display pictures of familiar signs with no words, such as "no smoking," "no littering," or "railroad crossing" and have students *interpret* the signs.

4 **WORD PARTS** Run your hand under the three word parts *in-ter-prets* as students read each part and then read the whole word.

transmit

1 To *transmit* something is to pass it along.

2 **EXAMPLES** Wash your hands after you blow you nose so you don't *transmit* germs. The weather forecaster will *transmit* a storm warning on television.

3 **APPLY TO THE INSTRUCTION** Have students demonstrate how to *transmit* a message or other information in either written or verbal form.

4 **SOUND-SPELLINGS** Identify the sound-spelling /tr/tr. Students can decode *transmit*.

visible

1 If something is *visible*, it can be seen.

2 **EXAMPLES** The ocean was *visible* from the top of the hill. The storm damage was *visible* as soon as we looked out the window.

3 **APPLY TO THE INSTRUCTION** Have students list things in the classroom that are *visible*.

4 **WORD PARTS** Run your hand under the three word parts *vis-i-ble* as students read each part and then read the whole word.

Oral Vocabulary Unit 4 Week 4

Let's Learn Amazing Words

Definitions, examples, applications, and **sound-spellings** to use with the Oral Vocabulary Routine each week.

Routine *Oral Vocabulary*

combine

1. When you *combine* things, you join two or more things together.
2. **EXAMPLE** The cook tried to *combine* all of the ingredients in one bowl.
3. **APPLY TO THE INSTRUCTION** Have students tell about two or more things you can *combine* to make something else.
4. **WORD PARTS** Run your hand under the two word parts *com-bine* as students read each part and then read the whole word.

conversation

1. *Conversation* is friendly talk between two or more people.
2. **EXAMPLES** The *conversation* between the friends lasted for over an hour. We had a long *conversation* about what we can do during our school vacation.
3. **APPLY TO THE INSTRUCTION** Have students suggest behavior tips for having a *conversation*.
4. **WORD PARTS** Run your hand under the four word parts *con-ver-sa-tion* as students read each part and then read the whole word.

dialect

1. A *dialect* is a form of a language spoken by a group of people from the same area.
2. **EXAMPLE** I could tell from her *dialect* that she was from the South.
3. **APPLY TO THE INSTRUCTION** Have students discuss how communication is affected when two people speak different *dialects* of the same language.
4. **WORD PARTS** Run your hand under the three word parts *di-a-lect* as students read each part and then read the whole word.

phrase

1. A *phrase* is a short group of words that have a meaning but don't form a complete sentence.
2. **EXAMPLES** "See you soon" is a popular *phrase*. "On the ball" is a *phrase* that can describe someone who completes a task quickly.
3. **APPLY TO THE INSTRUCTION** Have students make a list of common *phrases* they know.
4. **SOUND-SPELLINGS** Identify the sound-spelling /f/*ph*. Students can decode *phrase*.

region

1. A *region* is any place, space, or area.
2. **EXAMPLE** The team traveled to the southern *region* of the state for the championship game.
3. **APPLY TO THE INSTRUCTION** Have students name the *region* of the country in which they live. Have them describe characteristics of the *region*.
4. **WORD PARTS** Run your hand under the two word parts *re-gion* as students read each part and then read the whole word.

shouts

1. Someone who *shouts* calls or yells loudly.
2. **EXAMPLE** The coach *shouts* across the room in order to be heard.
3. **APPLY TO THE INSTRUCTION** Ask students when a person might *shout*, and why.
4. **SOUND-SPELLINGS** Identify the sound-spelling /sh/*sh*. Students can decode *shouts*.

symbols

1. *Symbols* are things that stand for or mean the same as something else.
2. **EXAMPLE** A dove and an olive branch are *symbols* of peace.
3. **APPLY TO THE INSTRUCTION** Have students identify familiar *symbols* and what they stand for.
4. **WORD PARTS** Run your hand under the two word parts *sym-bols* as students read each part and then read the whole word.

Oral Vocabulary Unit 4 Week 5

Let's Learn Amazing Words

Definitions, examples, applications, and sound-spellings to use with the Oral Vocabulary Routine each week.

Routine *Oral Vocabulary*

convince

1. If you *convince* others of something, you say or do something to make them believe it.

2. **EXAMPLES** Her mother tried to *convince* her that bringing an umbrella was a good idea. The magician could not *convince* us that the rabbit had really disappeared.

3. **APPLY TO THE INSTRUCTION** Ask: What would you say to *convince* someone to wear a jacket on a chilly day?

4. **WORD PARTS** Run your hand under the two word parts *con-vince* as students read each part and then read the whole word.

curious

1. If you are *curious*, you are eager to know something.

2. **EXAMPLE** The *curious* children searched for clues.

3. **APPLY TO THE INSTRUCTION** Ask: Is a *curious* person more likely to ask questions or draw a picture? Have students use *curious* in their answers.

4. **WORD PARTS** Run your hand under the three word parts *cur-i-ous* as students read each part and then read the whole word.

diver

1. A *diver* is a person who works underwater using special equipment.

2. **EXAMPLE** The *diver* helped to discover the shipwreck.

3. **APPLY TO THE INSTRUCTION** Have students list jobs that a *diver* might do.

4. **WORD PARTS** Students can identify the base word *dive* and the suffix -*er*. Students can decode *diver*.

evidence

1. *Evidence* is anything that shows what happened.

2. **EXAMPLE** My brother's dirty hands were *evidence* that he had been playing in the dirt.

3. **APPLY TO THE INSTRUCTION** Have students give examples of *evidence* that can show what someone has done.

4. **WORD PARTS** Run your hand under the three word parts *ev-i-dence* as students read each part and then read the whole word.

explorer

1. An *explorer* is someone who travels to unknown places to discover new things.

2. **EXAMPLES** The undersea *explorer* prepared for his dive down to the ocean floor. Christopher Columbus was an early *explorer*.

3. **APPLY TO THE INSTRUCTION** Ask: Where might an *explorer* travel to in the future?

4. **WORD PARTS** Students can identify the base word *explore* and the suffix -*er*.

investigate

1. When you *investigate* something, you examine it to find out more about it.

2. **EXAMPLE** In science class, the students began to *investigate* the soil samples.

3. **APPLY TO THE INSTRUCTION** Have students tell what they *investigate* when they do science experiments.

4. **WORD PARTS** Run your hand under the four word parts *in-ves-ti-gate* as students read each part and then read the whole word.

scrutiny

1. *Scrutiny* is close study or careful inspection.

2. **EXAMPLE** Use *scrutiny* when shopping for used clothing; otherwise, you might buy a stained item.

3. **APPLY TO THE INSTRUCTION** Ask: If you look at something with *scrutiny*: do you look quickly or slowly? Have students use *scrutiny* in their answer.

4. **WORD PARTS** Run your hand under the three word parts *scru-ti-ny* as students read each part and then read the whole word.

Oral Vocabulary Unit 5 Week 1

Let's Learn Amazing Words

Routine *Oral Vocabulary*

dangerous

1. If something is *dangerous*, it is not safe.

2. **EXAMPLE** It is *dangerous* to cross the busy street unless you cross at a traffic light.

3. **APPLY TO THE INSTRUCTION** Point out that some types of weather can be *dangerous*. Have students give examples.

4. **WORD PARTS** Run your hand under the three word parts *dan-ger-ous* as students read each part and then read the whole word.

destroyed

1. If something has been *destroyed*, it has been very badly damaged.

2. **EXAMPLES** The house was *destroyed* by the fire. The insects *destroyed* the farmer's crops.

3. **APPLY TO THE INSTRUCTION** Have students name one word that means the opposite of *destroyed*, and another word that means about the same as *destroyed*.

4. **WORD PARTS** Run your hand under the two word parts *de-stroyed* as students read each part and then read the whole word.

exciting

1. Something that is *exciting* causes strong, lively feelings.

2. **EXAMPLES** The action-adventure movie was very *exciting*. The rafting trip down the river was scary but *exciting*.

3. **APPLY TO THE INSTRUCTION** Have students name activities that they think are *exciting*, and explain why.

4. **WORD PARTS** Students can identify the base word *excite* and the ending *-ing*.

hazards

1. *Hazards* are dangers.

2. **EXAMPLES** The icy sidewalks were *hazards* to people walking on them. The smog was a *hazard* to the people living in the city.

3. **APPLY TO THE INSTRUCTION** Have students name potential *hazards* in their home or community.

4. **WORD PARTS** Run your hand under the two word parts *haz-ards* as students read each part and then read the whole word.

hero

1. A *hero* is someone admired for his or her bravery.

2. **EXAMPLE** The woman who dove into the water to save the drowning dog was a *hero*.

3. **APPLY TO THE INSTRUCTION** Have students list things a *hero* might do.

4. **WORD PARTS** Run your hand under the two word parts *her-o* as students read each part and then read the whole word.

profession

1. A *profession* is a job that requires special training and study.

2. **EXAMPLE** A veterinarian is a good *profession* for someone who likes animals.

3. **APPLY TO THE INSTRUCTION** Have students name different *professions* and share which one interests them most.

4. **WORD PARTS** Run your hand under the three word parts *pro-fes-sion* as students read each part and then read the whole word.

Oral Vocabulary Unit 5 Week 2

Let's Learn Amazing Words

Routine *Oral Vocabulary*

ancient

1. If something is *ancient*, it is very old; it belongs to times long past.
2. **EXAMPLE** In Mexico, you can see *ancient* ruins of a temple.
3. **APPLY TO THE INSTRUCTION** Have students name one word that means the opposite of *ancient* and another that means about the same.
4. **WORD PARTS** Run your hand under the two word parts *an-cient* as students read each part and then read the whole word.

artifacts

1. *Artifacts* are objects from the past that people made.
2. **EXAMPLE** The tools and toys in the museum are *artifacts* from a hundred years ago.
3. **APPLY TO THE INSTRUCTION** Have students describe any *artifacts* they have seen or read about.
4. **SOUND-SPELLINGS** Identify the sound-spelling /är/. Students can decode *artifacts*.

civilization

1. A *civilization* is a group of people who work together in many ways.
2. **EXAMPLE** The *civilization* responsible for building the city was very advanced.
3. **APPLY TO THE INSTRUCTION** Ask: Which of these would you find in most *civilizations*: a form of writing or cell phones? Why?
4. **WORD PARTS** Run your hand under the five word parts *civ-i-li-za-tion* as students read each part and then read the whole word

society

1. *Society* is people living together as a group. It can also mean all the people.
2. **EXAMPLE** Some people think our *society* puts too much emphasis on owning things like big TVs and big cars.
3. **APPLY TO THE INSTRUCTION** Have students tell something about the *society* we live in.
4. **WORD PARTS** Run your hand under the four word parts *so-ci-e-ty* as students read each part and then read the whole word.

statue

1. A *statue* is a figure made of stone, wood, or metal that looks like a person or animal.
2. **EXAMPLE** The *statue* of the lion stood next to the library steps.
3. **APPLY TO THE INSTRUCTION** Ask: Why might an artist create a *statue*? Have students use *statue* in their answers.
4. **WORD PARTS** Run your hand under the two word parts *stat-ue* as students read each part and then read the whole word.

theater

1. A *theater* is a place where people go to see movies, plays, or other performances.
2. **EXAMPLE** Many people filled the *theater* to see the play.
3. **APPLY TO THE INSTRUCTION** Ask students to describe how a *theater* and a museum are alike and different.
4. **WORD PARTS** Run your hand under the three word parts *the-a-ter* as students read each part and then read the whole word.

traditions

1. *Traditions* are beliefs and customs that have been handed down from parents to children.
2. **EXAMPLE** One of the family's *traditions* was to have a picnic on the first day of spring.
3. **APPLY TO THE INSTRUCTION** Ask volunteers to describe *traditions* from their own families.
4. **WORD PARTS** Run your hand under the three word parts *tra-di-tions* as students read each part and then read the whole word.

Oral Vocabulary Unit 5 Week 3

Let's Learn Amazing Words

Routine *Oral Vocabulary*

adventure

1 An *adventure* is an unusual or exciting experience.

2 **EXAMPLES** The whitewater rafting trip was an *adventure*. We thought it was an *adventure* to try foods from other cultures.

3 **APPLY TO THE INSTRUCTION** Ask: If you were going on a trip, would you prefer to have an *adventure* or do something more ordinary? Why?

4 **WORD PARTS** Run your hand under the three word parts *ad-ven-ture* as students read each part and then read the whole word.

expeditions

1 An *expedition* is a long, well-planned trip, usually for a special purpose.

2 **EXAMPLES** The scientists had been planning the *expedition* to the Arctic for many years. The rover collected important data on its *expedition* to Mars.

3 **APPLY TO THE INSTRUCTION** Have students list things they might pack on an *expedition* to either a very hot region or a very cold region.

4 **WORD PARTS** Run your hand under the four word parts *ex-pe-di-tions* as students read each part and then read the whole word.

forecasts

1 *Forecasts* are statements of what is going to happen.

2 **EXAMPLE** All the weather *forecasts* for the coming week called for cold temperatures.

3 **APPLY TO THE INSTRUCTION** Have volunteers give a pretend *forecast* for the next day's weather.

4 **SOUND-SPELLINGS** Identify the sound-spelling /fôr/ *fore*. Students can decode *forecasts*.

unfamiliar

1 If something is *unfamiliar* it is not well-known.

2 **EXAMPLES** When we realized that the landscape was *unfamiliar*, we knew we were lost. His face is *unfamiliar*; we do not know who he is.

3 **APPLY TO THE INSTRUCTION** Have students name one word or phrase that means the opposite of *unfamiliar* and another that means about the same as *unfamiliar*.

4 **WORD PARTS** Run your hand under the four word parts *un-fa-mil-iar* as students read each part and then read the whole word.

wilderness

1 The *wilderness* is a wild place or region with few or no people living in it.

2 **EXAMPLE** The cabin was surrounded by *wilderness*. As more houses are built, there are fewer areas of *wilderness*.

3 **APPLY TO THE INSTRUCTION** Have students give examples of things they might encounter in the *wilderness*.

4 **WORD PARTS** Run your hand under the three word parts *wil-der-ness* as students read each part and then read the whole word.

Oral Vocabulary Unit 5 Week 4

Let's Learn Amazing Words

Routine *Oral Vocabulary*

adapted

1. If something has *adapted*, it has changed to fit different conditions.

2. **EXAMPLES** We *adapted* the garage to use as a workshop. It can take a while to *adapt* to thin mountain air if you're not used to it.

3. **APPLY TO THE INSTRUCTION** Have students imagine they have moved from a hot climate to a cold one. Have them identify things in their lives that might need to be *adapted*, and tell why.

4. **WORD PARTS** Students can identify the verb ending *-ed*.

architecture

1. *Architecture* is a style or method of building.

2. **EXAMPLE** The modern *architecture* of the building was different from some of the older buildings in the city.

3. **APPLY TO THE INSTRUCTION** Ask: If you are reading a book about *architecture*, which of these might you read about: a skyscraper, a car, an arch, an airplane, an airport, a roof, a porch, a museum, a painting.

4. **WORD PARTS** Run your hand under the four word parts *ar-chi-tec-ture* as students read each part and then read the whole word.

burrow

1. A *burrow* is a hole dug in the ground by a person or animal for protection.

2. **EXAMPLES** The mouse hid from the heat of the day inside a *burrow*. The *burrow* protected the rabbits from predators.

3. **APPLY TO THE INSTRUCTION** Have students list animals that live in a *burrow*.

4. **SOUND SPELLINGS** Identify the sound-spelling /bėr/*bur*. Students can decode *burrow*.

extreme

1. If something is *extreme,* it is much more than usual.

2. **EXAMPLE** The *extreme* cold forced the skiers to return home early.

3. **APPLY TO THE INSTRUCTION** Have students name one word that means the opposite of *extreme* and another that means about the same as *extreme*.

4. **SOUND-SPELLINGS** Identify the sound-spelling /ex/*ex*. Students can decode *extreme*.

homesteaders

1. *Homesteaders* are people who built houses on the prairie long ago.

2. **EXAMPLE** The *homesteaders* built houses on land that was unsettled. *Homesteaders* faced many challenges during the long, cold winters and dry summers.

3. **APPLY TO THE INSTRUCTION** Ask: Would you want to be a *homesteader*? Why or why not?

4. **WORD PARTS** Students can identify the shorter word *home*.

prairie

1. A *prairie* is a large area of level or rolling land. It has grass, but few or no trees.

2. **EXAMPLES** The *prairie* seemed to stretch on for miles. The farmers cleared the grass and planted crops on the *prairie*.

3. **APPLY TO THE INSTRUCTION** Have students list the sights and sounds they might see and hear on the *prairie*.

4. **WORD PARTS** Run your hand under the word parts *prair-ie* as students read each part and then read the whole word.

Oral Vocabulary Unit 5 Week 5

Let's Learn **Amazing Words**

Routine *Oral Vocabulary*

astronaut

1. An *astronaut* is a person who has been trained to fly in a spacecraft.
2. **EXAMPLES** The *astronaut* prepared for the flight to the space station. Each *astronaut* trained for many years before going into space.
3. **APPLY TO THE INSTRUCTION** Have students list things *astronauts* can do.
4. **WORD PARTS** Run your hand under the three word parts *as-tro-naut* as students read each part and then read the whole word.

astronomers

1. *Astronomers* are scientists who study things in space.
2. **EXAMPLES** The *astronomer* observed the moon through the telescope. Ancient *astronomers* were the first to discover that Earth revolves around the sun.
3. **APPLY TO THE INSTRUCTION** Have students tell which of these are things *astronomers* might study: sun, moon, plants, stars, planets, fossils.
4. **WORD PARTS** Run your hand under the four word parts *as-tron-o-mers* as students read each part and then read the whole word.

craters

1. A *crater* is a hole in the ground shaped like a bowl.
2. **EXAMPLES** Some *craters* are deeper than others. The *crater* was the largest on that side of the moon.
3. **APPLY TO THE INSTRUCTION** Ask: Which word most closely describes the shape of a *crater*: square, round, or triangular?
4. **WORD PARTS** Students can identify the open syllable *cra-*. Students can decode *crater*.

mission

1. A *mission* is a task that people are sent somewhere to do.
2. **EXAMPLE** Their *mission* was to collect all of the bottles and cans in the neighborhood for the recycling drive.
3. **APPLY TO THE INSTRUCTION** Ask: Which of these words means almost the same as *mission*: job, game, assignment, vacation, errand?
4. **WORD PARTS** Run your hand under the two word parts *mis-sion* as students read each part and then read the whole word.

myths

1. *Myths* are legends or stories, usually made up to explain something in nature.
2. **EXAMPLES** Many *myths* explain how the world was created. Some ancient *myths* describe why birds fly.
3. **APPLY TO THE INSTRUCTION** Have students tell about *myths* they know.
4. **SOUND-SPELLINGS** Students can identify the sound-spelling /m/*m*.

satellite

1. A *satellite* is an object in space that revolves around a planet.
2. **EXAMPLES** The moon revolves around Earth; it is Earth's *satellite*. Artificial *satellites* are used to send weather and other information back to Earth.
3. **APPLY TO THE INSTRUCTION** Have students pantomime how a *satellite* revolves around a planet.
4. **WORD PARTS** Run your hand under the three word parts *sat-el-lite* as students read each part and then read the whole word.

Oral Vocabulary Unit 6 Week 1

Let's Learn Amazing Words

Routine *Oral Vocabulary*

circumstances

1 *Circumstances* are conditions that go along with some fact or event.

2 **EXAMPLE** The tennis player's *circumstances*, including his sore leg and lack of practice time, made it difficult for him to win.

3 **APPLY TO THE INSTRUCTION** Have students list possible *circumstances* that would cause an event to be canceled.

4 **WORD PARTS** Run your hand under the four word parts *cir-cum-stan-ces* as students read each part and then read the whole word.

conviction

1 A *conviction* is a strong belief.

2 **EXAMPLES** His *conviction* in his ability helped him to win the race. It is our *conviction* that he is right.

3 **APPLY TO THE INSTRUCTION** Ask: If a man speaks about something with *conviction*, do you think it will be easy or hard to get him to change his mind? Why?

4 **WORD PARTS** Run your hand under the three word parts *con-vic-tion* as students read each part and then read the whole word.

devised

1 If you *devised* something, you thought up some new way of doing something.

2 **EXAMPLES** The students *devised* a plan for organizing the classroom. We *devised* a new way to get to school that was faster than the old way.

3 **APPLY TO THE INSTRUCTION** Have students *devise* a new seating plan for the classroom.

4 **WORD PARTS** Run your hand under the two word parts *de-vised* as students read each part and then read the whole word.

model

1 A *model* is a small copy of something.

2 **EXAMPLES** The *model* ship sat on top of the boy's bookcase. They built a *model* of an old-fashioned car.

3 **APPLY TO THE INSTRUCTION** Have students describe different types of *models* they have built or seen.

4 **WORD PARTS** Run your hand under the two word parts *mod-el* as students read each part and then read the whole word.

procrastinates

1 If you *procrastinate*, you put off doing something until later.

2 **EXAMPLES** Their father always *procrastinates* about mowing the lawn. Some students *procrastinate* when they have homework to do.

3 **APPLY TO THE INSTRUCTION** Ask: If you have a project to do and you *procrastinate*, is it more likely to get done early or late? Why?

4 **WORD PARTS** Run your hand under the four word parts *pro-cras-ti-nates* as students read each part and then read the whole word.

suggested

1 To *suggest* something is to bring up an idea.

2 **EXAMPLES** She *suggested* that we all go to a movie. The waiter *suggested* that they try the chicken.

3 **APPLY TO THE INSTRUCTION** Have students *suggest* ideas for a field trip. Then have volunteers tell which of the *suggested* ideas they like best.

4 **WORD PARTS** Run your hand under the three word parts *sug-gest-ed* as students read each part and then read the whole word.

Let's Learn Amazing Words

Routine *Oral Vocabulary*

achieved

1. If you have *achieved* something, you have accomplished it.

2. **EXAMPLES** We *achieved* our goal of climbing to the top of the mountain. The skater *achieved* a perfect score during the competition.

3. **APPLY TO THE INSTRUCTION** Ask: Which word relates to *achieved*: success or failure? Have students explain their answers.

4. **WORD PARTS** Run your hand under the two word parts *a-chieved* as students read each part and then read the whole word.

furious

1. If you are *furious*, you are very angry.

2. **EXAMPLES** The owners were *furious* when they saw the mess that the painters left. We were *furious* when the concert was canceled.

3. **APPLY TO THE INSTRUCTION** Have students name one word that means the opposite of *furious* and another word that means almost the same as *furious*.

4. **WORD PARTS** Run your hand under the three word parts *fur-i-ous* as students read each part and then read the whole word.

hurdles

1. *Hurdles* are things that stand in your way.

2. **EXAMPLE** She overcame many *hurdles*, including being short, to become part of the basketball team.

3. **APPLY TO THE INSTRUCTION** Have students give examples of other *hurdles* they or people they know have overcome.

4. **SOUND-SPELLINGS** Identify the sound-spelling /hėr/*hur*. Students can decode *hurdles*.

perseverance

1. *Perseverance* is not giving up what you have set out to do.

2. **EXAMPLES** It was their *perseverance* that allowed the athletes to make it to the Olympics. Our *perseverance* got us through the hardest parts of the test.

3. **APPLY TO THE INSTRUCTION** Ask: Which of these words or phrases are close in meaning to *perseverance*: quit, stick to it, persist, give up?

4. **WORD PARTS** Run your hand under the word four parts *per-se-ver-ance* as students read each part and then read the whole word.

personality

1. Your *personality* is the individual quality that makes you different from everyone else.

2. **EXAMPLE** His warm, friendly *personality* makes him easy to like.

3. **APPLY TO THE INSTRUCTION** Have students list different *personality* traits.

4. **WORD PARTS** Students can identify the shorter word *person*.

timid

1. If you are *timid*, you are easily frightened or shy.

2. **EXAMPLES** The *timid* kittens would not leave their mother's side. At first, the new girl was *timid*, but she soon got to know people.

3. **APPLY TO THE INSTRUCTION** Have students tell one word that is the opposite of *timid*, and another word that means about the same as *timid*.

4. **SOUND-SPELLINGS** Identify the sound-spelling /tim/*tim*. Students can decode *timid*.

Oral Vocabulary Unit 6 Week 3

Let's Learn Amazing Words

Routine *Oral Vocabulary*

appreciate

1 If you *appreciate* something, you think highly of it; you value it.

2 **EXAMPLES** We *appreciate* the help of the volunteers. It is important to show your friends that you *appreciate* them.

3 **APPLY TO THE INSTRUCTION** Have students list ways that you can show someone that you *appreciate* him or her.

4 **WORD PARTS** Run your hand under the four word parts *ap-pre-ci-ate* as students read each part and then read the whole word.

awkward

1 If something is *awkward*, it is embarrassing.

2 **EXAMPLE** The dancer had an *awkward* moment when she stumbled in the middle of the performance.

3 **APPLY TO THE INSTRUCTION** Have students name one word that means the opposite of *awkward*, and another word that means about the same as *awkward*.

4 **WORD PARTS** Run your hand under the two word parts *awk-ward* as students read each part and then read the whole word.

barrier

1 A *barrier* is something that stands in the way.

2 **EXAMPLES** The fallen tree formed a *barrier* in the middle of the road. In France, not knowing French can be a *barrier* to communicating well.

3 **APPLY TO THE INSTRUCTION** Point out that a *barrier* can be something you can see, like a fence, or something you can't see, like a language *barrier*. Have students give examples of each.

4 **WORD PARTS** Run your hand under the three word parts *bar-ri-er* as students read each part and then read the whole word.

immigration

1 *Immigration* is the act of coming into a foreign country to live.

2 **EXAMPLE** Chinese restaurants are one result of the *immigration* of people from China to the United States.

3 **APPLY TO THE INSTRUCTION** Have students explain how *immigration* has helped the United States.

4 **WORD PARTS** Run your hand under the four word parts *im-mi-gra-tion* as students read each part and then read the whole word.

international

1 Something that is *international* is between two or more countries.

2 **EXAMPLES** The *international* chess competition featured players from all over the world. The flight from Japan to the United States was an *international* flight.

3 **APPLY TO THE INSTRUCTION** Ask: If you were going to travel, would you prefer *international* travel or travel within the United States? Why?

4 **WORD PARTS** Run your hand under the five word parts *in-ter-na-tion-al* as students read each part and then read the whole word.

occupations

1 An *occupation* is the work someone does to earn a living.

2 **EXAMPLE** The *occupations* of the different members of the group included teaching, retail sales, and caring for the sick.

3 **APPLY TO THE INSTRUCTION** Have students list various *occupations* of people they know.

4 **WORD PARTS** Run your hand under the four word parts *oc-cu-pa-tions* as students read each part and then read the whole word.

Let's Learn Amazing Words

Definitions, examples, applications, and sound-spellings to use with the Oral Vocabulary Routine each week.

Routine *Oral Vocabulary*

apply

1. To *apply* is to set to work and stick to it.

2. **EXAMPLE** I had to *apply* myself to researching and writing the report.

3. **APPLY TO THE INSTRUCTION** Have students give examples of ways they can *apply* themselves to complete a school project.

4. **WORD PARTS** Run your hand under the two word parts *ap-ply* as students read each part and then read the whole word.

determined

1. If you are *determined* to do something, you have your mind made up to do it.

2. **EXAMPLES** We were *determined* to get all the litter cleaned up before dark. The girl was *determined* to finish reading the book before bedtime.

3. **APPLY TO THE INSTRUCTION** Ask: If someone is *determined* to do something, would it be easy or hard to talk them out of it? Why?

4. **WORD PARTS** Run your hand under the three word parts *de-ter-mined* as students read each part and then read the whole word.

distinguishes

1. Someone who *distinguishes* one thing from another sees the differences between them.

2. **EXAMPLES** He *distinguishes* an oak tree from a maple tree. She *distinguishes* between the sound of a clarinet and a flute.

3. **APPLY TO THE INSTRUCTION** Ask: Which words are close in meaning to *distinguishes*: mimics, sets apart, confuses, or separates?

4. **WORD PARTS** Run your hand under the four word parts *dis-tin-guish-es* as students read each part and then read the whole word.

efficient

1. If you are *efficient*, you are able to do things without wasting time, energy, or materials.

2. **EXAMPLES** Using the dishwasher was more *efficient* than washing the dishes by hand. Planning our trip ahead of time was an *efficient* way to travel.

3. **APPLY TO THE INSTRUCTION** Ask: Would you rather have an *efficient* car or a fancy car? Why?

4. **WORD PARTS** Run your hand under the three word parts *ef-fi-cient* as students read each part and then read the whole word.

headway

1. To make *headway* is to move forward.

2. **EXAMPLES** The rowers didn't make much *headway* as they paddled against the current. In the past fifty years, science has made *headway* in the area of space exploration.

3. **APPLY TO THE INSTRUCTION** Say: Imagine you and a friend are filling bags with raked leaves. You have very few leaves in your bag and your friend's bag is almost full. Who is making *headway*? Explain.

4. **WORD PARTS** Students can identify the two smaller words *head* and *way* in the compound word.

progress

1. *Progress* is growth or improvement.

2. **EXAMPLES** They worked all weekend and made *progress* on their project for the science fair. The girl is showing a lot of *progress* in learning to play the piano.

3. **APPLY TO THE INSTRUCTION** Have students list things that are examples of *progress* they have made this year.

4. **WORD PARTS** Run your hand under the two word parts *prog-ress* as students read each part and then read the whole word.

Let's Learn Amazing Words

Definitions, examples, applications, and **sound-spellings** to use with the Oral Vocabulary Routine each week.

Routine *Oral Vocabulary*

complex

❶ Something that is *complex* is made up of a number of parts that work together. *Complex* can also mean "hard to understand."

❷ **EXAMPLES** The car's engine is *complex*. The math problem was *complex* and hard to solve.

❸ **APPLY TO THE INSTRUCTION** Have students name one word that means the opposite of *complex* and another word that means about the same as *complex*.

❹ **WORD PARTS** Run your hand under the two word parts *com-plex* as students read each part and then read the whole word.

futuristic

❶ If something is *futuristic*, it is like something in the future.

❷ **EXAMPLES** The story about a family traveling on a spaceship is *futuristic*. The science fair was full of *futuristic* inventions.

❸ **APPLY TO THE INSTRUCTION** Ask students to draw a *futuristic*-looking object or structure and tell about it.

❹ **WORD PARTS** Run your hand under the four word parts *fu-tur-is-tic* as students read each part and then read the whole word.

galaxy

❶ A galaxy is a group of billions of stars forming one system.

❷ **EXAMPLES** Our solar system is in the Milky Way *galaxy*. A large *galaxy* can have more than a trillion stars.

❸ **APPLY TO THE INSTRUCTION** Have students list space objects that can be found in our *galaxy*.

❹ **WORD PARTS** Run your hand under the three word parts *gal-ax-y* as students read each part and then read the whole word.

scientific

❶ Something that is *scientific* uses the facts and laws of science.

❷ **EXAMPLE** The group tried to reach a *scientific* conclusion about the rocks they were studying.

❸ **APPLY TO THE INSTRUCTION** Point out that global warming is a *scientific* discovery. Have students give examples of other *scientific* discoveries.

❹ **WORD PARTS** Run your hand under the four word parts *sci-en-tif-ic* as students read each part and then read the whole word.

telescope

❶ A *telescope* is a device you look through that makes objects far away appear nearer and larger.

❷ **EXAMPLES** The *telescope* allowed us to see the night sky clearly. Scientists have used a powerful *telescope* to view the surface of the moon.

❸ **APPLY TO THE INSTRUCTION** Have students list things they might be able to see through a *telescope*. Ask what time of day might be best for using a *telescope* to see those things, and why.

❹ **WORD PARTS** Run your hand under the three word parts *tel-e-scope* as students read each part and then read the whole word.

universe

❶ The *universe* is everything there is, including everything in space.

❷ **EXAMPLES** The planet Earth is one small part of the *universe*. Everything that exists is part of the *universe*.

❸ **APPLY TO THE INSTRUCTION** Ask: Can you name something that is not part of the *universe*? Have students use *universe* to explain their answers.

❹ **WORD PARTS** Run your hand under the three word parts *u-ni-verse* as students read each part and then read the whole word.

Unit 1 Word List

Unit 1 Week 1 Diversity

Closed Syllables with Short Vowels

absent	different	husbands	practice
admit	dinner	impress	project
bonnet	dollar	invent	puppet
bottle	dragons	lesson	ribbon
button	eggplant	listen	shepherds
children	followed	messages	velvet
cinnamon	fossil	mumbled	understanding
connect	gallons	mustard	weddings
cultural	hollow	pancakes	witness
customs	hundred	plantains	
differ	hundreds	plaster	

Concept Vocabulary

backgrounds
culture
ethnic
homesick
translated
understanding

Unit 1 Week 2 Exploration

Closed Syllables with Long Vowels

admire	confine	inhale	outrage
arrived	confused	inside	reptile
arrives	device	intone	subscribe
compete	escape	invite	tadpole
compute	escaped	mistake	trombone
concede	explore	mistakes	

Concept Vocabulary

area
confused
device
perspective
pioneers
territory
voyage

Unit 1 Week 3 Travel America

Plurals and Inflected Endings -s, -es, -ies

ants	hundreds	promises	views
attractions	landmarks	raises	volunteers
blisters	lanes	roads	walkers
bridges	looks	routes	walks
cars	lots	shoes	walls
changes	marshmallows	sights	weighs
coaches	miles	sounds	workers
congratulations	Millers	stations	
cousins	millions	stops	crosses
days	months	survivors	crutches
desserts	needs	televisions	
destinations	organizes	things	cities
dollars	parts	tons	companies
ears	passengers	tourists	families
flights	patients	towers	flurries
forms	pictures	towns	itineraries
friends	places	travelers	memories
groups	planes	travels	movies
headphones	pledges	treatments	stories
highways	postcards	valleys	worries
hours	pours	vehicles	

Concept Vocabulary

itineraries
journey
miles
mode
route
transportation
views

Unit 1 Word List

Unit 1 Week 4 The Southwest

Verb Endings

added	lived	tired	filming
asked	looked	turned	frightening
attached	loved	used	hiking
attracted	needed	visited	hoping
blamed	opened	waited	looking
called	painted	walked	parking
carved	passed	wanted	racing
changed	picked	watched	rising
chatted	pinned	whispered	running
created	pointed	wondered	shopping
destroyed	pounded	worked	sitting
died	pulled		sleeping
filmed	reached	baking	slipping
followed	remembered	biting	standing
grabbed	roamed	climbing	stunning
granted	searched	driving	swimming
herded	sobbed	enjoying	thrilling
hired	spotted	facing	
improved	starred	falling	
learned	striped	fighting	

Concept Vocabulary

arid
canyon
carved
cliffs
frontier
guide
hiking

Unit 1 Week 5 The West

Prefixes *un-, re-, in-, dis-*

unbelievable	unspoiled	reappear	disagree
unbroken	unspoken	redirect	disapprove
uncertain	unusual	reread	disconnect
unclear	unwelcoming	rerecord	dishonest
		indefinite	
		indirect	
		injustice	
		insincere	

Concept Vocabulary

astonishing
eruptions
formed
gigantic
naturally
unbelievable

Syllables with *r*-Controlled *ar, or, ore*

are	jar	fortune	portrait
artists	large	horizons	sport
bombard	largest	important	tornado
carpet	radar	inform	
carton	solar	information	explore
cartoons	stars	meteorologist	ignore
darling	tarnish	morning	more
darted		north	restore
garlic	for	or	wore
harbor	forgery	order	
hard	forget	performance	
	forgot	popcorn	

Concept Vocabulary
- awareness
- comprehend
- exhibit
- experience
- horizons
- interactive

Syllables with *r*-Controlled *er, ir, ur*

another	larger	printer	thirty
better	later	quarterback	virtue
certain	members	remember	
certainly	never	reporter	curtain
deliver	newspaper	scenery	future
determined	other	servant	nursery
disaster	others	soccer	pursue
father	percussion	teacher	treasure
gathering	perfect	together	turkey
grandmother	perfume		turn
her	person	circle	turning
interested	players	circus	turtle
ladder	posters	thirteen	

Concept Vocabulary
- accomplished
- collaboration
- cooperate
- members
- orchestra
- teamwork

Comparative Endings *-er, -est*

angrier	louder	fastest	safest
bluer	stronger	funniest	scariest
crazier	sturdier	greatest	silliest
earlier	wider	hardest	simplest
fancier		highest	sturdiest
harder	craziest	largest	surest
higher	earliest	lightest	widest
longer	fanciest	longest	

Concept Vocabulary
- extraordinary
- fantastic
- inspiration
- sculptures
- skillful

Unit 2 **Week 4** **A Job Well Done**

Open (V/CV) and Closed (VC/V) Syllables

				Concept Vocabulary
amazed	locate	animals	living	career
apart	making	body	model	contribution
before	music	closet	money	energy
began	nature	columns	planet	gear
camel	never	drawings	positive	option
famous	notice	elevated	project	workers
female	paper	experienced	promise	
fever	papers	family	second	
finally	pilot	finish	study	
humor	Rosie	finished		
Jamie	safer	glamorous		
legal	solution	knowing		
lemon	super	linen		

Unit 2 **Week 5** **Our Nation's Capital**

Suffixes -ly, -ful, -ness, -less

				Concept Vocabulary
daily	frightful	awareness	breathless	capital
neatly	joyful	bitterness	countless	Capitol
sadly	powerful	kindness	heartless	dedicated
slowly	thoughtful	laziness	timeless	executive
smoothly	wonderful	sweetness		memorabilia
surprisingly				museum
wildly				

Unit 3 Word List

Unit 3 Week 1 Nature's Designs

Long a Spelled *ai, ay*

available	painted	always	Saturday
claim	plain	birthday	say
contain	proclaim	clay	subway
exclaim	rain	crayfish	today
explain	rainbow	days	way
explained	raindrop	may	
fainted	rained	maybe	
gain	regain	layered	
paint	wait	replay	

Concept Vocabulary

arrangement
available
landscape
patterns
repeats
reveal
snowfall

Unit 3 Week 2 Animal Journeys

Long e Spelled *e, ee, ea*

be	feet	three	heaters
because	free	tree	leading
before	freezer	trees	leaves
ecology	freedom		leaving
equator	freezing	clean	ordeal
even	geese	downstream	reach
maybe	keep	each	read
remember	need	eagerly	reason
	needed	easier	seasons
between	see	easily	southeast
deep	seeds	eastern	streams
deeper	seen	eat	
feed	sheep	heat	
feeders	sleepless	heater	

Concept Vocabulary

migrate
observe
refuges
shelter
zones

Unit 3 Week 3 Our Spinning Planet

Contractions

it's	we'll	couldn't	won't
let's	I'll	didn't	wouldn't
that's	you'll	doesn't	
		mustn't	could've
I'm	aren't	shouldn't	would've
	can't		

Concept Vocabulary

dazed
hemisphere
nocturnal
revolution
rotation
vacation

Unit 3 Word List

Unit 3 Week 4 Storms

Long o Spelled *oa, ow*

approaching	floating	bowling	snow
bloated	foamy	follow	swallow
charcoal	loaded	outgrow	swallowed
coast	tugboat	rainbow	
coastal		slowly	

Concept Vocabulary
behavior
coast
inland
phenomenon
tsunami
unpredictable

Unit 3 Week 5 Going Green

Prefixes *mis-, non-, over-, pre-, mid-*

misfortune	overactive	precaution	midseason
misunderstand	overpriced	premature	midstream
	oversized	prepaid	midway
nonfiction		preview	midweek
nonrenewable			
nonstop			

Concept Vocabulary
benefits
cells
electricity
hydrogen
resources
solar

Unit 4 Word List

Unit 4 Week 1 Perception

Compound Words

anything	gentleman	sometimes	watercolor
cannot	handcuffed	stovetop	waterfall
Englishman	handcuffs	tabletop	workman
fireman	handmade	underground	
Frenchman	something	underwater	

Concept Vocabulary

illusion
invisible
magician
mysterious
perception
vanish

Unit 4 Week 2 Wild Things

Long *i* Spelled *igh, ie,* Final *y*

brightest	cries	deny	python
fighting	fireflies	dragonfly	satisfy
frightened	lie	dry	shy
higher	replied	fly	shyness
might	terrified	fry	skylight
nighttime		hydrant	try
sighing	cry	July	why
	crying	lullaby	

Concept Vocabulary

communication
instinct
protect
relationships
response
sense
young

Unit 4 Week 3 Secret Codes

Consonant + *le*

able	cradle	puzzle	stifle
angle	doubles	rifle	stumble
babble	example	ripple	tumble
Bittle	gentle	scrambles	twinkle
bubble	giggle	shuffle	uncle
bugle	middle	simple	unscramble
cable	noble	single	visible
crackle	possible	stable	

Concept Vocabulary

conceals
creative
exchange
interprets
transmit
visible

Unit 4 Word List

Unit 4 Week 4 Communication

Diphthongs *ou, ow /ou/*

around	surround	clowns	powerful
couches	thousand	coward	touchdown
countless	touchdown	download	towel
foundation	without	downstairs	township
grounded		downtown	
hourly	allowance	flowering	
shout	breakdown	frowning	

Concept Vocabulary

combine
conversation
dialect
phrase
region
shouts
symbols

Unit 4 Week 5 Finding Clues

Suffixes *-er, -or, -ish, -ous*

biker	collector	childish	curious
builder	director	foolish	dangerous
diver	editor	impish	joyous
explorer	inventor	Scottish	monstrous
officer	investigator	selfish	mysterious
reporter	senator	sheepish	nervous
			venomous

Concept Vocabulary

convince
curious
diver
evidence
explorer
investigate
scrutiny

Unit 5 Word List

Unit 5 Week 1 Emergencies

Diphthongs *oi, oy*

avoid	pointing		employer
broiler	poisonous	annoying	enjoying
coins	recoil	boy	oysters
moisture	sirloin	boyish	royal
noisiest	viewpoint	destroyed	royalty
point	voice	disloyal	toys

Concept Vocabulary

dangerous
destroyed
exciting
hazards
hero
profession

Unit 5 Week 2 Past Times

Common Syllables *-ion, -tion, -sion, -ture*

champion	civilizations	traditions	architecture
companion	Constitution	vacation	creature
region	generations		future
religion	irrigation	admission	lecture
	location	division	mature
attractions	pollution	fusion	picture
celebration	station	permission	pictures
civilization	tradition		

Concept Vocabulary

ancient
civilization
society
statue
theater
traditions

Unit 5 Week 3 Adventures and Heroes

Syllables with Vowel Combinations *oo, ew, ue*

bamboo	spoon	knew	blueberry
boots	too	news	clueless
food	toolbox	outgrew	clues
foolish	toolboxes	renew	continued
groom	troop	view	glue
moon		withdrew	true
rooftop	cashew		untrue
scoop	dew	avenue	
soon	few	blue	

Concept Vocabulary

adventure
expeditions
forecasts
unfamiliar
wilderness

Unit 5 **Word List**

Unit 5 Week 4 Extreme Homes

Vowel Sound in *ball: a, al, au, aw, augh, ough*

water	hallway	assault	awful	
waterproof	install	Australia	hawkish	
	smallest	Australian	jawbone	
all	stalking	Australians	outlaw	
also	tall	caution	straw	
boardwalk	walking	faulty		
called	walls	hauled	daughter	
fallen		laundry	coughing	
		pauper		

Concept Vocabulary

adapted
architecture
burrow
extreme
homesteaders
prairie

Unit 5 Week 5 The Moon

Suffixes -hood, -ment, -y, -en

adulthood	embarrassment	lucky	earthen
brotherhood	enjoyment	messy	golden
childhood	improvement	salty	wooden
		shadowy	
amazement	cloudy		
contentment	dirty	ashen	

Concept Vocabulary

astronaut
astronomers
craters
mission
myths
satellite

Unit 6 Word List

Unit 6 Week 1 Opportunity Knocks

Syllables with Short e Spelled ea

breakfast	headline	ready	unhealthy
breath	heaven	spread	wealth
feather	heavier	steady	weather
gingerbread	instead	sweating	
head	read	threatening	

Concept Vocabulary

circumstances
conviction
devised
model
procrastinates
suggested

Unit 6 Week 2 Challenges

Syllables with Vowels oo in foot, u in put

barefoot	crooked	underfoot	pushed
book	driftwood	unhook	put
boyhood	football		putting
cookbook	goodness	input	
cookie	outlook	output	

Concept Vocabulary

achieved
furious
hurdles
perseverance
personality
timid

Unit 6 Week 3 American Journeys

Syllables with Long i: -ind, -ild, Long o: -ost, -old

find	rewind	almost	behold
findings		ghostly	cold
grinder	childhood	hostess	household
kind	mildly	most	resold
kindness	wildlife	outpost	
remind		utmost	

Concept Vocabulary

appreciate
awkward
barrier
immigration
international
occupations

Unit 6 Word List

Unit 6 Week 4 Grand Gestures

Syllables V/V

created	idea	piano	rodeo
diary	Indiana	poetry	ruined
diet	iodine	quiet	science
doing	librarian	radio	sundial
experience	meteor	react	triumph
flying	museum	real	video
fuel	nutrient	realize	violets

Concept Vocabulary

apply
determined
distinguishes
efficient
headway
progress

Unit 6 Week 5 Space

Related Words

astronomer	imaginary	scenery	telegraph
astronomy	imagination	scenes	telepathy
discover	imagine	scenic	telephone
discovered	real	science	telescope
discovery	realistic	science fiction	television
future	relate	scientific	universal
futuristic	relationship	scientist	universe
imagery	relative	telecommute	university
images	scenario	telegram	

Concept Vocabulary

complex
futuristic
galaxy
scientific
telescope
universe

Student's Name _____   Date _____

Observation Checklist

Use this checklist to record your observations of students' reading skills and behaviors.

	Always (Proficient)	Sometimes (Developing)	Rarely (Novice)
Applies knowledge of letter-sounds to decode words			
Uses word structure and syllabication to decode longer words			
Reads at an appropriate reading rate			
Reads with appropriate intonation and stress			
Uses concept vocabulary in discussion			
Previews and uses prior knowledge to understand text			
Asks questions while reading			
Recognizes main ideas			
Recognizes sequence			
Makes comparisons and contrasts			
Draws conclusions to understand text			
Understands story structure (character, setting, plot)			
Summarizes plot or main ideas accurately			
Responds thoughtfully to the text			

General Comments

Word Parts

Students need to become familiar with meaningful parts of words so they can recognize them instantly as they read. This will improve both their reading fluency and the size of their vocabulary. Teach the meaning and pronunciation of these common word parts whenever students encounter them in words they are reading.

Common Prefixes	Meaning	Examples
bi-	two	bicycle
bio-	life	biology
dis-	not; opposite	disagree, disarm, disobey, disrespect
geo-	earth	geology
in-, im-, il-, ir-	not	injustice, insane, impolite, impossible, illegal, illiterate, irregular, irresponsible
micro-	small	microscope
mid-	during; middle	midnight, midsummer, midyear
mis-	bad; not; wrongly	misbehave, misfire, misspell, misunderstand
mono-	one	monologue, monorail
non-	not	nonfiction, nonstop, nonviolent
out-	surpassing	outbid, outdo, outlive
over-	over; too much	overdo, overlook, overpriced
photo-	light	photocopy, photosynthesis
post-	after	postwar
pre-	before	preview
re-	again	redo, retell, return, rewrite
tele-	far; distant	telescope, telephone, telegraph, television
tri-	three	triplets
un-	not	undo, unkind, uncut, unhappy, unsafe, unlucky
under-	below; less than	underpriced, underground, undercover

Common Suffixes	Meaning	Examples
-er, -or	doer; one who	teacher, painter, writer, actor, sailor, visitor, inventor
-ful	full of	careful, hopeful, helpful, wonderful
-hood	state or quality of	childhood, falsehood, adulthood
-ish	relating to	foolish, childish, selfish
-ism, -ist	belief in; one who believes in; one who is	communism, capitalism, capitalist
-less	without	fearless, careless, hopeless, harmless
-ly	like; characteristic of	quickly, happily, briefly, gently, sadly
-ment	action or process	enjoyment, government, amazement
-ness	state of; quality of	kindness, laziness, happiness, goodness
-ous, -eous, -ious	full of	dangerous, joyous, nervous, curious, delicious, courageous

Greek and Latin Roots	Meaning	Examples
astr, aster	star	astronomy, asterisk
aud	hear	audible, audience, audio, inaudible, auditorium
tract	drag; pull; draw from	tractor, attraction, detract, subtract
spect	look	inspect
port	carry	porter, portable, export
dict	to say	dictate, diction, dictionary, edict, predict, verdict
rupt	to break	erupt, rupture, abrupt, disruptive, bankrupt
scrib, scrip	to write	scribble, describe, postscript
ped	foot	pedestrian, pedal
equi	equal	equal, equate, equation, equitable
pop	people	popular, population

Name

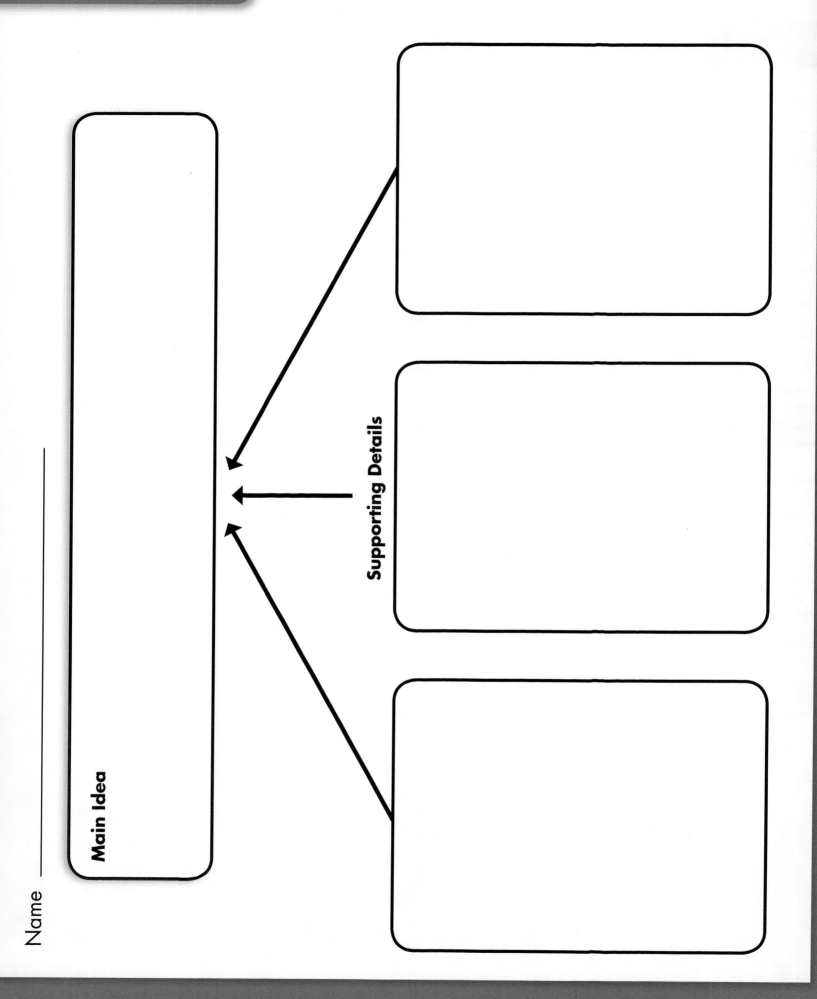

Main Idea

Supporting Details

Name _____

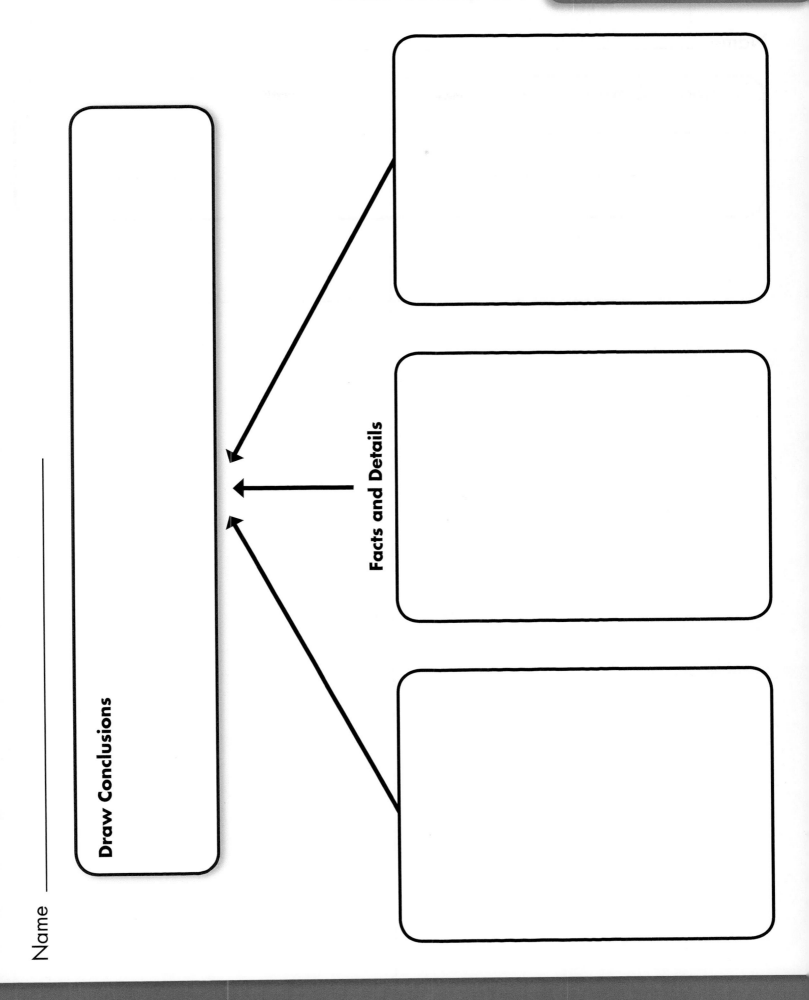

Draw Conclusions

Facts and Details

Name _____

Compare/Contrast Words

_____   _____   _____   _____

_____   _____   _____   _____

Name _____

Compare/Contrast Words

_____   _____   _____   _____

_____   _____   _____   _____

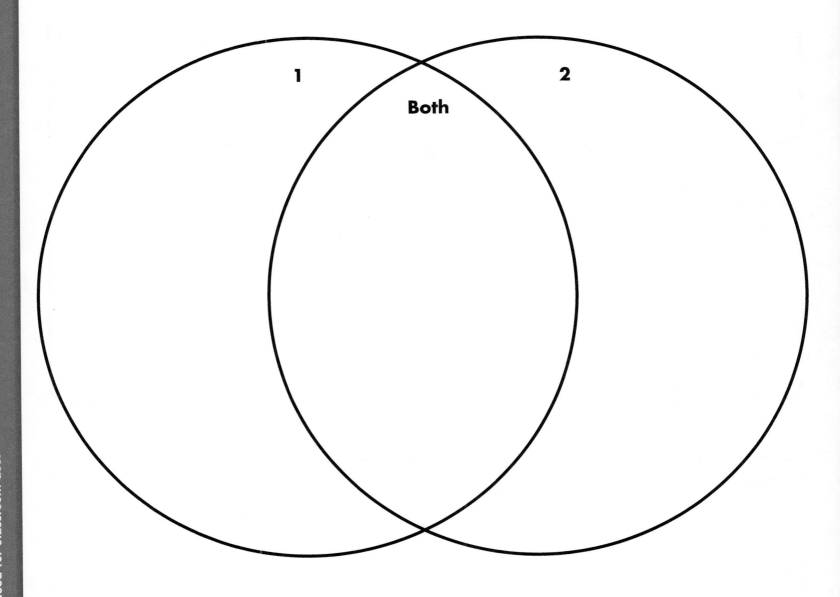

1

Both

2

Name _____

Sequence Words

_____   _____   _____   _____

_____   _____   _____   _____

Beginning

Middle

End

Name _____

Sequence Words

_____ _____ _____ _____

_____ _____ _____ _____

Steps:

1

2

3

4

5

Bookmarks

Fiction

- Who are the characters?

- Where does the story take place?

- When does the story take place?

- What is the problem or goal?

- How is the problem solved or the goal reached?

Nonfiction

- What did I learn?

- What is this mainly about?

Connections Between *My Sidewalks* and Scott Foresman *Reading Street*

My Sidewalks is designed to parallel essential elements in *Scott Foresman Reading Street.*
Connections between the two programs are reflected in the indexes of the Teacher's Guides.

- Corresponding **priority skills** ensure that students receive instruction in the critical elements of reading—phonemic awareness, phonics, fluency, vocabulary, and comprehension.

- Parallel **concepts and themes** enable smooth transitions between *My Sidewalks* and *Reading Street.*

- Consistency of **scaffolded instruction** promotes familiarity with routines and terminology.

- Alignment of **before, during, and after reading strategies** reinforces successful reading habits.

- **Comprehension** skill links provide Tier III readers with additional instruction and practice with main idea, compare/contrast, sequence, and drawing conclusions.

- **Vocabulary** links provide Tier III readers with additional instruction and practice with oral vocabulary.

- Consistent procedures for **corrective feedback** promptly reveal and address student needs, providing guidance for error correction.

- Connected **writing** modes offer student opportunities to respond to literature.

- **Cross-curricular** links lay out the same science and social studies foundations for Tier III readers as for students in the core program.

Index

A

Activate prior knowledge. *See* Comprehension, Strategies.

Advertisement. *See* Graphic sources.

Affixes. *See* Word structure, prefixes, suffixes.

After reading comprehension strategies. *See* Comprehension, Strategies.

Animal fantasy. *See* Genres.

Antonyms. *See* Vocabulary, Development.

Assessment

Assessment Book, *Welcome to My Sidewalks,* 13; *V1* 61, 121, 181; *V2* 61, 121, 181

Benchmark Readers, *Welcome to My Sidewalks,* 13; *V1* vi; *V2* vi

classroom-based, *Welcome to My Sidewalks,* 13; *V1* 5, 6, 7, 9, 12, 17, 18, 19, 21, 24, 29, 30, 31, 33, 36, 41, 42, 43, 45, 48, 53, 54, 55, 57, 60, 65, 66, 67, 69, 72, 77, 78, 79, 81, 84, 89, 90, 91, 93, 96, 101, 102, 103, 105, 108, 113, 114, 115, 117, 120, 125, 126, 127, 129, 132, 137, 138, 139, 141, 144, 149, 150, 151, 153, 156, 161, 162, 163, 165, 168, 173, 174, 175, 177, 180; *V2* 5, 6, 7, 9, 12, 17, 18, 19, 21, 24, 29, 30, 31, 33, 36, 41, 42, 43, 45, 48, 53, 54, 55, 57, 60, 65, 66, 67, 69, 72, 77, 78, 79, 81, 84, 89, 90, 91, 93, 96, 101, 102, 103, 105, 108, 113, 114, 115, 117, 120, 125, 126, 127, 129, 132, 137, 138, 139, 141, 144, 149, 150, 151, 153, 156, 161, 162, 163, 165, 168, 173, 174, 175, 177, 180

diagnosis and placement, *Welcome to My Sidewalks,* 12, 14–15

DIBELS, *Welcome to My Sidewalks,* 12

End-of-Unit Test, *Welcome to My Sidewalks,* 13; *V1* 61, 121, 181; *V2* 61, 121, 181

exit criteria, *Welcome to My Sidewalks,* 13; *V1* 188; *V2* 188

fluency. *See* Fluency.

formal, *V1* 13, 25, 37, 49, 61, 73, 85, 97, 109, 121, 133, 145, 157, 169, 181; *V2* 13, 25, 37, 49, 61, 73, 85, 97, 109, 121, 133, 145, 157, 169, 181

progress monitoring, *Welcome to My Sidewalks,* 13; *V1* 5, 6, 7, 9, 12, 17, 18, 19, 21, 24, 29, 30, 31, 33, 36, 41, 42, 43, 45, 48, 53, 54, 55, 57, 60, 65, 66, 67, 69, 72, 77, 78, 79, 81, 84, 89, 90, 91, 93, 96, 101, 102, 103, 105, 108, 113, 114, 115, 117, 120, 125, 126, 127, 129, 132, 137, 138, 139, 141, 144, 149, 150, 151, 153, 156, 161, 162, 163, 165, 168, 173, 174, 175, 177, 180; *V2* 5, 6, 7, 9, 12, 17, 18, 19, 21, 24, 29, 30, 31, 33, 36, 41, 42, 43, 45, 48, 53, 54, 55, 57, 60, 65, 66, 67, 69, 72, 77, 78, 79, 81, 84, 89, 90, 91, 93, 96, 101, 102, 103, 105, 108, 113, 114, 115, 117, 120, 125, 126, 127, 129, 132, 137, 138, 139, 141, 144, 149, 150, 151, 153, 156, 161, 162, 163, 165, 168, 173, 174, 175, 177, 180

Audio-assisted reading. *See* Fluency.

Author's craft. *See* Literary craft.

Authors, program

Juel, Connie, *Welcome to My Sidewalks,* 8; *V1* viii; *V2* viii

Paratore, Jeanne R., *Welcome to My Sidewalks,* 8; *V1* viii; *V2* viii

Simmons, Deborah, *Welcome to My Sidewalks,* 8; *V1* viii; *V2* viii

Vaughn, Sharon, *Welcome to My Sidewalks,* 8; *V1* viii; *V2* viii

Automaticity. *See* Fluency.

B

Background, build. *See* Concept development.

Base words without spelling changes. *See* Word structure.

Base words with spelling changes. *See* Word structure.

Before reading comprehension strategies. *See* Comprehension, Strategies.

Benchmark Readers. *See* Assessment.

Bibliography, research. *See* Research.

Biography. *See* Genres.

Blending sounds. *See* Phonics.

C

Calendar. *See* Graphic sources.

Caption. *See* Graphic sources, illustration.

Character. *See* Comprehension, Strategies, story structure.

Charts/tables. *See* Graphic sources.

Chunking. *See* Word structure, multisyllabic words.

Comparative, superlative endings. *See* Spelling, word structure; Word structure, endings.

Compare and contrast. *See* Comprehension, Skills.

Compound words. *See* Spelling, word structure; Word structure.

Comprehension

Skills

compare and contrast, *V1* 42, 44, 46, 48, 54, 68, 70, 72, 102, 162, 164, 168, 174; *V2* 18, 20, 22, 24, 30, 32, 34, 36, 70, 78, 80, 82, 84, 94, 96, 174, 176, 178, 180

draw conclusions, *V1* 18, 22, 78, 80, 82, 84, 90, 92, 94, 96, 138, 150, 152, 154, 156, 166; *V2* 54, 56, 58, 60, 114, 118, 120, 138, 140, 142, 144, 150, 152, 154, 156

main idea and supporting details, *V1* 56, 58, 60, 114, 116, 118, 120, 140, 142, 144, 156, 176, 178; *V2* 42, 44, 46, 48, 102, 104, 106, 108, 116, 162, 164, 166, 168

sequence, *V1* 6, 8, 10, 12, 20, 24, 30, 32, 34, 36, 66, 104, 106, 108, 126, 128, 130, 132; *V2* 6, 8, 10, 12, 66, 68, 72, 90, 92, 126, 128, 130, 132

Strategies

activate prior knowledge, *V1* 4, 16, 28, 40, 52, 64, 76, 88, 100, 112, 124, 136, 148, 160, 172; *V2* 4, 16, 28, 40, 52, 64, 76, 88, 100, 112, 124, 136, 148, 160, 172

answer questions, *V1* 5, 7, 9, 11, 12, 17, 19, 21, 23, 24, 29, 31, 33, 35, 36, 41, 43, 45, 47, 48, 53, 55, 57, 59, 60, 65, 67, 69, 71, 72, 77, 79, 81, 83, 84, 89, 91, 93, 95, 96, 101, 103, 105, 107, 108, 113, 115, 117, 119, 120, 125, 127, 129, 131, 132, 137, 139, 141, 143, 144, 149, 151, 153, 155, 156, 161, 163, 165, 167, 168, 173, 175, 177, 179, 180; *V2* 5, 7, 9, 11, 12, 17, 19, 21, 23, 24, 29, 31, 33, 35, 36, 41, 43, 45, 47, 48, 53, 55, 57, 59, 60, 65, 67, 69, 71, 72, 77, 79, 81, 83, 84, 89, 91, 93, 95, 96, 101, 103, 105, 107, 108, 113, 115, 117, 119, 120, 125, 127, 129, 131, 132, 137, 139, 141, 143, 144, 149, 151, 153, 155, 156, 161, 163, 165, 167, 168, 173, 175, 177, 179, 180

41, 43, 45, 47, 53, 55, 57, 59, 65, 67, 69, 71, 77, 79, 81, 83, 89, 91, 93, 95, 101, 103, 105, 107, 113, 115, 117, 119, 125, 127, 129, 131, 137, 139, 141, 143, 149, 151, 153, 155, 161, 163, 165, 167, 173, 175, 177, 179

paired reading, *V1* 7, 11, 19, 23, 31, 35, 43, 47, 55, 59, 67, 71, 79, 83, 91, 95, 103, 107, 115, 119, 127, 131, 139, 143, 151, 155, 163, 167, 175, 179; *V2* 7, 11, 19, 23, 31, 35, 43, 47, 55, 59, 67, 71, 79, 83, 91, 95, 103, 107, 115, 119, 127, 131, 139, 143, 151, 155, 163, 167, 175, 179

phonics, *V1* 6, 18, 66, 78, 126, 138, 162; *V2* 18, 42, 66, 78, 90, 102, 126, 138, 150

word structure, *V1* 18, 30, 42, 54, 90, 102, 114, 150, 174; *V2* 6, 30, 54, 114, 162, 174

See also Fluency; Phonics.

Creative/dramatic activities. *See* Fluency, Readers' Theater.

Critical thinking. *See* Comprehension, Skills.

Cultures, appreciating. *See* Multicultural connections.

Derivations, word. *See* Vocabulary, Development, etymologies; Word structure, related words.

Descriptive writing. *See* Writing, writing purpose.

Diagram. *See* Graphic sources.

Dictionary/glossary, *V1* 4, 16, 28, 40, 52, 64, 76, 88, 100, 112, 124, 136, 148, 160, 172; *V2* 4, 16, 28, 40, 52, 64, 76, 88, 100, 112, 124, 136, 148, 160, 172

Differentiated instruction, *Welcome to My Sidewalks,* 10–11; *V1* xiv–xv; *V2* xiv–xv

Discussion. *See* Oral language.

Drama. *See* Fluency, Readers' Theater.

Draw conclusions. *See* Comprehension, Skills.

During reading comprehension strategies. *See* Comprehension, Strategies.

ELL

English Language Learners, *V1* xvi–xvii; *V2* xvi–xvii

Endings. *See* Spelling, word structure; Word structure.

Entertaining article. *See* Genres.

Error correction. *See* Corrective feedback.

ESL (English as a Second Language). *See* ELL.

Etymologies. *See* Vocabulary, Development.

Evaluation. *See* Assessment.

Expository nonfiction. *See* Genres.

Expository writing. *See* Writing, writing purpose.

Family involvement. *See* School-home connection.

Fantasy. *See* Genres.

Fine Arts. *See* Content-area texts.

Fix-up strategies. *See* Comprehension, Strategies.

Flexible grouping. *See* Differentiated instruction.

Fluency

accuracy, *V1* 13, 25, 37, 49, 61, 73, 85, 97, 109, 121, 133, 145, 157, 169, 181, 184–185; *V2* 13, 25, 37, 49, 61, 73, 85, 97, 109, 121, 133, 145, 157, 169, 181, 184–185

assessment (WCPM), *V1* 13, 25, 37, 49, 61, 73, 85, 97, 109, 121, 133, 145, 157, 169, 181; *V2* 13, 25, 37, 49, 61, 73, 85, 97, 109, 121, 133, 145, 157, 169, 181

audio-assisted reading, *V1* 5, 7, 9, 11, 17, 19, 21, 23, 29, 31, 33, 35, 41, 43, 45, 47, 53, 55, 57, 59, 65, 67, 69, 71, 77, 79, 81, 83, 89, 91, 93, 95, 101, 103, 105, 107, 113, 115, 117, 119, 125, 127, 129, 131, 137, 139, 141, 143, 149, 151, 153, 155, 161, 163, 165, 173, 175, 177, 179; *V2* 5, 7, 9, 11, 17, 19, 21, 23, 29, 31, 33, 35, 41, 43, 45, 47, 53, 55, 57, 59, 65, 67, 69, 71, 77, 79, 81, 83, 89, 91, 93, 95, 101, 103, 105, 107, 113, 115, 117, 119, 125, 127, 129, 131, 137, 139, 141, 143, 149, 151, 153, 155, 161, 163, 165, 167, 173, 175, 177, 179

automaticity, *V1* 13, 25, 37, 49, 61, 73, 85, 97, 109, 121, 133, 145, 157, 169, 181, 184–185; *V2* 13, 25, 37, 49, 61, 73, 85, 97, 109, 121, 133, 145, 157, 169, 181, 184–185

corrective feedback, *V1* 5, 7, 9, 11, 17, 19, 21, 23, 29, 31, 33, 35, 41, 43, 45, 47, 53, 55, 57, 59, 65, 67, 69, 71, 77, 79, 81, 83, 89, 91, 93, 95, 101, 103, 105, 107, 113, 115, 117, 119, 125, 127, 129, 131, 137, 139, 141, 143, 149, 151, 153, 155, 161, 163, 165, 167, 173, 175, 177, 179; *V2* 5, 7, 9, 17, 19, 21, 23, 29, 31, 33, 35, 41, 43, 45, 47, 53, 55, 57, 59, 65, 67, 69, 71, 77, 79, 81, 83, 89, 91, 93, 95, 101, 103, 105, 107, 113, 115, 117, 119, 125, 127, 129, 131, 137, 139, 141, 143, 149, 151, 153, 155, 161, 163, 165, 167, 173, 175, 177, 179

fluency probes. *See* Fluency, assessment.

modeling by teacher, *Welcome to My Sidewalks,* 28; *V1* 5, 17, 29, 41, 53, 65, 77, 89, 101, 113, 125, 137, 149, 161, 173; *V2* 5, 17, 29, 41, 53, 65, 77, 89, 101, 113, 125, 137, 149, 161, 173

oral reading, *Welcome to My Sidewalks,* 28–29; *V1* 5, 7, 9, 11, 17, 19, 21, 29, 31, 33, 41, 43, 45, 53, 55, 57, 65, 67, 69, 71, 77, 79, 81, 83, 89, 91, 93, 95, 101, 103, 105, 107, 113, 115, 117, 119, 125, 127, 129, 131, 137, 139, 141, 143, 149, 151, 153, 155, 161, 163, 165, 167, 173, 175, 177, 179; *V2* 5, 7, 9, 17, 19, 21, 23, 29, 31, 33, 35, 41, 43, 45, 47, 53, 55, 57, 59, 65, 67, 69, 71, 77, 79, 81, 83, 89, 91, 93, 95, 101, 103, 105, 107, 113, 115, 117, 119, 125, 127, 129, 131, 137, 139, 141, 143, 149, 151, 153, 155, 161, 163, 165, 167, 173, 175, 177, 179

paired reading, *V1* 7, 11, 19, 23, 31, 35, 43, 47, 55, 59, 67, 71, 79, 83, 91, 95, 103, 107, 115, 119, 127, 131, 139, 143, 151, 155, 163, 167, 175, 179; *V2* 7, 11, 23, 35, 47, 59, 67, 71, 79, 83, 91, 95, 103, 107, 115, 119, 127, 131, 139, 143, 151, 155, 163, 167, 175, 179

Readers' Theater, *V1* 11, 23, 35, 47, 59, 71, 83, 95, 107, 119, 131, 143, 155, 167, 179; *V2* 11, 23, 35, 47, 59, 71, 83, 95, 107, 119, 131, 143, 155, 167, 179

repeated reading, *Welcome to My Sidewalks,* 28–29; *V1* 5, 7, 9, 11, 17, 19, 21, 29, 31, 33, 41, 43, 45, 53, 55, 57, 65, 67, 69, 71, 77, 79, 81, 83, 89, 91, 93, 95, 101, 103, 105, 107, 113, 115, 117, 119, 125, 127, 129, 131, 137, 139, 141, 143, 149, 151, 153, 155, 161, 163, 165, 167, 173, 175, 177, 179; *V2* 5, 7, 9, 17, 19, 21, 23, 29, 31, 33, 35, 41, 43, 45, 47, 53, 55, 57, 59, 65, 67, 69, 71, 77, 79, 81, 83, 89, 91, 93, 95, 101, 103, 105, 107, 113, 115, 117, 119, 125, 127, 129, 131, 137, 139, 141, 143, 149, 151, 153, 155, 161, 163, 165, 167, 173, 175, 177, 179

word reading, *Welcome to My Sidewalks,* 20

Fluency probes. *See* Fluency, assessment.

Focus. *See* Writing, writing elements.

Generate questions. *See* Comprehension, Strategies, ask questions.

Genres

animal fantasy, *V1* 23; *V2* 11

Graphic and semantic organizers

Graphic sources

Greek and Latin roots. *See* Word structure.

Grouping students for instruction. *See* Differentiated instruction.

Guided oral reading. Guided oral reading is part of every lesson plan.

Health. *See* Content-area texts.

Higher order thinking skills. *See* Comprehension, Strategies.

Historical fiction. *See* Genres.

Historical nonficton. *See* Genres.

Home-school connection. *See* School-home connection.

Homework. *See* School-home connection.

How-to article. *See* Genres.

Idioms. *See* Vocabulary, Development.

Illustrations. *See* Graphic sources.

Immediate corrective feedback. *See* Corrective feedback.

Inference. *See* Comprehension, Skills, draw conclusions. Inferential thinking questions appears throughout each lesson.

Inflected endings. *See* Spelling, word structure; Word structure, endings, inflected.

Informal assessment. *See* Assessment, classroom-based.

Informational article. *See* Genres.

Judgments, make. *See* Comprehension, Skills, draw conclusions.

Language, oral. *See* Oral language.

Latin and Greek roots. *See* Word structure.

Legend. *See* Genres.

Letter. *See* Genres.

List. *See* Graphic sources.

Listening comprehension

Literal comprehension. Literal comprehension questions appear throughout each lesson.

Literary craft

    author's craft, *V1* 83; *V2* 35

Literary devices

    point of view, *V1* 71; *V2* 11

    See also Sound devices and poetic elements.

Main idea and supporting details. *See* Comprehension, Skills.

Make connections. *See* Connections, make.

Make judgments. *See* Comprehension, Skills, draw conclusions.

Map. *See* Graphic sources.

Mapping selection. *See* Graphic and semantic organizers, story map.

Math. *See* Content-area texts.

Metacognition. *See* Comprehension, Strategies, self-monitor.

Modeling. Teacher modeling and think alouds are presented throughout the lessons.

Monitor Progress. *See* Assessment, progress monitoring.

Multicultural connections, *V1* 4, 5, 7, 9, 11, 12, 13, 72, 167; *V2* 23, 47, 115, 149, 151, 155, 156

Multisyllabic words. *See* Word structure.

Music. *See* Content-area texts.

Mystery. *See* Genres.

Myth. *See* Genres.

Narrative nonfiction. *See* Genres.

Narrative writing. *See* Writing, writing purpose.

New Literacies. *See* Content-area texts, technology.

Nonfiction. *See* Genres.

Note-taking. *See* Comprehension, Strategies, fix-up strategies.

Oral language

discussion, *V1* 4, 13, 16, 25, 28, 37, 40, 49, 52, 61, 64, 73, 76, 85, 88, 97, 100, 109, 112, 121, 124, 133, 136, 145, 148, 157, 160, 169, 172, 181; *V2* 4, 13, 16, 25, 28, 37, 40, 49, 52, 61, 64, 73, 76, 85, 88, 97, 100, 109, 112, 121, 124, 133, 136, 145, 148, 157, 160, 169, 172, 181

questions, *V1* 5, 7, 9, 11, 12, 17, 19, 21, 23, 24, 29, 31, 33, 35, 36, 41, 43, 45, 47, 48, 53, 55, 57, 59, 60, 65, 67, 69, 71, 72, 77, 79, 81, 83, 84, 89, 91, 93, 95, 96, 101, 103, 105, 107, 108, 113, 115, 117, 119, 120, 125, 127, 129, 131, 132, 137, 139, 141, 143, 144, 149, 151, 153, 155, 156, 161, 163, 165, 167, 168, 173, 175, 177, 179, 180; *V2* 5, 7, 9, 11, 12, 17, 19, 21, 23, 24, 29, 31, 33, 35, 36, 41, 43, 45, 47, 48, 53, 55, 57, 59, 60, 65, 67, 69, 71, 72, 77, 79, 81, 83, 84, 89, 91, 93, 95, 96, 101, 103, 105, 107, 108, 113, 115, 117, 119, 120, 125, 127, 129, 131, 132, 137, 139, 141, 143, 144, 149, 151, 153, 155, 156, 161, 163, 165, 167, 168, 173, 175, 177, 179, 180

retelling, *V1* 13, 25, 37, 49, 61, 73, 85, 97, 109, 121, 133, 145, 157, 169, 181; *V2* 13, 25, 37, 49, 61, 73, 85, 97, 109, 121, 133, 145, 157, 169, 181

summary, *V1* 7, 12, 19, 24, 31, 36, 43, 48, 55, 60, 67, 72, 79, 84, 91, 96, 103, 108, 115, 120, 127, 132, 139, 144, 151, 156, 163, 168, 175, 180; *V2* 7, 12, 19, 24, 31, 36, 43, 48, 55, 60, 67, 72, 79, 84, 91, 96, 103, 108, 115, 120, 127, 132, 139, 144, 151, 156, 163, 168, 175, 180

Oral reading. *See* Fluency.

Oral vocabulary

concept words, *V1* 4, 6, 8, 10, 16, 18, 20, 22, 28, 30, 32, 34, 40, 42, 44, 46, 52, 54, 56, 58, 64, 66, 68, 70, 76, 78, 80, 82, 88, 90, 92, 94, 100, 102, 104, 106, 112, 114, 116, 118, 124, 126, 128, 130, 136, 138, 140, 142, 148, 150, 152, 154, 160, 162, 164, 166, 172, 174, 176, 178; *V2* 4, 6, 8, 10, 16, 18, 20, 22, 28, 30, 32, 34, 40, 42, 44, 46, 52, 54, 56, 58, 64, 66, 68, 70, 76, 78, 80, 82, 88, 90, 92, 94, 100, 102, 104, 106, 112, 114, 116, 118, 124, 126, 128, 130, 136, 138, 140, 142, 148, 150, 152, 154, 160, 162, 164, 166, 172, 174, 176, 178

Organization. *See* Writing, writing elements.

Organizing information. *See* Graphic and semantic organizers.

Paired reading. *See* Comprehension, Strategies; Fluency.

Personal narrative. *See* Writing, writing purpose.

Phonics

blend sounds to decode words, *V1* 9, 21, 33, 45, 57, 81, 105, 117, 129; *V2* 9

corrective feedback, *V1* 6, 18, 66, 78, 126, 138, 162; *V2* 18, 42, 66, 78, 90, 102, 126, 138, 150

multisyllabic words. *See* Word structure.

vowel digraphs

ai, ay, *V1* 126, 128, 129

ea, ee, *V1* 138, 140

ie, igh, *V2* 18, 20

oa, ow, *V1* 162, 164

oo, /ü/, *V2* 90, 92

oo, u, /ü/, *V2* 138, 140

vowel diphthongs

oi, *V2* 66, 68

ou, *V2* 42, 44

ow, *V2* 42, 44

oy, *V2* 66, 68

vowel patterns, less common

a, al, *V2* 102, 104

au, aw, *V2* 102, 104

ew, ue, *V2* 90, 92

vowels, long

e, y, *V1* 138, 140

i, y, *V2* 18, 20, 21, 150, 152

o, *V2* 150, 152

vowels, r-controlled

ar, *V1* 66, 68

er, ir, ur, *V1* 78, 80, 81

or, *V1* 66, 68

vowels, short

ea /e/, *V2* 126, 128

word parts. *See* Word structure.

Photo essay. *See* Genres.

Pictures. *See* Comprehension, Strategies, pictures clues; Graphic sources, illustrations.

Plurals. *See* Spelling, word structure; Word structure.

Poetic devices. *See* Sound devices and poetic elements.

Poetry. *See* Genres.

Point of view. *See* Literary devices.

Research

Spelling

Text structure. *See* Comprehension, Strategies.

Think alouds. *See* Comprehension, Strategies; Concept development.

Tiers of intervention, *Welcome to My Sidewalks,* 4; *V1* iv; *V2* iv

Timed reading. *See* Fluency, assessment.

Time line. *See* Graphic and semantic organizers; Graphic sources.

Trade books. *See* Self-selected reading.

Unfamiliar words. *See* Vocabulary, Strategies.

Venn diagram. *See* Graphic and semantic organizers.

Vocabulary

Development

antonyms, *V2* 46, 94

concept vocabulary, *Welcome to My Sidewalks,* 23; *V1* 2, 4, 6, 8, 10, 12, 14, 16, 18, 20, 22, 24, 26, 28, 30, 32, 34, 36, 38, 40, 42, 44, 46, 48, 50, 52, 54, 56, 58, 60, 62, 64, 66, 68, 70, 72, 74, 76, 78, 80, 82, 84, 86, 88, 90, 92, 94, 96, 98, 100, 102, 104, 106, 108, 110, 112, 114, 116, 118, 120, 122, 124, 126, 128, 130, 132, 134, 136, 138, 140, 142, 144, 146, 148, 150, 152, 154, 156, 158, 160, 162, 164, 166, 168, 170, 172, 174, 176, 178, 180; *V2* 2, 4, 6, 8, 10, 12, 14, 16, 18, 20, 22, 24, 26, 28, 30, 32, 34, 36, 38, 40, 42, 44, 46, 48, 50, 52, 54, 56, 58, 60, 62, 64, 66, 68, 70, 72, 74, 76, 78, 80, 82, 84, 86, 88, 90, 92, 94, 96, 98, 100, 102, 104, 106, 108, 110, 112, 114, 116, 118, 120, 122, 124, 126, 128, 130, 132, 134, 136, 138, 140, 142, 144, 146, 148, 150, 152, 154, 156, 158, 160, 162, 164, 166, 168, 170, 172, 174, 176, 178, 180

etymologies, *V1* 47

Greek and Latin roots. *See* Word structure.

idioms, *V2* 24, 47

synonyms, *V2* 61, 94

Strategies

concept definition map. *See* Concept development, concept definition mapping.

context clues, *V1* 107, 141, 153, 165, 177; *V2* 93, 119, 141, 177

cumulative review, *V1* 12, 24, 36, 48, 60, 72, 84, 96, 108, 120, 132, 144, 156, 168, 180; *V2* 12, 24, 36, 48, 60, 72, 84, 96, 108, 120, 132, 144, 156, 168, 180

dictionary/glossary. *See* Dictionary/glossary.

semantic map (concept web). *See* Concept development, semantic map (concept web).

Tested Vocabulary Cards, *Welcome to My Sidewalks,* 20, *V1* 4, 16, 28, 40, 52, 64, 76, 88, 100, 112, 124, 136, 148, 160, 172; *V2* 4, 16, 28, 40, 52, 64, 76, 88, 100, 112, 124, 136, 148, 160, 172

unfamiliar words, *V1* 107, 141, 153, 165, 177; *V2* 93, 119, 141, 177

Web. *See* Graphic and semantic organizers, concept web.

Word Reading. *See* Fluency.

Word structure

base words

without spelling changes, *V1* 42, 44, 90, 92

with spelling changes, *V1* 30, 32, 42, 44, 90, 92, 93, 106

compound words, *V1* 10, 21; *V2* 6, 8, 9, 33, 57

contractions, *V1* 150, 152

corrective feedback, *V1* 18, 30, 42, 54, 90, 102, 114, 150, 174; *V2* 6, 30, 54, 114, 162, 174

endings, comparative/superlative, *V1* 90, 92, 93

endings, inflected, *V1* 30, 32, 42, 44, 45

Greek and Latin roots, *V2* 70, 118, 130

multisyllabic words, *V1* 4, 9, 16, 21, 28, 33, 40, 45, 52, 57, 64, 66, 68, 69, 76, 88, 100, 112, 124, 136, 148, 160, 172; *V2* 4, 16, 28, 33, 40, 45, 52, 57, 64, 69, 76, 88, 100, 112, 124, 136, 148, 160, 172

plurals, *V1* 30, 32, 106

prefixes, *V1* 54, 56, 82, 94, 130, 153, 154, 166, 174, 176, 178, 179

related words, *V1* 106, 118, 142; *V2* 22, 34, 106, 142, 174, 176

root words, *V1* 22, 58, 178; *V2* 82

suffixes, *V1* 34, 70, 114, 116, 117; *V2* 10, 54, 56, 58, 114, 116

syllable patterns

closed with long vowels, *V1* 18, 20

closed with short vowels, *V1* 6, 8

common, *V2* 78, 80

consonant + *le,* *V2* 30, 32

VC/CV, *V1* 66, 68

VC/V; V/CV, *V1* 102, 104, 105

V/V, *V2* 162, 164

Word study. *See* Phonics; Vocabulary; Word structure.

Writing

journal, *V1* 5, 17, 29, 41, 53, 65, 77, 89, 101, 113, 125, 137, 149, 161, 173; *V2* 5, 17, 29, 41, 53, 65, 77, 89, 101, 113, 125, 137, 149, 161, 173

response to literature, *V1* 5, 7, 8, 11, 13, 17, 19, 21, 23, 25, 29, 31, 33, 35, 37, 41, 43, 45, 47, 49, 53, 55, 57, 59, 61, 65, 67, 69, 71, 73, 77, 79, 81, 83, 85, 89, 91, 93, 95, 97, 101, 103, 105, 107, 109, 113, 115, 117, 119, 121, 125, 127, 129, 131, 133, 137, 139, 141, 143, 145, 149, 151, 153, 155, 157, 161, 163, 165, 167, 169, 173, 175, 177, 179, 181; *V2* 5, 7, 8, 11, 13, 17, 19, 21, 23, 25, 29, 31, 33, 35, 37, 41, 43, 45, 47, 49, 53, 55, 57, 59, 61, 65, 67, 69, 71, 73, 77, 79, 81, 83, 85, 89, 91, 93, 95, 97, 101, 103, 105, 107, 109, 113, 115, 117, 119, 121, 125, 127, 129, 131, 133, 137, 139, 141, 143, 145, 149, 151, 153, 155, 157, 161, 163, 165, 167, 169, 173, 175, 177, 179, 181

writing elements

conventions *V1* 35, 71, 91, 103, 131, 175, 179; *V2* 11, 107, 131, 151, 167

focus, *V1* 23, 55, 107, 119, 139, 143, 155, 167, 179; *V2* 11, 35, 59, 83, 95, 119, 131, 139, 143, 175

organization, *V1* 11, 35, 37, 83, 107, 115, 119, 131, 163, 179; *V2* 11, 35, 71, 107, 127, 131, 179

support, *V1* 19, 23, 31, 43, 55, 59, 67, 71, 79, 83, 95, 127, 139, 143, 151, 155, 163, 167, 175, 179; *V2* 7, 19, 23, 31, 43, 47, 55, 67, 71, 79, 83, 91, 103, 115, 119, 127, 155, 163, 167, 179

writing purpose

descriptive writing, *V1* 23, 47, 71, 83, 155; *V2* 35

expository writing, *V1* 35, 95, 119, 179; *V2* 23, 47, 59, 83, 95, 107, 119, 143, 167

narrative writing, *V1* 11, 107, 131, 167; *V2* 11, 131, 179

personal narrative writing, *V1* 59, 143; *V2* 71, 155

Teacher Notes

Teacher Notes

Teacher Notes

Teacher Notes